Celebrate Canada's sesqu[illegible] by celebrating Canadian creativity!

In this exciting new book, noted author and cultural scholar D. Paul Schafer tackles the subject of Canadian creativity in every field of human endeavour, from the arts and entertainment through transportation, communications and industry to science, technology, sports, and conservation of the natural environment. As Schafer notes, creativity has been the foundation both of Canada's high standard of living and its much admired quality of life. In the years ahead, Canadian creativity can serve as a model and inspiration for other nations, and as the principal means of ensuring Canada's future shines as brightly as its past. Accomplishments profiled in *Celebrating Canadian Creativity* include:

- The remarkable achievements of Canada's Indigenous peoples in transportation (the canoe), shelter (the igloo, teepee, and longhouse), foodstuffs (maple syrup and pemmican) and many other fields
- How Canada helped feed the world through the development of Marquis wheat
- Little-known Canadian pioneers in the development of the electric light bulb, radio, and the electronic music synthesizer
- Alexander Graham Bell's little-known achievements in early aeronautics and the development of the hydrofoil boat
- Canada's role in shaping the modern sporting world through the invention of basketball and contributions to curling and to the country's national sport of hockey
- Strategic breakthroughs in medicine and health care by William Osler, Emily Stowe, Tommy Douglas, Frederick Banting, Charles Best, James Till, Ernest McCulloch, and many others
- Canada's remarkable role in the early development of Hollywood and Broadway as well as recent contributions to pop music through such talents as Céline Dion, Michael Bublé, Drake, and many other singers and songwriters
- Canadian writers who have achieved global recognition, from Thomas Chandler Haliburton, Stephen Leacock, Lucy Maud Montgomery, Gabrielle Roy, Robert Service, and Morley Callaghan to Margaret Atwood, Carol Shields, Lawrence Hill, and Nobel prize-winner Alice Munro

CELEBRATING CANADIAN CREATIVITY

CANADA 150 EDITION

D. Paul Schafer

To Milan and Family
I hope you enjoy this book and its companion The True North
Paul

Rock's Mills Press
Oakville, Ontario

PUBLISHED BY
Rock's Mills Press

ILLUSTRATION CREDITS: Building a canoe (Library and Archives Canada/C-079651); Building an igloo (NFB/LAC/PA-117147); Inuit sculptor photographed by Gar Lunney (NFB/LAC/PA-180267); Canada Dry plant photographed by Conrad Poirier (Bibliothèque et Archives nationales du Québec/P48,S1,P13355); Avro Arrow artist's conception (NFB; LAC/PA-111546); electric organ and inventor Frank Morse Robb (Wikimedia Commons); Canadarm (NASA); BlackBerry (Bart Everson/flickr); Oil Springs photograph by W.J. Bolton (LAC/PA-031112); Robertson screw advertisement (LAC); Hugh Le Caine photograph by Etan Tal (Wikimedia Commons); Electronic Sackbut photograph by David Carroll (Wikimedia Commons; flickr); Expo 67 photograph (Shawn Nystrand/flickr); Combine photograph by Gar Lunney, NFB (LAC/PA-159648); Model of Bell's first telephone (LAC); Dr. and Mrs. Bell (LAC/PA-089114); Canadian Museum of Human Rights (Ccyyrree/Wikimedia Commons); Jack Miner (Jack Miner Bird Foundation); Grey Owl photograph by Karsh (LAC/R613-459, e010751811); Stratford Festival photographs by Walter Curtin, NFB (LAC); Dawson Curling Club photograph by H.J. Goetzmann (LAC/PA-052869); Five-pin bowling (Sam/flickr); Team Canada during opening ceremonies at 2010 Olympics, photograph by Tim Hipps (www.defense.gov/PhotoEssays); Jacques Plante (LAC/PA-195211); Marie-Philip Poulin (hockeyMedia & The Want List/flickr); Sandford Fleming portrait by John Wycliffe Lowes Forester (LAC/Accession 1951-566-1); Abraham Gesner halftone from William Francis Ganong Collection (1987.17.498); Adam Beck (OPG); Adelaide Hunter Hoodless (Wikimedia Commons); Thomas Ahearn photograph by William James Topley (LAC/PA-012222); Arthur McDonald photograph by Bengt Nyman (Wikimedia Commons); Samuel Cunard lithograph from the Canadian Portrait Gallery, Toronto (LAC/C-7044); William Stephenson (Intrepid Society); Reginald Fessenden (Fessenden.ca); J.-A. Bombardier, photograph from NFB (LAC); Nellie McClung photograph by Cyril Jessop (LAC/PA-030212); Elizabeth McMaster (Sick Kids Foundation); William Osler (LAC/Accession 1962-120-1); Tommy Douglas (Saskatchewan Archives Board/R-A5739-3); Banting and Best (University of Toronto/Wikimedia Commons); Terry Fox photograph by Jeremy Gilbert (Wikimedia Commons); Lucy Maud Montgomery (University of Guelph); Clara Hughes photograph by Robert Scoble (Wikimedia Commons); Alice Munro photograph by Arnaud Maggs (LAC/R7959-2742ff.); Margaret Atwood photograph by Mario Biondi (Wikimedia Commons); Céline Dion photograph by Anirudh Koul (Wikimedia Commons); Oscar Peterson photograph by D.G. Langford (LAC); James Naismith (Wikimedia Commons).

Library and Archives Canada Cataloguing in Publication is available from the publisher.
Email Rock's Mills Press at customer.service@rocksmillspress.com.

ISBN-13: 978-1-77244-057-7 (Canada 150 Edition)

Contents

Illustrations follow Chapter Two and Chapter Six.

Foreword

Celebrating Canadian Creativity is a major piece of writing by a man who loves his country, its people, and its culture. It is the most inclusive, horizontally connected, informative, and inspirational work about the pervasiveness and uniqueness of the human creative urge in Canada that I have ever encountered.

Since the book deals with the everyday life of Canadians, it will arouse a nostalgia in many older citizens that will warm and delight. We need to know that we have lived in an exciting country and much that we have witnessed within our borders has influenced the lives of people well beyond Canada's shores. In short, we need to know that the stereotype of Canada as being full of dull, unimaginative, and uncreative people does not deserve a moment's thought. It simply doesn't exist.

For the young and those who have come to Canada from far-off lands, this book contains the most significant history lesson that could be devised. Rather than a story of meaningless and forgettable dates and pointless and obscure references to past events, the book provides surprising and admirable evidence of a splendid commitment on the part of a sizeable coterie of Canadians determined to give attention to matters that affect the survival, comfort, and well-being of countless people in Canada and other parts of the world. Canada can claim to have been the homeland of men and women of deep concern about the problems facing humanity, who were and are driven to find solutions to these problems with little concern for monetary reward and often at great personal sacrifice.

The concept of creativity is used here in the broadest terms, to include those things that affect the daily course of every person's life. In so doing, Schafer has made the creative response a reachable expectation for virtually everyone, young and old, rich and poor, men and women. If, indeed, creativity is the spark of the divine in each of us, this book has theological implications that defy all the limitations of the individual human being. With appropriate learning and experience we can all be "creators."

One of the most important outcomes of reading *Celebrating Canadian Creativity* is the realization that the lack of creativity produces missed opportunities that diminish our lives, hopes, and dreams for the future. The most obvious example is our continuing reliance on public and private systems that once represented a valuable step forward in the ordering of human affairs but now seem incapable of coming to grips with the difficult problems confronting humanity in general and Canadians in particular. As John Ralston Saul has observed, our parliamentary system once provided the stage for an extraordinarily unique accommodation of French and English in post-Conquest Canada, but the late twentieth century and the early years of the twenty-first have witnessed an inadequate response to the enormous challenges posed by inequalities in income and wealth, climate change, and environmental deterioration—challenges that threaten the very existence of future generations of Canadians. Only creative thinking and innovative responses now seem capable of dealing with these problems.

In the complex world of international affairs, we have seen Canada's role greatly diminished, and have learned through recent experiences that when we eschew the wisdom of the past, we invariably follow the paths of other countries less capable of dealing with diversity. Our historic achievements are forgotten and we define ourselves as followers rather than leaders. We look back with nostalgia to a Lester Pearson who creatively changed the direction of affairs in the Middle East by defying the traditional logic of dying empires. In so doing, he prevented yet another journey into death and destruction by people inhabiting a particularly volatile part of the planet, and was recognized with the Nobel peace prize for his efforts.

This book is much more than an account of Canada's inventive contributions to the world's knowledge. It is not merely a collection of accolades honouring inventors of products and activities that have enriched our presence on a troubled planet. It is a challenge to every Canadian citizen engaged in the frustrating struggle to make sense of the human condition. It is a celebration of those who have committed themselves to the task of bettering the daily lives of the world's inhabitants. The examples that Paul Schafer describes should inspire us to expand and enhance our own creativity in the cause of a desperate world in need of new ideas, timely interventions, effective institutions, and more compassion.

Walter Pitman
2016

Preface

This is a book about Canadian creativity. I have written it because I found during the course of my research on Canadian culture that Canadians are an extremely creative people and that creativity has played a crucial role in the country's development. Unfortunately, the extent of this creativity is not well known in Canada or in other parts of the world, in itself providing one of the most important reasons for writing this book.

Canadian creativity is not limited to hockey, insulin, basketball, standard time, and the telephone. On the contrary, it is spread liberally across every area of the country's cultural life. Over the centuries, Canadians have been compelled to be highly creative in order to deal with many complex problems and unique opportunities. What is particularly fascinating about Canadian creativity is the degree to which it is intimately connected to the country's colossal size, cold climate, and small population. It is no coincidence that Canadians have been highly creative in the development of transportation and communications, health care and social security systems, and in such industries as pulp and paper, mining, petrochemicals, hydroelectricity, and a host of other fields and endeavours. The size, nature, and demands of the country have necessitated it.

In coming to grips with these challenges, Canadian creativity has flowed from small towns and rural areas as well as large cities. Individuals and groups, men and women, recent immigrants and long-time residents have all played vital roles. There is hardly a region, community, or ethnic group anywhere in the country that has not made an enduring contribution in this regard. Equally fascinating is the fact that Canadian creativity has benefited countless people in other parts of the world.

There is no better time to be focusing on Canadian creativity than the present. Not only is there a great deal of interest today in creativity, but growing numbers of educators, business leaders, and politicians are coming to the conclusion that creativity is the key to improving living standards around the world, as well as coming to grips with the planet's most difficult, demanding, and debilitating problems.

But there is another, equally compelling reason for focusing on Canadian creativity. It is an ideal vehicle for telling important aspects of the Canadian story. For just as is it impossible to tell the story of the Canadian economy without reference to the crucial role that natural resources have played in it, so it is impossible to tell the story of Canadian culture *as a whole* without dealing with the quintessential role of creativity.

To illustrate this fact, it is necessary to include in the book many events and developments that are not necessarily creative as such, but nevertheless form an essential part of the context needed to understand how creativity has evolved in Canada, why it is so deeply engrained in the country's cultural life, and how it has contributed to Canadian development. Creativity does not take place in a vacuum. It is the product of very specific historical, environmental, cultural, and human circumstances, and a response to many different needs, pressures, and possibilities.

It is impossible to write a book like this without encountering some very contentious issues, including how terms like "creativity" and "Canadian" are to be used, as well as how dates, places, and "firsts" of one type or another are addressed.

In the first instance, I have used the term creativity very broadly as encompassing the origination of things that have never existed before, that have broken new ground in some way, or that are original or unique. Used this way, creativity is an expansive notion that includes innovation, invention, exploration, discovery, and application—what Thomas Homer-Dixon meant when he used the word "ingenuity," and what Northrop Frye called "the imagination." While this is a broader use of the term creativity than the standard dictionary definition, it is consistent with how the concept is viewed today.

Equally problematic is the term "Canadian." By "Canadian" I mean people who were born in Canada and developed much of their creativity here, and by "Canada" I mean not only the country as it presently exists but those lands and colonies which would eventually make up Canada, including the independent Dominion of Newfoundland prior to its joining Canada in 1949. Many creative Canadians moved to other countries to carry out most or all of their life's work, but I still consider their contributions as being representative of Canadian creativity. I have also included the contributions of those born in other parts of the world who came to Canada at some point in their lives and did a significant part of their creative work here.

With respect to the equally difficult problem of dates, places, and "firsts," I have consulted many different sources of information, and have tried to follow the consensus among researchers working in this field. I would like to pay tribute here to the pioneering contributions made to this fascinating field by J.J. Brown, Thomas Carpenter, Roy Mayer, Ralph Nadir, Ken McGoogan, John Melady, Bob McDonald, Susan Hughes, Lisa Wojna, Maxine Trottier, and John Andraos, as well as by Research Matters, Historica.ca, and its recent *Canadian Made* series. I would also like to acknowledge the fact that the book *Canada from Sea unto Sea*, published by the Loyalist Press in 1968, was very helpful in my own research.

It remains to thank a number of people who have made specific contributions to this book, or have supported my efforts over the years to broaden and deepen knowledge and understanding of Canadian culture and creativity in all their diverse forms and manifestations. Included here are my immediate and extended family—Nancy, Charlene, Susan, Alan, brother Murray and his wife Eleanor, and my children's godparents Attila and Elfriede—as well as André Fortier, Tom Symons, Mavor Moore, Bill McWhinney, John Meisel, John Hawco, Ian Morrison, Steven Thorne, Leslie Oliver, George Tillman, Don McGregor, John and Francine Gordon, Barry Witkin, Joyce Zemans, Frank Pasquill, Peter Sever, and many others.

Most of all, I would like to express my gratitude to Walter Pitman, James Gillies, John Hobday, and Sheila Jans for the valuable contributions they made to the book and to my work in the cultural field in general. Most of all, I would like to thank my good friend David Stover for the key role he played in the design, editing, and publication of this book. While the book has been in the making for many years, it simply would not exist without David's crucial contribution to it.

D. Paul Schafer
2016

. . . every house had a draw-well near it, which differed in the contrivance for raising the water from those I had seen in the old country. The plan is very simple: —a long pole, supported by a post, acts as a lever to raise the bucket, and the water can be raised by a child with very trifling exertion. This method is by many persons preferred to either rope or chain, and from its simplicity can be constructed by any person at the mere trouble of fixing the poles. *I mention this merely to show the ingenuity of people in this country, and how well adapted all their ways are to their means.*

—Catharine Parr Traill, *The Backwoods of Canada* (1836)

CHAPTER ONE

Setting the Stage

I was walking in the magnificent forests of York Region one day when I happened to meet a fellow Canadian out with his dogs.

After exchanging the usual comments about the weather—discussing the weather is, I believe, the single most common characteristic of Canadian culture!—and discovering we both had grown up in Toronto and knew several people in common, my fellow walker asked me about my work. I said I had been working for many years on a book on Canadian creativity. He stopped dead in his tracks and exclaimed, "You mean Canadians are creative!"

My response shocked him even more. "Not only are Canadians creative," I replied, "but they have manifested an incredible amount of creativity over the centuries." He said he found this difficult to believe. Canadians are so conventional, so conservative. He could understand someone describing Americans as creative because they are dynamic, aggressive risk-takers. But Canadians? Surely there must be some mistake.

—There is no mistake. The evidence confirms—and confirms convincingly—that Canadians are a highly creative people, and have been from the beginning of their history to the present day.

CREATIVITY AND HOW IT MANIFESTS ITSELF IN CANADA

Regardless of how creativity is understood or defined, all creativity begins with a vision or an idea. It is usually a vision or idea that is different from the ones that are already in existence, or that builds on them in some original, unique, or fundamental way.

But having a vision or idea is not enough. It must be made real in some way, such as when Joseph-Armand Bombardier produced motorized vehicles that could glide over the snow. He had a vision of such vehicles, but true creativity emerged only when he actually designed and built such a vehicle—the snowmobile.

Most people think of the arts and artists when they hear the word creativity. This is understandable in view of the strong connections between the arts, artists, and creativity that date back to classical times. A country's artists are often deemed to be creative because they produce things that are original or unique or break new ground. One Canadian example is the Group of Seven, who created a style of painting that was distinctively Canadian (although influenced, of course, by other non-Canadian trends in painting, including Impressionism).

But creativity is not limited to artists. It also exists in science and among scientists. Surely scientists are creative when they originate new ideas and theories, or invent new products or devices as a result of their experimentation and research. The best-known Canadian example of scientific creativity may be the discovery of insulin by Frederick Banting, Charles Best, C. P. Collip, and J. J. R. Macleod in the early 1920s. Not only was their research original, but it took the world by storm because it produced a treatment for the dreaded disease of diabetes.

What is true of science is also true of business, politics, education, sports, social policy, and many other areas, and of the men and women who devote their lives to those fields. Was K. C. Irving not creative when he built a huge commercial empire in the Maritimes where nothing existed before? Was Sir John A. Macdonald not creative when he devised a strategic plan to counter American expansion and establish Canada as an independent country? Was Pierre Elliott Trudeau not creative when he forged Canada's Charter of Rights and Freedoms and the country's official policy of multiculturalism? Was Harold Innis not creative when he formulated his "staples thesis" to explain the development of the Canadian economy? Was James Naismith not creative when he invented basketball? And was Doris Anderson not creative when she transformed *Chatelaine* into a ground-breaking magazine concerned with women's rights and important social issues, not just fashion and cooking?

Surely all these Canadians—and many others, as we shall see in the pages ahead—have been creative when they have broken new ground, produced things that are original or unique, and devised policies and practices that have had a profound effect on the country, its citizens, and the rest of the world. So without wanting to put too fine a point on the matter or to get involved in an endless semantic debate, the term *creativity* will be used in this book to embrace contributions in many different fields and by many different types of people and not just artists and the arts.

Creativity manifests itself in a variety of ways. In some cases, it emerges in the creation of products, devices, and works of one kind or another. In others, it manifests itself in the creation of new activities, institutions, fields, industries, and firsts of many other types. There are no hard and fast boundaries for creativity and how it manifests itself in Canada or in other parts of the world.

The pacemaker, Pablum, Marquis wheat, the telephone, the walkie-talkie, kerosene, insulin, the caulking gun, the alkaline battery, artificial vanilla extract, Kraft dinner, the foghorn, the batteryless radio, the zipper, and the BlackBerry are all examples of Canadian creativity that manifested itself in the form of products and devices. Interestingly, when the CBC was confronted with the task of putting together a list of Canada's greatest creative achievements for its television program *The Greatest Canadian Invention* some years ago, it had no trouble coming up with a list of 50 items that were created by Canadians and had an important influence on the country, its citizens, and people in other parts of the world. Even the electric oven, which most people assume was invented by Thomas Edison in the United States, was actually devised by a Canadian.

But creativity is not limited to new products, works, and devices. It also manifests itself in a variety of activities, institutions, industries, and fields. The most obvious Canadian examples are lacrosse, basketball, the petrochemical industry, the pulp and paper industry, automation, and the creation of organizations like L'Arche and the Cirque du Soleil. But Canada and Canadians have also made highly creative contributions in many other fields, including ice hockey, curling, transportation, communications, medicine, health care, technology, resource development, the arts, entertainment, social welfare, comedy, and so forth. Canadian fingerprints are all over developments in all these areas, and often in highly innovative and imaginative ways.

Creativity also (though not always) manifests itself in firsts of one kind or another. This occurs most frequently in sports and other forms of competitive activity. Consider the examples of Canadian hockey players and curlers winning many world and Olympic championships, Canadian skiers winning numerous international competitions, and the Toronto Blue Jays winning two consecutive World Series. A great deal of creativity went into these accomplishments, not only in terms of how the athletes prepared but also in terms of the strategies devised to win.

Regardless of how creativity manifests itself, there are times when it occurs at very specific points in time, and other times when it is the product of work that continues over a long period.

The invention of the telephone and the discovery of insulin are excellent examples of Canadian creativity that occurred at a very specific point in time. The telephone was invented in 1876 and insulin was discovered in 1921, although in both cases a great deal of preliminary research was necessary to lay the foundations for the critical breakthrough. In fact, many of Canada's creative achievements have been of this sort. Years of painstaking research and experimentation are required before a sudden breakthrough is realized. And usually many more years are required to make such discoveries and inventions useful in a practical sense and bring them to market.

This pattern contrasts sharply with creativity that is evident over a long period of time. The creation of ice hockey falls into this category. As the producers of the CBC's popular television program *Hockey: A People's History* were at pains to point out, there is no specific point in time when hockey was "invented." Indeed, quite the reverse is true. This sport developed over an extended period and involved antecedents and precedents that can be traced back to classical times and that first appeared in different forms in different parts of the world. However, once the necessary requirements were in place, Canadians made hockey their own by introducing so many creative contributions to its organization, development, and play that it quickly became known as "Canada's game" throughout the world.

Canadian creativity has also been individual as well as collective. In some cases, it can be traced to a single individual, working in total or relative isolation, or with only a few people assisting in the background. In other cases, creativity is the product of a group or team, with no one person the sole discoverer or inventor.

Generally speaking, however, most creativity in Canada has been the product of individuals rather than groups. For example, John Patch, Samuel Cunard, Charles Fenerty, Abraham Gesner, Sandford Fleming, Charles Saunders, Edward Samuel Rogers, Archibald Huntsman, and William Knapp are generally recognized as, respectively, the creators of the screw propeller, the first Atlantic steamship, newsprint from pulpwood, kerosene, standard time, Marquis wheat, the batteryless radio, frozen food for commercial use, and Buckley's cough syrup. But this is not to deny groups their due. For instance, Canadian pediatricians Frederick Tisdall,

Theodore Drake, and Alan Brown, as well as nutritionist Ruth Herbert, created Pablum working together with American chemists. A host of engineers and aviation specialists developed the Avro Arrow, at one time the fastest plane in the world. And numerous teams of researchers and scientists at the National Research Council have created many innovations that have had a significant effect on Canada, Canadians, and the world as a whole.

HEARTACHES, HEADACHES, AND REWARDS

Like creativity anywhere, Canadian creativity is not without its share of heartaches and headaches. But it has also produced countless benefits and rewards.

The heartaches and headaches are easy to understand. They are part and parcel of what creativity is all about and what is required to achieve it. It is simply not possible to be creative without putting in many long hours, expending a great deal of energy and effort, and experiencing numerous setbacks and obstacles along the way. What may look like instant creativity from the outside usually turns out to be the result of years of painstaking work, research, hardship, experimentation, and effort when examined up close. Even composers, poets, and scientists, who are often said to experience creative impulses and sudden inspirations, usually spend countless hours working through the implications of these impulses and inspirations before their creative work is done.

Despite such difficulties, the rewards of creativity can be, and often are, very great. Indeed, one of the most important aspects of Canadian creativity is the way it has generated countless benefits and opportunities for people in other parts of the world and not just Canadians.

Many examples come to mind. Had John Patch, Robert Foulis, and Samuel Cunard not created the screw propeller, the fog horn, and the Cunard steamship line, the history of sea travel would be very different, since these achievements are generally regarded as being revolutionary. If Walter Rupert Turnbull had not invented the variable pitch propeller in the early twentieth century, the history of aviation would have turned out much differently, as his breakthrough opened the doors to the development of commercial aviation. And these examples only scratch the surface of the benefits derived from Canadian creativity.

Nevertheless, there have been numerous obstacles and setbacks along the way. Many of Canada's most highly acclaimed creative talents have been forced to live and work elsewhere in the world, primarily because of the lack of research facilities and funding in Canada, as well as the small size of the Canadian market. The result has too often been the sale of patents and inventions to foreign companies, and heavy reliance on European and especially American capital, commercial expertise, and business acumen. Investors elsewhere have been only too willing to exploit Canadian creativity and make it commercially viable and financially profitable.

One can find many examples of this. Henry Woodward, a Canadian who is credited by many people with the invention of the incandescent light bulb, was forced to sell his patent to Thomas Edison, now generally regarded as its inventor. Abraham Gesner, inventor of kerosene, was forced to move to the United States where his unique invention was used to fund the development of the North American Gaslight Company, the forerunner of Standard Oil of New Jersey. However, the two individuals who best epitomize the problems experienced by many of Canada's creative talents are undoubtedly Reginald Aubrey Fessenden and Alexander Graham Bell.

Fessenden, who played a key role in developing concepts and inventions that eventually led to radio and television broadcasting, did much of his pioneering work at Thomas Edison's Llewellyn Park Laboratory in the United States. He also worked at a subsidiary of the Westinghouse Company, taught at Purdue University and the University of Pittsburgh, established a major research facility at Brant Rock in Massachusetts, and frequently travelled between Canada and the United States. He is considered by many to be one of Canada's greatest inventors, since he was also involved in the creation of nickel, iron, and silicon steel alloy, tracer bullets, sonar, the fathometer, and many other devices.

Fessenden's life was filled with heartache and tragedy because many of his inventions were exploited by American businesses that were anxious to take commercial advantage of his ideas while at the same time ignoring his patents. As a result, Fessenden was compelled to spend a great deal of time in court fighting costly legal battles, and trying without much success to win credit for his inventions and receive proper remuneration for them.

Although Alexander Graham Bell fared much better, he also faced many problems. This world-famous inventor of the telephone, who also played important roles in the development of the hydrofoil boat, gramophone, film soundtrack, electric eye, iron lung, and many other devices, was forced to spend much of his working life in the United States.

In fact, one of the few Canadian inventors prior to the middle of the twentieth century who was able to remain in Canada, undertake his research here, and profit from the development of his creativity in the Canadian marketplace was Edward Samuel (Ted) Rogers, inventor of the batteryless radio. By inventing a radio receiver that used house current rather than expensive batteries that tended to wear out, Rogers gave a boost to the Canadian broadcasting industry when it needed it the most.

As these examples illustrate, dependence on foreign and especially American capital, markets, and research facilities has been a persistent theme in the story of Canadian creativity. As J. J. Brown points out in his book, *Ideas in Exile*, the problem has never been creativity itself, which Brown believed Canadians possess in abundance, but, rather, unwillingness on the part of Canadian investors to support the commercial development of this creativity. As Brown put it:

> Time after time we have gotten there first after a magnificent sprint, and then stood around idly for years waiting to collect the risk capital required to get an industry going. Usually by the time we have solved the financial problem, other less torpid nations have caught up with and passed us. This happened with the variable-pitch propeller, with the hydrofoil boat, with the Jetliner, with automatically controlled machine tools, with the electronic organ. Our inventors presented us with a world's first and a clear head start. But because of our conservative bent, and chronic financial ineptitude, we were unable to do anything with it.

This problem, still not solved, must be addressed if Canadian creativity is to prosper in the future.

PERIODS AND CHARACTERISTICS OF CANADIAN CREATIVITY

Looking back over the history of Canadian creativity, it divides neatly into three distinct periods: pre-colonial, colonial, and post-colonial. These periods have tended to follow the general contours of Canadian development over the centuries, from initial concern with the basics of food, clothing, and shelter to the more recent emphasis on high standards of living and a better quality of life.

From the arrival of the Indigenous peoples until the beginning of the eighteenth century, the problem was survival, clear and simple. A whole series of creative achievements were needed to ensure that people had enough food to eat, appropriate clothing to wear, and adequate shelter to protect themselves from the elements. A creative base was laid that paved the way for future developments. This was especially true of the creativity of the Indigenous peoples, who were compelled to rely on their own ingenuity and resources in virtually every area of life.

Following European settlement, the country plunged into a long colonial period during the eighteenth, nineteenth, and early twentieth centuries. Most creativity during this era was channelled into developing the natural resources of the country, as well as exporting those resources to other parts of the world. This necessitated creating an effective system of transportation and communications and establishing numerous political, legal, and educational institutions and mechanisms.

Canada's political, legal, and educational systems were modelled largely, if not exclusively, on those in vogue in Great Britain, France, and the United States. Nevertheless, a number of creative achievements were realized during this time, including progress in the timber trade and extraction industries, the construction of ships, canals, and railroads, advances in pulp and paper production, agricultural breakthroughs, and the development of sports like hockey, baseball, basketball, football, rowing, and curling.

Though Canadians have continued to build up their creative capabilities in all these areas, their ingenuities were channelled into additional pursuits by the middle of the twentieth century. Much effort centred on the need to create an effective health care and social security system, as well as to achieve higher standards of living and a superior quality of life for the country's increasingly diverse and rapidly expanding population.

Canadian creativity has been particularly profuse in areas that have to do with the major challenges and unique opportunities Canadians have faced over the centuries. It is not surprising that Canadians have been at the cutting edge of many breakthroughs in transportation and communications over the last two centuries, given the vast size of the country they inhabit. Likewise, it would have been impossible to take advantage of the unique opportunities Canadians have been presented with—most notably the abundance of natural resources and basic staples—without manifesting a high degree of creativity in these fields.

This fact highlights one of the most interesting and important things about Canadian creativity. Not only does it manifest itself most obviously in terms of the particular problems and possibilities confronting Canadians over the centuries, but it is intimately connected to the character and circumstances of "the land." It should come as no surprise that Canadians originated the snowmobile, the screw propeller, retractable stadium roofs, standard time zones, and many other concepts and inventions. Nor is it surprising that Canada boasts the world's longest street, highway, recreational trail, and outdoor skating rink, or that Canadians are pioneers in the creation of indoor shopping centres and underground pedestrian walkways. All these creative accomplishments were at least in part a response to the unique needs of Canada's climate and geography.

Many of the country's most cherished athletic achievements and artistic creations have also been concerned with, or strongly influenced by, the natural environment and the seasons. This is true not only of winter sports, including hockey and curling, in which Canadians have long excelled, but also of music, literature, and painting, where the seasons (and particularly winter) have often played a starring role. Whether it is a memoir such as Susanna Moodie's *Roughing It in the Bush*, a musical composition like Jean de Brébeuf's *Huron Carol*, or a painting such as Tom Thomson's *The West Wind,* more often than not Canada's writers, musicians, and artists have been preoccupied with the country's geography, climate, and landscape.

Also worth noting is the fact that many creative contributions have come from immigrants and their descendants, something which is understandable in view of the fact that Canada is often referred to as a "land of immigrants." Examples can be cited in virtually every domain of the country's cultural life. Canada's rural and remote areas have also contributed greatly to the country's creativity, which has not been restricted to big cities or the populous provinces of central Canada.

To this should be added the fact that Canadian creativity has often come in "clusters" or "bursts," rather than as isolated events. The invention of Marquis wheat provides one such example. No sooner was this miracle grain created than a whole series of innovative achievements poured forth in agriculture, such as the invention of the self-propelled combine harvester. Similarly, the railroad boom that gripped Canada in the late nineteenth and early twentieth centuries gave rise to numerous creative achievements, such as the creation of the sleeping car, air-conditioned coach, locomotive braking system, and rotary snowplough. Echoes of the great era of the railways persist in Canadian culture to this day. When Gordon Lightfoot composed his classic *Canadian Railroad Trilogy* to celebrate the country's centennial in 1967, who would have thought that it would still be popular with many Canadians today?

All this makes for a fascinating story. Now that the stage has been set, it's possible to delve deeply into the way Canadian creativity has manifested itself over the centuries, in everything from food, clothing, and shelter to the arts, recreation, and the environment. In the process, we will discover just how creative Canadians really are.

CHAPTER TWO

Food, Clothing, and Shelter

Survival is paramount for every country and culture. No matter where a country is located in the world, a great deal of time and energy go into ensuring its people have enough food to eat, clothing to wear, and adequate shelter to protect themselves against the elements. Even in countries where food is more readily available, few seasonal changes in clothing are required, and shelter can be provided without encountering too many obstacles, considerable time, energy, and effort must go into ensuring that "the basics" are attended to properly. But survival means something very different in countries confronted with difficult geographic and climatic conditions. This is especially true for northern countries like Canada.

Technological advances have made surviving in harsh climates easier today than was once the case. But adverse conditions can still pose serious problems. Food supplies can be disrupted by inclement weather, heating systems and furnaces may fail, and ice storms can trigger power outages with devastating consequences. Today, fortunately, most Canadians do not need to worry about bare-bones survival except in unusual circumstances, although that challenge continues to haunt those lacking income and resources.

But it wasn't always this way. In fact, throughout most of Canadian history, most Canadians were compelled to think about survival every minute of every day.

This was especially true for the Indigenous peoples. It is impossible to imagine how challenging the problem of surviving in an inhospitable climate and geography must have been for them. Whether they were pushed out of their original homelands in Asia because of lack of the basic necessities of life, or were drawn to North America by the possibility of an easier, more satisfying existence, it is difficult to conjure up what life must have been like for these courageous people as they set out for a new land, not knowing if they would survive until the next day, let alone the next month or year.

But survive they did, and eventually reached the northwest shores of North America. It is not known exactly when they arrived, and it really doesn't matter. What *does* matter is that once here, they survived and carved out an effective way of life for themselves, their families, and their descendants, fanning out across the vast expanses of North and South America in the centuries that followed.

CANADA'S CREATIVE BASE SET EARLY

The Indigenous peoples travelled from north to south and west to east across what eventually became Canada, looking for suitable living conditions and establishing pockets of population wherever settlement proved feasible and desirable. In the process, they established a strong, creative base for the development of Canada and future generations of Canadians—a base that was enlarged considerably by those who followed in their footsteps.

This base was erected on three fundamental premises: effective use of all the natural resources of the country; an original and ingenious response to an extremely difficult climate and geography; and, strange as it may sound, the fact that the newcomers couldn't rely on people "back home" to solve their problems or come to their rescue. The high degree of creativity the Indigenous peoples manifested in their new land can be traced back to these three premises in one form or another, and goes to the heart and soul of what Canada and Canadians are all about. While Canada's political origins can be traced back to Confederation and the colonial settlements that were brought together by the British North America Act in 1867, the origins of Canada in a creative sense date back to the Indigenous peoples and their quest to survive, innumerable centuries earlier.

While little specific is known about the creativity of the Indigenous peoples in the early centuries, the main contours of this creativity are well known. It is a creativity that manifested itself across the full spectrum of cultural life, from food, clothing, and shelter to transportation, communications, social arrangements, political affairs, spiritual endeavours, recreation, and the realization of distinctive ways of life.

Indeed, not being able to depend on people and resources back home compelled the Indigenous peoples to be highly creative in addressing the challenges of their new land. Historical accounts reveal that they took advantage of everything nature had to offer. In addition to the three staples—corn, beans, and squash—the evidence indicates that Indigenous diets included roasted reindeer and polar bear meat, moose meat soup, pickled beaver, squirrel, and woodchuck, stuffed whale breast, steamed muskrat, boiled porcupine and caribou, dried buffalo meat, acorn bread, rhubarb, blueberries, cranberries, wild rice, artichokes, fiddleheads, and many other types of game, vegetables, berries, and fruit. The evidence also indicates that the Indigenous peoples used the natural resources of the country for both food and medicinal purposes, and were very skilled at curing, smoking, and preserving fish, game, and meat. It is a skill that is still preserved in many Indigenous communities today, especially along the east and west coasts of Canada where First Nations people excel at the art of curing, smoking, and preserving salmon, trout, caribou, and other delicacies.

Even maple syrup, one of the country's most iconic products, did not escape their attention. Long before the arrival of the Europeans, the Indigenous peoples waited patiently for the "sugar moon" to arrive, as this was an indication that the magic sap was flowing once again in the country's maple trees. They celebrated this unique time of year with feasting, thanksgiving, telling tales, and sharing legends. Not only did they use maple syrup to sweeten many of their meats, puddings, soups, and dishes, but they were also skilled at kneading the congealed syrup by hand and paddle, as well as preserving it in moulds as maple sugar, to be eaten at festive occasions and numerous other events throughout the year.

What is true for food is equally true for clothing. The Indigenous peoples demonstrated an uncanny knack for creating clothes that were suitable to a northern geography and cold climate, once again taking advantage of everything nature had to offer. Fur and animal skins were especially popular—seal and caribou in the far north and beaver and muskrat farther south—since they provided a great deal of warmth in winter and helped to counteract the elements. Many different types of clothing were created, including parkas, mittens, hats, boots, moccasins, snowshoes, mukluks, and so forth. Parkas, mittens, and hats were imperative for withstanding the cold and the wind; snowshoes were needed to walk in the forests, woods, and clearings during the winter months; and moccasins and mukluks provided warmth and allowed hunters to sneak up on game without being detected. Parkas generally consisted of an outer garment and an inner garment. Some Indigenous groups preferred wearing parkas made of seal skin during the spring, summer, and fall, and ones made from caribou skins in the winter. Footwear was usually made from different types of seal skin—haired for winter use and hairless for spring and summer use, the latter being waterproof. Mukluks were especially popular, since they extended farther up the legs than moccasins; mukluks were made of moose hide or reindeer skin, and lined with rabbit or fox fur.

But it is probably in the area of shelter that the creativity of the Indigenous peoples shone through most brightly. In the Arctic, the Inuit constructed igloos made of ice and snow—using ice and snow to combat ice and snow, so to speak—since these materials were excellent insulation against the strong northerly and westerly winds and inclement weather. The entrances to igloos were tunnelled out and curved, in order to block the cold from the dwelling's interior. A raised "sleep platform" was also constructed; it faced the low entrance, since heat rises. The platform was usually covered by caribou skins to provide extra warmth. In constructing the igloo, blocks of ice and snow were placed next to one another in an upward spiral, each block tipped slightly more inward to narrow the gap until a circular dome was created that eliminated the need for scaffolding. Insulation of the interior of the dwellings was often enhanced by lining the walls and ceiling with caribou hides and seal skins.

Farther south, teepees and wigwams made of animal skins were constructed by the Plains Indians and Algonquians. They were conical in shape with entrances facing east or south to provide as much warmth as possible and render protection against the strong northern and western winds. These dwellings were designed to be easy to pack up and move from one area to another in search of food. A tailored buffalo hide was usually draped over the poles that held up the dwelling, and was then staked and weighed down with stones along the bottom edge. A smoke hole in the top of the teepee or wigwam allowed smoke from the fire to escape from the interior.

The longhouses of the Hurons and the Iroquois, on the other hand, were built of saplings and covered with bark, another indigenous material found in large quantities throughout the country. These longhouses often housed eight to ten families—there is warmth in numbers as well as strength; stretched more than half a football field in length; and included sweat lodges, the early forerunners of steam baths in North America. The plank houses of the Salish, Kwakiutl, Haida, and West Coast peoples were constructed of cedar planks, often accommodated extended families of twenty to thirty people, and usually incorporated totem poles adjacent to the houses to commemorate the dead and express crucial cultural, spiritual, and religious beliefs.

To this range of dwellings should be added "pit houses" and "quiggly holes," both popular in the interior of British Columbia. What an ingenious response they were to Canada's difficult geography and climate! These houses and holes were much like inverted bowls, made of wood and covered with an insulating layer of earth. You entered these unique dwellings by climbing down a ladder. But what perfect protection they provided against the elements and the cold.

The high degree of creativity manifested by the Indigenous peoples in developing food, clothing, medicine, and shelter suitable for a cold climate and punishing geography proved indispensable to the first Europeans. In fact, without this, the first European explorers, fishermen, trappers, traders, and settlers would likely not have survived. What is often described as a one-way relationship between the Indigenous peoples and the first Europeans was in fact a two-way relationship that benefited the Europeans much more than the Indigenous peoples. As Gustave Lanctot pointed out in his book, *A History of Canada*:

> The Indians greatly helped the European in exploring and adapting himself to his Canadian environment. They extended a warm welcome to the first white men; they helped them by teaching them their inventions and their whole body of knowledge and experience of the wilderness. . . . They taught the Europeans the way of the forest, how to keep their bearings and how to live off the land.

A HARD ACT TO FOLLOW

Europeans did not demonstrate the same degree of creativity in developing food, clothing, and shelter suitable for the New World. There are two reasons for this. In the first place, there wasn't the same need to be creative, as the Indigenous peoples had already come up with many of the necessities. In the second place, the people who came to North America from the fifteenth century onward were able to draw on skills, expertise, and resources back home to a significant extent. Nevertheless, there were a number of areas in which the new settlers built upon the creativity of the

Indigenous peoples, or came up with their own ingenious solutions as conditions and circumstances warranted. This is particularly true with respect to various foods and foodstuffs discovered originally by the Indigenous peoples, especially fiddleheads, rhubarb, leeks, wild rice, cranberries, and maple syrup. As Catharine Parr Traill observed in 1860 in *The Canadian Settler's Guide*, "The rising of the sap is felt in the forest trees; frosty nights and sunny days call forth the activity of the settlers in the woods; the sugar making is now at hand, and all is bustle and life in the shanty." Not only were maple-syrup products created in many parts of the country, but they also gave rise to several well-known recipes and the creation of an export industry that has done much to enhance Canada's reputation at home and abroad, particularly after Denis Desilets invented an effective method for collecting maple sap using plastic tubes in 1970. What Canadian has allowed a visitor or relative from another part of the world to leave Canada without a jar of maple syrup or a package of wild rice in their hand or in their suitcase?

Maple syrup and wild rice were not the only foodstuffs originally discovered by the Indigenous peoples that were used to advantage and exploited commercially by those who followed in their footsteps. The Indigenous peoples also introduced the Europeans to pemmican. It was made of dried elk, buffalo, or deer meat, pounded into a fine powder, mixed with dried berries like raspberries, blueberries, and gooseberries, packed into bags and containers, and sealed with grease. Easy to carry, light in weight, resistant to spoilage, and very nourishing, it was a staple in the diets of fur-traders and trappers since it freed up a lot of space in their canoes, thus leaving more room for furs and the equipment necessary on long voyages.

Cod was another foodstuff that was used to great advantage by European settlers in highly inventive and original ways. Every part of the cod was used, as Dorothy Duncan points out in her book *Canadians at Table*: "As we follow the cod from the water to the kitchen to the dinner table, we find the ingenious recipes developed by enterprising cooks over the centuries that used virtually every part of the fish: Fried Cod Roe, Fried or Baked Cod Tongues, Stewed or Fried Cods' Heads, Fish Hash (made from fresh or salt codfish), Codfish Balls, Cod Sounds (membrane lying along the backbone, first simmered in water, then baked in a casserole with onions, grated cheese, and thin strips of salt pork), Toast and Fish, Roasted Scrawd (small cod culled from the catch), Fish and Brewis, Salt Fish and Potatoes, Boiled Rounders (small codfish with soundbone intact), and many more!" Both cod and salmon remain very popular fish in Canada, as well as ones that elicited a creative response from Canadian cooks over the centuries.

But it is probably the McIntosh apple and Marquis wheat that are the best-known examples of food-related creativity in Canada. The McIntosh apple was created in 1796 by John McIntosh, who discovered a number of apple trees growing on his farm near Dundela in central Ontario. He transplanted several of the trees and found that one of them produced excellent fruit. After experimenting for many years, his son Allan perfected the art of grafting and began producing McIntosh apples commercially. They became extremely popular because of the profuse and luscious nature of the fruit and the sturdy and resilient character of the trees. It is interesting to note in this regard that the original tree, which gave rise to all the others, bore fruit for more than ninety years before it died in 1908. It boggles the mind to think of how many millions of McIntosh apples have been harvested and sold over the years.

But Canada's greatest claim to creative fame in the area of food and foodstuffs is undoubtedly Marquis wheat. It was invented by Charles E. Saunders in 1908 and played a pivotal role in "filling up the West," a venture which Sir John A. Macdonald saw as key to resisting imperialist pressures from the United States, attracting immigrants from other parts in the world, and to ensuring Canada's survival. Doing so was not possible, however, without creating agricultural products that could withstand the Prairies' long winters, cold climate, early frosts, and short growing season.

Charles Saunders was a cerealist at the Dominion Department of Agriculture in Ottawa when he invented Marquis wheat. Prior to this time, the most common variety of wheat grown in Canada was Red Fife. It was rust resistant, and was created by David Fife in Ontario in 1843. While this particular type of wheat served many parts of the country well where the growing season was longer, it was not suitable to the West with its shorter growing season. Capitalizing on research undertaken by his father, William Saunders, the first director of the Central Experimental Farm in Ottawa,* Charles Saunders invented Marquis wheat by crossing Red Fife with another variety called Red Calcutta. Since Marquis wheat matured in a shorter period of time, produced significantly higher yields, and was

* The Central Experimental Farm was established in 1889. It is in itself a rather remarkable achievement; it grew to an area of more than 400 hectares.

more resistant to disease, it proved to be a bonanza for Western farmers and the Canadian economy.

Like his father, Charles Saunders was an interesting individual. He was a shy, modest, and self-effacing person who taught music at Havergal Ladies College in Toronto for a time, played the flute, studied French, wrote poetry, married a beautiful and talented soprano named Mary Blackwell, and served as music critic for the *Toronto Globe* (forerunner of the *Globe and Mail*) for a number of years. But his real talent lay in horticulture and agricultural research. Urged on by his father, he became a giant of biological engineering, becoming an "experimentalist" in the cereals department of the experimental farm in 1903 and Dominion cerealist in 1905, a position he held until his retirement in 1922. He was very systematic and methodical in his research. Not only did he test a huge number of grains and bake the flours into small loaves to assess their quality, but he also chewed many varieties of grain himself to determine their gluttonous properties.

Saunders' unique variety of wheat was an instant success. It matured a full week to ten days sooner than Red Fife, and yielded five more bushels per acre. In 1911, this "miracle grain" from Canada was awarded the gold prize at the World's Fair in New York as the best wheat grown in the world. Canada soon became a major wheat exporter, with people in many different countries depending on the miracle grain from Manitoba, Saskatchewan, and Alberta. By 1920, ninety percent of the Canadian wheat crop was Marquis, and the strain was soon used elsewhere in the world where the growing season was short and quality was essential. Following his development of Marquis, Saunders went on to produce several other varieties of wheat that were also rust resistant, including Ruby, Carnet, and Reward. In 1921, he was made a fellow of the Royal Society of Canada, and in 1933 he was knighted by King George V for his contribution to world agriculture. He was quick to point out that this honour would not have been possible without important contributions by his brother Percy, his father William, and his associate Will Macoun.

While many Canadians know of Marquis wheat, far fewer know about the miracle of canola oil and the comparable amount of creativity and hard work required to develop it. Like Marquis wheat, it is a miracle foodstuff that is produced largely on the Prairies and especially in Saskatchewan.

Rapeseed, from which canola oil is derived, has been known for centuries. However, it was traditionally a very low acreage crop, largely because it was deemed to be toxic in character and had a poor "meal quality." Even after it was discovered to be useful as an industrial oil because it adhered well to metals, its production was limited. In Canada, for example, acreage devoted to rapeseed diminished from 20,000 acres to only 400 acres by the 1950s.

It was about this time that Burton Craig and Keith Downey arrived on the scene. Believing that rapeseed possessed vast potential, they experimented for years with various types, much as Charles Saunders had with different types of wheat, until they eventually produced a "LEAR" variety in 1964 that began rapeseed's transformation into canola. By 1977, they had solved two major drawbacks associated with rapeseed—high erucic acid content and too much glucinaolate—and produced an excellent variety that yielded a high quality oil and had excellent meal properties. They coined the name "canola oil" because it sounded like "Canadian oil," and the rest is history. By 1981, these two inventive individuals and others had turned rapeseed into pure gold, transforming the colour of the Canadian prairies when the canola crop ripens and giving rise to a billion-dollar industry. Interestingly, canola surpassed wheat as Canada's most valuable crop in 1994. It is now used extensively throughout the world for edible-oil production, although some researchers still claim it possesses certain toxic residues as a result of its derivation from rapeseed.

Pumpkins may not be vital to the world food supply in the same way as wheat and canola, but they also present a unique example of Canadian creativity. It's all because of Howard Dill, the son of a farmer born in 1934. While young, he entered many pumpkin-growing competitions in the Hants County Exhibition in Windsor, Nova Scotia—one of North America's oldest agricultural exhibitions, if not *the* oldest. After a long period testing various pumpkin seeds and pollination techniques, in 1966 Dill produced a pumpkin that weighed over 100 pounds. He went on to produce the largest pumpkin in the world in 1984—a 493½-pounder, according to the *Guinness Book of World Records*—after setting four consecutive world records for growing the heaviest pumpkins. He called his pumpkins "Atlantic Giants" to commemorate their birthplace in the Atlantic provinces, and started marketing Atlantic Giant pumpkin seeds in Canada, the United States, the United Kingdom, and elsewhere. While his world record was eventually broken by producers in the United States, his incredible seeds now yield pumpkins weighing more than 1,000 pounds each.

§ § § § §

If food is one area of fascinating creative achievements, clothing is another. This was especially true for the early years of European settlement. For example, French Canadians created many types of apparel, including footwear shaped like moccasins called *bottes* or *soulier sauvages*, as well as leather or fabric leggings that were very popular with the *couriers de bois*, fur traders, and habitant farmers.

But the most creative and popular clothing item was the cloak or *blanket capot*. It was designed specifically for Canada's cold winters, and eventually included a hood made of thick grey homespun wool. The Métis, who wrapped blankets around themselves to form cloaks, played an important role in the development of these items. The most popular blankets were made by the Hudson's Bay Company, beginning in the late eighteenth century. They proved to be extremely popular with the Indigenous peoples, since they came in many colours—especially white and green, which were popular with Indigenous chiefs—and were called "point blankets" because they were manufactured in accordance with a highly elaborate system of points developed in France to differentiate between various levels of quality.

Capots were especially popular with French Canadians, and usually had white and blue bands near the hemline with matching bands at the wrist. They also had upright collars and were closed in front by a series of ties in red or blue or both colours combined. They eventually evolved into the Hudson's Bay coat, which was popular in most parts of Canada and elsewhere in the world because it was fashionable and colourful as well as warm.

Beaver hats and coats were yet another area where Canadian creativity was quick to manifest itself. They were all the rage in Europe for more than a century, and (along with cod) rapidly became one of Canada's biggest exports. Harold Innis, the country's great political economist, wrote about the way the Canadian economy was grounded in the production of such staples in his books on the fur trade and the cod fisheries.

While beaver, seal, and fur generally have lost much of their appeal in the modern era because of pressure from animal rights' groups and others, they reveal a great deal about the development of clothing in Canada in the seventeenth, eighteenth, and nineteenth centuries. After the founding of the Hudson's Bay Company in 1670—making it the oldest company in North America—the Company went on to become the largest and most successful manufacturer of clothing in Canada for many years. Over the course of its history, this innovative institution has produced many different types of apparel. However, none has been more popular than Hudson's Bay coats and blankets with their vivid colours, evocative Indigenous designs, and ecological motifs. More recently, coats and mittens marketed in conjunction with the Winter Olympics have been a mainstay of the Hudson's Bay Company.

As the fur trade diminished in importance and Canada became more settled and urbanized, European fashions began to predominate. Clothing styles became less creative and more colonial in character. In Quebec, French and Italian fashions were extremely popular, much as they still are today. In other parts of the country, British fashions were the order of the day, particularly Victorian fashions that required many layers of clothing and a strong commitment to "lacing up" and especially "covering up." Long-laced boots, corsets, slips, and floor-to-neck dresses were popular with women; high-cut boots, trousers, breeches, ties, shirts, suits, and jackets with men. However, just as British and French architectural styles gave away to American architectural styles in the latter nineteenth and early twentieth centuries, so British and French clothing styles gave way to American styles at about the same time. By this point, many Jewish immigrants had arrived in Canada and were establishing themselves in the garment and tailoring trades in Montreal, Toronto, and Winnipeg, either because they had learned these trades back home, or, more often, were prevented from entering other professions and found that they could establish a niche for themselves in the clothing business.

It was also around this time that the T. Eaton Company was created. Founded by Timothy Eaton in Toronto in 1869, Eaton's went on to build numerous department stores across the country that in the early years specialized primarily in men's and women's clothing. The firm's reputation was built on fixed prices, cash sales, and allowing customers to return items if they were not satisfied. These policies made it possible for Eaton's to capture the clothing market in many parts of Canada—except in the West where the Hudson's Bay Company continued to dominate—especially after it opened its catalogue business in 1884. Such a business was ideally suited to Canada, where the population was widely dispersed and travel was difficult during the winter months.

While the T. Eaton Company was very successful, it experienced stiff competition from the Hudson's Bay Company in the West and Simpson's in the East. For many years, these two department stores played a major role in Canadian retailing, engaging in a rivalry much like that between Macy's and Gimbels in United States. Both stores have now disappeared from the Canadian scene: Eaton's was eventually forced into bankruptcy due to poor management and stiff competition, and Simpson's was taken over by the Hudson's Bay Company. Sears, the huge American retail conglomerate, had since the 1950s run a joint venture with Simpson's, called Simpsons-Sears, that included a catalogue business as well as retail stores; Simpsons-Sears was renamed Sears Canada following the sale of Simpson's itself. Though Sears thrived in Canada for many years because of its numerous stores, strong customer service, and successful mail order business, it eventually fell on hard times as well, closing many of its stores. Even the country's oldest retailer, the Hudson's Bay Company, changed hands several times though in recent years it has expanded its operations with the acquisition of U.S. department stores Saks Fifth Avenue and Lord and Taylor.

It is in the area of shelter, however, that Canadians proved to be most inventive during the long period of colonialism. When settlers arrived in large numbers from France, Great Britain, and other parts of Europe and the world, protection from the elements was vital. Wood was used most frequently in the early years, because it was ubiquitous in most parts of the country and was readily available. Wooden houses made of huge logs hewn from the country's forests were commonplace. Various styles included the Red River Frame, the Hudson's Bay Frame, and especially the log house and log cabin. This latter type of dwelling was extremely popular with trappers, fur traders, settlers, and pioneers because it was built with squared logs placed horizontally between vertical posts, thereby sealing in the heat effectively. Interestingly, homes and cottages of wood and constructed in the log-cabin style are still popular among Canadians today.

While wood remained popular throughout the colonial period, stone came into wider use because it was also readily available, extremely durable, and not as prone to fire. As a result, many homes, blockhouses, and public buildings were built of stone in Ontario, Quebec, and especially Nova Scotia, where many Scottish tenant farmers had settled and built stone huts or crofters' cottages reminiscent of those of the Scottish Highlands.

Since stone and wood were not readily available on the prairies, other materials had to be used. Sod proved ideal for this purpose. It was broken into sod bricks, placed grass side down, and stacked in rows. This made it possible to create sod homes—"soddies"—that were extremely popular because the walls were thick and the homes were fireproof. They provided warmth in winter, coolness in summer, and avoided the risk of fire common with wood dwellings.

Most Canadians were engaged in farming during this period, and farmhouses were built with increased frequency across the country. Built of stone, wood, and occasionally brick, most of these farmhouses were heated with huge wood stoves, usually located in the kitchen. Since this was the warmest room in the house, most socializing, entertaining, and family functions took place in this room: the eating of meals; the education of children; conversations with family and friends; and various types of celebrations. The invention in 1892 of the electric oven by Thomas Ahearn—a Canadian from Ottawa about whom much will be said later—helped to reinforce this tradition.

In Quebec, the farmhouses of the *habitants* were unique and required a great deal of creativity in their design and development. They were initially low, broad-based structures, built of wooden planks with a high-pitched shingled roof and gable verges. They were usually rectangular in shape and divided into two rooms of unequal size, with a large masonry chimney rising from the cross wall. Eventually, a unique style of farmhouse emerged with a steeply pitched "cayou roof." The overall style was French, but cleverly adapted to suit Canada's wintry weather and snowy conditions. A *cayou* is an extension fastened to the ends of the roof beams, with planking covering this extension to form an overhang that helps to carry the run-off from melting snow and ice away from the dwelling. The curved roof was often covered with brightly painted orange and green sheet metal, particularly in more recent renderings, thereby making this traditional *maison Québécoise* a colourful symbol of Quebec, and one that can still be seen and enjoyed in many parts of that province today.

Housing was also evolving in towns and cities across the country. Row houses, the forerunners of today's town homes, were popular in St. John's and elsewhere; joined together, they economized on construction costs and heating. While they were patterned after styles popular in England and elsewhere in Europe, they were adapted to Canada's conditions. And while they appeared somewhat later, duplexes, with separate upstairs and downstairs entrances, were extremely popular in places like Montreal. Many of these duplexes had external wrought-iron staircases that not only saved valuable space inside the dwellings, but also added variety and character to Montreal's rapidly evolving streetscapes.

Cities and towns were also the places where Canadians started to become aware of architectural styles popular in other parts of the world. Since France and Great Britain exerted an extremely powerful influence on Canada and Canadians in the seventeenth, eighteenth, and nineteenth centuries, French and British architectural styles had a particularly strong impact. In the late seventeenth century, for example, many religious and government buildings were built in the French baroque style. As the British influence began to assert itself more strongly in the eighteenth and nineteenth centuries, British styles began to predominate, particularly Georgian, Palladian, Edwardian, Victorian, and Gothic Revival styles.

There were, however, some notable exceptions to the dominant British and Italian architectural styles. In the late nineteenth and early twentieth centuries, the French influence returned to Canada, not only in the Beaux-Arts Movement and the emergence of the Art Deco style after the Paris Exposition of 1925, but also in the popular "château style." The Canadian Pacific Railway built a number of huge hotels across the country—"railroad hotels" as they were called—that closely resembled the châteaux of the Loire Valley in France. These included the Banff Springs Hotel and Château Lake Louise in Alberta, the Empress Hotel in Victoria, the Château Laurier in Ottawa, the Fort Garry in Winnipeg, and, most notably because of its incredible setting overlooking the St. Lawrence River and colossal size, the Château Frontenac in Quebec City. What was particularly innovative about these hotels was not so much their architectural style, which was predominantly French, but rather the imagination, audacity, and ingenuity required to create and build them. What other country in the world possesses five such majestic railroad hotels situated at strategic points across the country, evoking such character and panache?

THE SEARCH FOR MORE INDIGENOUS FORMS OF EXPRESSION

While creativity in Canada during colonial times was concerned more with adapting styles of food, clothing, and shelter popular in Europe to Canada's specific climatic conditions and geographical circumstances, these areas began to move in some new and innovative directions during the twentieth century and especially after the Second World War.

For one thing, the native foodstuffs of the country were beginning to make their way into an increasing number of homes in Canada, as well as onto the menus of restaurants and hotels across the country and indeed around the world. As a result, Canada started to become well-known internationally for the quantity and quality of its ocean, fresh-water, and shell fish: Atlantic and Pacific salmon, crab, Arctic char, cod, eel, clams, oysters, mussels, lobsters, mackerel, sturgeon, gold eye, white fish, mullet, pickerel, bass, pike, and trout. Many of these delicacies were packed and shipped, fresh, smoked, or frozen, to destinations in other parts of the world.

This was especially true of frozen fish. And why not? Canadians had been fishing off the coasts of the country for centuries, and both the dry and green methods of preserving and curing fish were developed off the east coast by French and English fishermen respectively. It is not surprising, therefore, that it was a Canadian—Archibald Huntsman—who first invented "frozen food" for commercial use in general and "frozen fish" in particular. This occurred in 1929, when Huntsman, a marine scientist on the Biological Board of Canada in Halifax—later the Fisheries Research Board—created his famous "ice fillets." In so doing, he became the first person to package quick-frozen food for commercial sale to the general public. And sell the fillets did. Within a few years, the Biological Board of Canada, in conjunction with two private companies—the Lunenburg Sea Products Company and the Lockeport Company—were selling tons of ice fillets to Canadians, mostly in the Toronto area. However, since the Board and these companies failed to capitalize on this unique commercial opportunity, or were not financially able to do so, this opened the door to Colonel Clarence Birdseye in the United States to create the billion-dollar frozen food industry, particularly after he was successful in acquiring financial support from the Postum Company. This would not be the first nor the last time Canadians created something new and different, only to see it commercially exploited by others.

Along with the country's fish, distinctively Canadian meats and game, including partridge, quail, pheasant, duck, buffalo, and caribou, began to appear with increased frequency on menus in Canada and abroad. So, too, did many of the country's vegetables, berries, and fruit, especially wild rice and fiddleheads (both international favourites), rhubarb, cranberries, corn, peaches, plums, pears, potatoes, blueberries, and apples. It is not surprising that the largest processor of potatoes and French fries in the world is Canadian—McCain Foods Ltd. of Florenceville, New Brunswick. Nor is it surprising that Canada possesses a number of world-famous fruit orchards in the Okanogan Valley of British Columbia and the Annapolis Valley of Nova Scotia, as well as in Ontario and Quebec. These orchards now produce more than fifty varieties of apples, such as Spys, Red Delicious, Cortlands, Wolf Rivers, Granny Smiths, Gravensteins, Russets, Ida Reds, and many others. However, the favourite remains the McIntosh.

Dietary and culinary practices have changed considerably in Canada over the last fifty years. Like many countries in the world, Canada has become a fast-food nation, with more and more Canadians anxious to "eat on the run." As a result, the country boasts its fair share of fast food chains and restaurants, including the Canadian-owned Harvey's and A&W as well as such well-known international brands as McDonald's, Burger King, Wendy's, Kentucky Fried Chicken, and so forth. Nevertheless, the favourite is still Tim Hortons. As many Canadian know, it is named after a famous Canadian hockey player, Tim Horton, who started the company before his untimely death. Canadians have demonstrated a remarkable loyalty to this fast-food chain, despite that fact that the chain was taken over by U.S. fast food giant Wendy's in the 1990s. Wendy's eventually divested Tim Hortons, but in 2014 the coffee chain was acquired by the Brazilian-controlled parent company of Burger King and once again passed into foreign hands. However, regardless of ownership, "Tim's" remains one of the most popular institutions in the country.

Given the intimate connection between food and climate, geography, and the natural environment in Canada, it is not coincidental that one of Canada's largest food producers and retailers—Loblaws—predicated much of its growth for many years on pre-packaged and frozen foods, bringing to mind Archibald Huntsman's creative achievements with frozen-fish fillets. Beginning in the 1980s, Loblaws created a whole series of frozen and pre-packaged foods evocative of the diverse peoples, countries, cultures, and cuisines of the world, thereby capitalizing on another well-known Canadian characteristic—the country's multiethnic and multicultural diversity. Loblaws' President's Choice brands, which include everything from tandoori chicken to Szechwan sauce, became so successful that they forced competitors to follow suit by creating their own private-label brands.

Every region of Canada has its own culinary specialties, adding to the diverse character of the country as a whole. The Prairie provinces are best known for their meats and grains, Ontario for its pork, bacon, cheddar cheese, and maple syrup, and the Atlantic Provinces, British Columbia, the Northwest Territories, the Yukon, and Nunavut for their "fruits of the sea." However, it is Quebec that is most renowned for its regional specialties and distinctive cuisine, not only in Canada but also in many other parts of the world. This is not surprising, given that Quebec inherited a rich agricultural and gastronomic tradition from France, and can trace its culinary roots and traditions back to the seventeenth century when the Order of Good Cheer was created to celebrate good food, drink, and entertainment.

As a result, Quebec gastronomic specialties and creative achievements abound—Brome Lake duck, Rougemount apples, Matane shrimps, honey salmon, Habitant pea soup, sugar pie, tortière—a pork pie made of ground pork, pastry, and spices— Oka and Ermite cheese, which are produced in a number of monasteries in the province, and *queues de castor*, quite literally "beavertails," or slabs of sweet dough formed in the shape of a beaver tail and drenched with sugar. But the most popular and famous specialty of Quebec is undoubtedly poutine—French fries smothered in cheese and gravy—which was invented by Fernand Lachance in 1957.

Canadians have begun to win more and more international awards for their creative accomplishments in the culinary arts. For instance, the restaurants at the long-established railroad hotels have won a number of prestigious international awards for recipes that are unique to Canada, which have come about as a result of going back to the country's culinary roots and gastronomic traditions. The "100-Mile Diet" is also worth noting. It was invented by two Canadian health specialists from Vancouver and has attracted a great deal of attention throughout the world in recent years.

Among those who have contributed to Canada's culinary heritage are Jehane Benoît, who popularized cooking and gastronomic achievements in Canada and especially Quebec, championed microwave cooking, and wrote the *Encyclopaedia of Canadian Cuisine*; Edward Asselbergs, head of food processing at the Food Research Institute in Ottawa, who invented "instant" pre-prepared meat, chicken, and cheese products, and especially instant mashed potatoes in the mid-1960s; Gary Johnston at the University of Guelph, who developed Yukon Gold potatoes with their buttery, yellow flesh in 1966 and named them after the Yukon Gold Rush; Michael Stadtländer, who emigrated from Germany and played a seminal role in generating interest in Canada's indigenous foods and foodstuffs; and Adrienne Clarkson and John Ralston Saul, who did so much to promote interest in Canadian cuisine and Canada's creative culinary traditions by serving unique Canadian dishes and wines at official functions when they lived at the Governor-General's residence in Ottawa.

There are some fascinating historical precedents here as well. James H. Ganong founded a small bakery and candy store in St. Stephen, New Brunswick in 1892 that eventually grew to become Ganong Brothers Limited, one of the largest manufacturers of candy and chocolate in the world. Arthur Ganong is credited with creating the first chocolate bar in 1910, originally to take on fishing trips because it was easy to transport. There is also James Lewis Kraft and Kraft Dinner, one of Canada's and the world's most cherished and devoured foods. James Lewis Kraft was originally from Fort Erie, Ontario, but went to Chicago, where he invented and was granted a patent for a method of processing a specific type of cheese in dried form. It eventually provided the basis for Kraft Dinner, as well as the underpinnings of Kraft Foods, the company in the United States that still bears James's last name. This company recently merged with Heinz to become the Kraft Heinz Company, one of the largest suppliers of foodstuffs in the world.

What is true for food is also true for drink. While drink is an essential part of every country's cuisine—think of what tea means to China and Japan, beer means to Germany and the United States, and wine means to France—Canada does not have a long tradition in this area. However, Canadians have made some highly original contributions. Included on the list would undoubtedly be Crown Royal whisky, Molson's beer, and the Caesar cocktail, first created by Walter Chell in 1969. But the country's best-known beverage is ginger ale. It was invented by John J. McLaughlin, a chemist and pharmacist who produced flavoured extracts for the soda water bottling plant he established in Toronto and began mass producing soft drinks for sale beyond the traditional soda fountains in drug stores. In 1904, this company introduced a Pale Dry Ginger Ale with a label depicting a beaver sitting on top of a map of Canada. Then, in 1907, McLaughlin trademarked his famous Canada Dry Ginger Ale and starting manufacturing it commercially at a plant on Sherbourne Street in Toronto, calling it "the champagne of ginger ales." It took the country and the world by storm and is now consumed by millions of people around the world.

More recently, Canadians have become well-known throughout the world for their creativity in making wine, not only as a result of their ability to blend domestic and foreign grapes to produce some of the best wines available—thanks to outstanding wineries in Ontario, British Columbia, and elsewhere—but also for their innovative contributions to "ice wine." In making ice wine, Canadians have demonstrated a remarkable capacity for taking advantage of specific climatic, geographic, and topographical conditions and turning them to best advantage. Ice wine is produced by picking the grapes at a precise time of year, after a hard freeze, and then crushing and aging them. The climatic conditions necessary for producing ice wine have made Canada one of the world's leading producers of this unique vintage.

It is impossible to complete this portrait of Canadian creativity in food, foodstuffs, and cuisine without commenting on the contemporary impact of Canada's diverse population and multicultural character. Not only are many new fruits, vegetables, and other foodstuffs becoming popular, but many recipes and dishes are now considered Canadian that would not have been several decades ago. This interesting mixture of different cuisines has led to a great deal more experimentation, especially by the nation's culinary masters.

Residents and visitors alike find this mixing of cusines one of the most attractive things about Canada. As a result, it is possible to see food practices moving in two contradictory but highly interrelated and exciting directions. On the one hand, the country is fashioning an indigenous cuisine of its own after a long period of colonialism and dependence on the culinary traditions of others. On the other hand, Canada is becoming known for embracing cuisines from many other countries. This augers well for the future, since it means that Canadians and visitors alike will be able to benefit from many unique and indigenous Canadian dishes while simultaneously being able to enjoy a variety of dishes from virtually every part of the world.

Clothing is another area where fundamental changes are occurring. What is most distinctive about Canadian clothing, however, is not how creative it is, but rather how much there is of it! In many parts of the world, especially those characterized by two seasons—a "wet season" and a "dry season"—people need a much narrower range of clothing. In Canada, however, with its four seasons, and with all seasons dominated by just one—namely winter—a broad range of clothing types and styles is required.

This becomes apparent as soon as one enters any Canadian household. No sooner are you inside the front door than you encounter a closet full of jackets, windbreakers, galoshes, boots, gloves, mittens, scarves, top coats, rain coats, hats, umbrellas, toques, caps, and so forth. And this is not all. Look in any bedroom and the same pattern repeats itself —closets and chests of drawers full of many different types of short- and long-sleeved shirts, light and heavy sweaters, summer pants, winter pants, blouses, shorts, long and short underwear, shoes, and so on. For most Canadians, this is merely the price that has to be paid for living in a northern country with wide seasonal variations—a country and climate where often it's impossible to know what type of clothing will be required later the same day, let alone the next day.

The fact that clothing styles in Canada tend to follow those popular in Europe and the United States means that Canadians have made fewer creative contributions in this area over the last century or so. However, examples of creativity and invention can still be found. It may come as a surprise to many Canadians to know that it was a Canadian—Moses (Moe) Nadler, founder and major owner of the Canadian Lady Corset Company—who is often credited with playing a key role in creating the Wonderbra in 1939 (Louise Poirier actually produced the first Wonderbra in 1964, despite the fact that the name was trademarked in the United States as early as 1935). And while it's not really clothing, it was a Canadian, Olivia Poole, who invented the Jolly Jumper baby swing in 1959. (She was part Ojibway, and the invention was inspired by her memory of seeing Indigenous mothers working in the fields suspend their babies in papooses from trees, occasionally rocking them to soothe them.)

However, the country's greatest claim to creative fame in clothing is likely the zipper, which was created by Gideon Sundback. Sundback was born in Sweden and worked at the Westinghouse Electric plant in Pittsburgh before coming to Canada to become president of the Lightning Fastener Company in St. Catharines, Ontario. Although he remained an American all his life, most of his work on the "hookless fastener"—the first version of the zipper without any design flaws that was developed between 1912 and 1914 and renamed the "zipper" by the B. F. Goodrich Company in 1923—was undertaken in Canada. Sundback's claim to be the inventor of the zipper and his 1917 Canadian patent for it were later challenged in court, but the Privy Council upheld his claim and he is now generally acknowledged as the person who invented the zipper.

To this should be added a number of creative contributions Canadians have made to fashion. The impetus for this came in 1967, when Fashion Canada was created, and in 1974, when the Fashion Designers Association of Canada was founded. Included among the original members of this latter organization were such well-known designers and creative talents as Leo Chevalier, John Warden, Michel Robichaud, and Hugh Garber of Montreal, and Alfred Sung, Ellen Henderson, Claire Haddad, and Pat McDonaugh of Toronto.

Peter Nygård and Joe Mimran should also be added to this list. Nygård was the son of Finnish immigrants who settled in Deloraine, Manitoba. It was there that Peter founded Nygård International, a major player in the world fashion industry and for many years a pioneer in women's clothing throughout the world. Like Nygård, Mimran was an immigrant whose parents came to Canada from Morocco when he was just four years old. They settled in Toronto and immediately got involved in the fashion and garment business. Joe and his brother Saul eventually created Club Monaco—a cross-border retail powerhouse later purchased by Ralph Lauren Co.—and more recently, in conjunction with Loblaws, the Joe Fresh line. However, despite industry leadership, it hasn't all been smooth sailing for Mimran; the company was one of those singled out when the Bangledeshi factory that produces some Joe Fresh merchandise collapsed in 2013, killing more than a thousand people.

Like Joe Mimran and Peter Nygård, Thomas John Bata came to Canada from another part of the world but ended up making a highly creative contribution to the production and manufacture of clothing in Canada. In his case, it was shoes. Son of Thomas Bata, in 1894 the founder of the world's largest shoe manufacturing company, which was located in Zlin, a city now part of the Czech Republic, Thomas John Bata brought the company to Canada, where he established a whole shoe-making industry and indeed an entire town—Batawa, Ontario—that played a major role in the manufacture of shoes. At its peak, the company had factories, stores, and retail outlets in more than 90 countries, employed more than 85,000 people, and as "the world's largest shoemaker" sold more than a million pairs of shoes a day. And this is not all. Bata's wife Sonja created the world-famous Bata Shoe Museum in Toronto. It is the largest museum in the world devoted entirely to showcasing shoes from every part of the world and every period in history—some 10,000 in all.

But for many Canadians, Canada's most creative contribution to the field of clothing is that of Roots Canada. Spearheaded by Michael Budman and Don Green, who claim to have come up with the idea when they were sitting around a campfire in Algonquin Park, Roots Canada is known throughout the world for its imaginative designs, comfortable clothing, and Olympic sportswear. It has created its reputation by capitalizing on such well-known Canadian symbols as the beaver and the maple leaf, popular Canadian recreational activities like camping, and such traditional clothing staples as the toque, the parka, and the cape.

Another highly creative company that has taken advantage of Canadian symbols—and the long Canadian winter—is Canada Goose. Its origins can be traced back to Sam Tick, a Polish immigrant who came to Canada and created Metro Sportswear in the mid-1950s when he was unable to find employment in his original field as a manufacturer of dentures. While he started by making woollen garments and snowmobile suits for Canada's long winters, his family switched to making jackets and parkas in the 1970s. Since that time, the company has grown steadily. Growth accelerated when Sam's grandson took over the marketing and management of the company, to the point where each year it now produces and sells more than half-a-million exclusive down-filled, very fashionable jackets bearing its distinctive red-blue-and-white insignias in more than fifty countries. Although it has been criticized by some for inhumane treatment of animals in recent years, and the majority stake in the company was sold to a U.S. private equity firm in 2013, Canada Goose still plans to continue manufacturing all its products in Canada.

When most people think of clothes, clothing, and fashion, they don't think of perfume. Here as well, however, Canadians have made some creative contributions. This is particularly true of Steven Michel Bailey, who was born in Quebec in 1964 to bilingual parents and changed his name to Michel Germain when he created a perfume that has been competitive with the likes of Calvin Klein, Oscar de la Renta, Yves St. Laurent, and Elizabeth Arden. The perfume is called *séxŭal*, and Germain invented it and began manufacturing it commercially in 1994, following an intensive research in Canada, the United States, and France. Inspired by Germain's wife Norma, the perfume is a blend of exotic florals as well as cinnamon, myrrh, sandalwood, and vanilla, and now ranks among the top perfumes in the world.

And this brings us, via a rather circuitous route, to the final element in our triumvirate of basic requirements for survival, namely shelter. It is only in the last half-century that Canadians have begun to demonstrate some creative achievements in this domain following the long period of colonialism.

As people flocked to towns and cities looking for work, new types of accommodation, architectural design, and housing began to appear in Canada. Apartments and prefabricated homes were popular during the Second World War because they were less expensive, as were bungalows and Victory homes. It was around this time that the federal government became actively involved in the housing business because of the shortage of affordable homes. In 1935, it passed the Dominion Housing Act, and then, in 1946, it created the Central Mortgage and Housing Corporation, forerunner of the Canada Mortgage and Housing Corporation. Both these initiatives were designed to provide low-cost housing for those who needed it, as well as financial assistance to homeowners and regulation of the housing market and industry in general.

After World War II, architectural styles and influences from the United States and other parts of the world began to predominate. Like many other countries in the world, Canada was "going modern." By the middle of the twentieth century, the modernist architectural style of the skyscraper era began to assert itself, although this era did not become prominent in Canada until the construction between 1964 and 1968 of the Toronto-Dominion Centre, designed by the world-famous Bauhaus architect, Mies van der Rohe, in conjunction with his Canadian partner, John Parkin.

While Canadian architects distinguished themselves throughout the long colonial period, Expo and the centennial celebrations in 1967 allowed them a world stage on which to display their creativity. Many Canadian architects and architectural firms received important commissions to design buildings for the Expo site as well as elsewhere in the country. The architectural firm of Affleck, Desbarats, Dimakopoulos, Lebensold, and Sise, for instance, designed a number of major theme pavilions for Expo, as well as the Place Bonaventure Hotel in Montreal and the National Arts Centre in Ottawa. Arthur Erickson, one of the country's most distinguished architects and the principal architect of Simon Fraser University in British Columbia, the Canadian Embassy in Washington, and the Tacoma Glass Museum in Washington State, also designed a number of superb exhibition facilities for Expo. Nevertheless, the most notable architectural edifice created for Expo was *Habitat*. It was designed by Moshe Safdie, and was built in component parts and multi-layers ideally suited for the Expo site.

These opportunities helped immeasurably in providing the impetus required for the emergence of a number of highly creative Canadian architects, including Raymond Moriyama and Ted Teshima, who designed the Ontario Science Centre and the new Metro Reference Library in Toronto; Ron Thom, who designed Trent University in Peterborough and Massey College in Toronto, albeit with decidedly West Coast themes; Frank Gehry, who designed the Guggenheim Museum in Bilbao, Spain, and made major architectural changes to the Art Gallery of Ontario and the Ontario College of Art and Design; and Carlos Ott and Jack Diamond, who designed new opera houses for Paris and Toronto respectively—to name but a few.

But it may be that Canada's most distinctive creative contribution to architecture, shelter, and the "built environment" is not buildings as such, but rather indoor malls, shopping centres, and underground pedestrian walkways. Such environments make a great deal of sense in Canada, since Canadians must spend a considerable amount of time indoors during the winter months. It was in 1961 that Canada's first fully enclosed indoor shopping centre—Wellington Square in downtown London, Ontario—opened its doors for business. Developments in this area have since escalated rapidly. Eberhardt Zeidler and his firm designed the iconic Eaton Centre in Toronto; in addition, there is the world-famous West Edmonton Mall in Edmonton, Plus 15 in Calgary, Place Ville Marie in Montreal, and many other indoor malls and shopping centres across the country. But the most striking achievement of all may be the extensive underground pedestrian walkways in Toronto and Montreal. Business people and shoppers are able to walk, talk, and shop for hours along the countless kilometres of underground walkways that honeycomb the centres of these cities. In Toronto, for instance, the city's so-called PATH system of subterranean walkways—the "city beneath the city" as some refer to it—is expected to total some sixty kilometres when it is completed, and will stretch all the way from Lake Ontario to College Street.

Surely one of the greatest things about architecture in Canada is that it is still possible to see most of the different architectural styles and types that have characterized the country over the centuries—churches, cathedrals, government buildings, squares, farm houses, silos, barns, grain elevators, log cabins, and the like—as one travels across the country. This is true both for styles indigenous to Canada, as well as those imported from other countries and parts of the world.

If there is one place where many of these styles and types converge and can be seen in close physical proximity, surely it is Ottawa. Standing cheek-by-jowl in the very centre of the city are the Parliament Buildings and the Château Laurier Hotel, so representative of English and French influences on architecture during the colonial era. Standing slightly to one side of the Parliament Buildings and the Château Laurier are the National Gallery of Canada—built almost entirely of glass, much like Buckminster Fuller's geodesic dome at Expo 67 but with a totally different design and purpose—and the American Embassy. These buildings are reminders of the more recent American influence on housing and architectural styles in Canada, as well as the strong relationship that exists between Canada and the United States. Standing kitty corner across the street from the Château

Laurier is the Rideau Centre. An enclosed mall with several hundred shops and numerous restaurants, it is symbolic of something much more fundamental in Canada, namely the need to provide protection from the cold, wind, ice, and snow.

And the symbolism does not end here. One doesn't have to travel far "off the Hill" to see housing and architectural styles on the streets and neighbourhoods of Ottawa and vicinity that are representative of those found in other parts of the country and earlier periods of Canadian history. Moreover, across the Ottawa River in Gatineau, Quebec, stands the Canadian Museum of History, formerly the Canadian Museum of Civilization. Designed by Douglas Cardinal of Indigenous and Métis descent and one of the country's most distinguished architects, it is constructed in curvilinear fashion using indigenous materials and domestic rather than foreign themes and sources of inspiration. It serves as a reminder of the quest in Canada to establish a style of architecture that is distinctively Canadian—from the construction of homes and public buildings to the creation of malls, shopping centres, subterranean walkways, and other facilities suitable for a northern climate, geography, and culture. It is a style increasingly familiar to Canadians as a result of the work of organizations like Heritage Canada, which has done much to stimulate interest in architectural achievements on "main street Canada" and the country's smaller towns and cities; the Society for the Study of Architecture in Canada; and especially the Canadian Centre for Architecture, which is doing so much to generate interest in Canada's own architects and architectural achievements.

This completes our portrait of creativity as it relates to food, clothing, and shelter in Canada. While this portrait reveals that it was the Indigenous peoples who were most creative in coming to grips with the basics of survival—largely because they had to rely on their own ingenuity in an unknown land without help from the outside world—it also demonstrates that later generations of Canadians have manifested a considerable amount of creativity in this area as well.

It has also revealed something else. Canadians derive a great deal of their identity and "sense of place" from the quest to come to grips with the most elementary needs for survival. In the process of scouring the country looking for the wherewithal needed to provide food, create clothing, and build homes and other dwellings capable of sealing in the warmth and keeping out the cold, Canadians have over the centuries been compelled to work out a very specific and highly creative accommodation with the natural environment, the climate, and "the land."

Canadian Creations and Creators

Building a canoe, October 1872, Lake of the Woods, Ontario
(Chapter Two)

ABOVE: Building an igloo, 1934.
RIGHT: Eetooloopak working on a soapstone carving in an igloo, 1956
(Chapter Two)

Construction of Canada Dry plant in St. Laurent, Quebec, May 1946
(Chapter Two)

Artist's conception of Avro Arrow jet fighter (Chapter Three)

Canadarm used during Space Shuttle Discovery mission to deploy satellite, September 1993 (Chapter Three)

ABOVE: Early version of BlackBerry (Chapter Three)

RIGHT: Oil field near Oil Springs, Ontario, 1923 (Chapter Four)

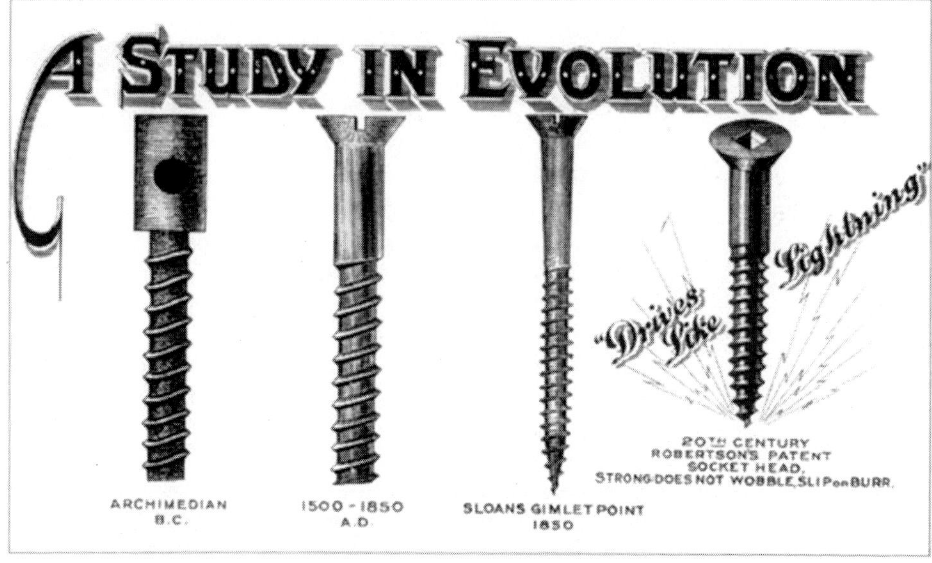

ABOVE: Promotional materials for the Robertson screw (Chapter Four)
BELOW LEFT: Inventor Hugh Le Caine, 1962 (Chapter Four)
BELOW RIGHT: One of Le Caine's music synthesizers, the "Sackbut" (Chapter Four)

Expo 67 (Chapter Seven)

Self-propelled combine harvester in a wheat field, about 40 miles north of Swift Current, Sask., in September 1952
(Chapter Four)

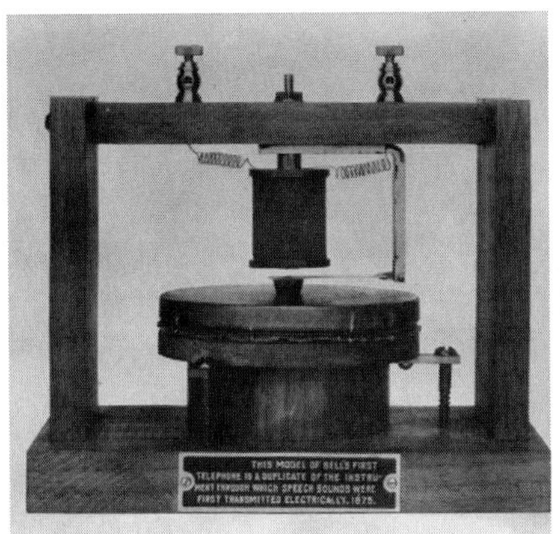

ABOVE: Model of Bell's first telephone (Chapter Three)
RIGHT: Dr. and Mrs. Alexander Graham Bell in their motorboat near Baddeck, N.S., in 1914
(Chapter Three)

Canadian Museum of Human Rights, Winnipeg (Chapter Five)

Jack Miner, naturalist, with a friend (Chapter Eight)

ABOVE: Grey Owl, naturalist (Chapter Eight)

LEFT AND BELOW: Stratford Festival, 1953: erecting tent, early play, artistic director Tyrone Guthrie (Chapter Seven)

Dawson Curling Club's championship game, April 1901
(Chapter Eight)

Five-pin bowling a uniquely Canadian game (Chapter Eight)

ABOVE: Team Canada at opening ceremonies of the 2010 Winter Olympics in Vancouver, B.C. (Chapter Eight)

BELOW LEFT: Jacques Plante, who developed and wore pioneering versions of the goalie's mask in the NHL (Chapter Eight)

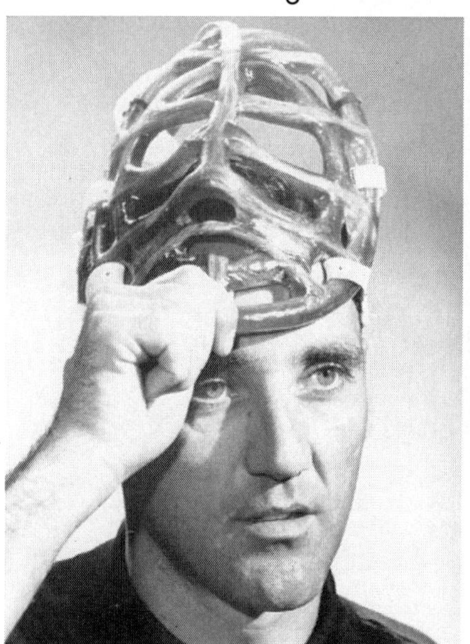

ABOVE: Women's hockey star Marie-Philip Poulin, who scored the winning goal in the championship game at the 2014 Winter Olympics (Chapter Eight)

CHAPTER THREE

Transportation and Communications

Transportation and communications are vital to any country's existence. Just as people must have food to eat, clothing to wear, and shelter to protect themselves against the elements, so, too, must they be bound together in space and time if they are to function as something more than a scattering of isolated individuals. But transportation and communications have special significance for a country like Canada, one that is colossal in size and confronts its people with many difficult spatial and temporal challenges to overcome. That's why over the centuries enormous creativity has gone into building Canada's transportation and communications systems. That the country and its citizenry have been more than equal to the challenge is affirmed by a few interesting facts and figures:

- Canada has the longest national highway in the world—the Trans-Canada Highway, which is 7,821 kilometres in length.
- Canada has the longest street in the world—Yonge Street, which runs 1,896 kilometres from the Lake Ontario shoreline in Toronto to the town of Rainy River, at the Ontario-Minnesota border.
- For many years, Canada boasted the tallest free-standing structure in the world—the CN Tower, which is 553 metres high.
- The longest recreational trail in the world, the Trans-Canada Trail, already stretches more than 15,000 kilometres and will be no less than 23,000 kilometres long when completed.
- Appropriately for a northern nation, Canada also has the longest and largest outdoor skating rinks in the world. According to the *Guinness Book of World Records*, Winnipeg boasts the longest outdoor skating rink, extending 9.3 kilometres along the Red and Assiniboine rivers.

However, a section of the Rideau Canal in Ottawa, although "only" 7.8 kilometres in length, is the largest skating rink in the world by area.

Canada has also produced some of the most creative and famous communications scholars in the world, including Marshall McLuhan, Northrop Frye, and Harold Innis. Marshall McLuhan set the world ablaze with his theories of "hot" and "cold" media and his famous catchphrase "the medium is the message"; Northrop Frye spent much of his life unraveling the mysteries of the Bible, one of the world's greatest books, as well as writing about the importance of creativity and the imagination in Canadian culture; and Harold Innis developed a comprehensive theory of human development grounded in patterns of communications and transportation. Only someone familiar with Canada's innumerable transportation, communications, and spatial challenges could likely have devised such a theory.

Nor is this all. Canadians probably own more transportation and communications devices, equipment, and vehicles per person—trucks, vans, cars, snowmobiles, skidoos, canoes, rowboats, sailboats, radios, telephones, mobile phones, BlackBerries, television sets, printers, computers, iPads, iPhones, tablets, and so forth—than any other people in the world. They are also among the world's most frequent computer users, with almost 90 percent of Canadians connected to the Internet in 2013. Surveys suggest on average Canadians spend 17 hours a week online. Canadians are also among the world's most frequent senders of text messages, and are leading users of Facebook, Twitter, and other social media. It is facts like these that caused Bruce Powe, one of the country's most respected contemporary communications scholars, to contend that Canada is first and foremost a "communications culture," as well as the world's first "wired nation."

Indigenous creativity revisited

As with food, clothing, and shelter, Canadian creativity in transportation and communications can be traced back to the Indigenous peoples. While there is uncertainty about when such transportation devices as the kayak, the umiak, and the canoe were first invented, there is no debate over the fact that First Nations peoples made many highly creative contributions in the realm of transportation.

Take the kayak, for instance. This highly ingenious device was ideally suited to Canada's northern geography, cold climate, and rugged landscape. Most often made of whalebone or driftwood with a flat bottom covered with sealskins, it had just enough room for a single passenger wielding a double paddle, usually a hunter. The kayak was light in weight, and highly portable. The kayak's much bigger "cousin," the umiak, was open rather than closed, and capable of carrying heavy loads and up to 15 or 20 people.

However, it is the canoe that was the most creative transportation vehicle developed in Canada prior to modern times. It was very light, resilient, waterproof, and easy to carry, making it possible for the Indigenous peoples to overcome a vast range of transportation barriers. This was especially true for the *birchbark canoe.* Its light weight facilitated portaging and carrying heavy loads over long distances. Small wonder it formed the basis of the Canadian economy for more than a century. As authorities at the Canadian Canoe Museum in Peterborough point out, the canoe is a Canadian icon and Canada exists primarily as a result of the canoe. It helped determine national boundaries and carried Canadian sovereignty to the northern half of North America.

If the Indigenous peoples were clever at creating devices that made transportation over long distances possible, they were equally clever at creating all the accompanying accoutrements.

Snowshoes were indispensable. They were made of a strip of wood bent in half so that it could be rounded at one end and drawn to a point at the other. The wooden frames were woven with deer gut or some other sturdy material, and then strapped on to the bottom of one's feet. While archaeologists and anthropologists still argue about the origins of snowshoes, there is no doubt about their usefulness. In the far north, *sun goggles* were also popular. These were ingenious devices made of whalebone, ivory, or wood, with tiny slits cut in them to protect the eyes from the harmful ultraviolet rays of the sun. They were quite possibly the early forerunners of today's sunglasses.

Inuit hunters in the far north solved the problem of transporting heavy loads during the winter by inventing the *komatik.* It was a long, flat sledge with wood or bone crossbars that lay between two handlebars usually made of caribou antlers. To prevent themselves from slipping on the ice when pulling their komatiks and other heavy loads, the Inuit invented *ice creepers.* These were strips of bone or ivory that acted like treads attached to the bottom of their moccasins, giving them the traction they needed. Further south, toboggans made of tamarack or birch were used. They consisted of thin hardwood boards joined together by horizontal strips of wood. Eventually came the *cariole*, a large toboggan with enclosed sides and back and a covered top not unlike certain types of sleighs. It was the perfect vehicle for transporting fur and people, and was usually pulled by a team of dogs with the driver at the back, much like a dogsled. Interestingly, toboggans are still very popular throughout Canada today, but largely for recreation rather than transportation.

TRANSPORTATION BY WATER, RAIL, AIR, AND OVER SNOW

Like the Indigenous peoples, the country's first European explorers—from Champlain, la Vérendrye, Hearne, Radisson, and Groseilliers, to Thompson, Mackenzie, Fraser, and others—were very skilled at spanning space. They relied heavily on the country's major waterways. While much has been made of their desire to find a trade route to the Orient, they were also (and especially as time went on) driven by a desire to explore the vast territories and exquisite landscapes of the North American continent. It must have been impossible for explorers to resist the temptation to go farther than any European had gone before, especially as they were constantly being beckoned by what lay beyond the next lake, river, mountain, or forest.

Until the nineteenth century, waterways were the backbone of the Canadian transportation system—the mighty St. Lawrence River and the Great Lakes in the eastern and central parts of the country, and the Coppermine, Peace, Kootenay, and Columbia rivers, Great Slave Lake, Hudson Bay, and James Bay in the western and northern parts of the country. Capitalizing on the impetus and expertise provided by the greatest maritime nation of all—England—a significant amount of attention was devoted to linking up the lakes and rivers of Canada. A remarkable east-west water transportation axis had been created.

But this was not the only place where Canadians were making their mark. They were also doing so on the high seas.

A great deal of trade had developed between the "Old World" of Europe and the "New World" of the Americas, and this spurred new achievements in transportation. The first steamship in North America, for example, was built in eastern Canada. The *Accommodation* was built in 1809 by John Molson, who emigrated to Canada from England at the age of 19 and eventually wound up founding Molson's Brewery, making numerous trips up and down the St. Lawrence River, and through the launching of the *Accommodation*, drastically reducing the amount of time required to travel from Quebec City to Montreal.

And how's this for a creative idea? Ever heard of a "disposable boat"? A Canadian named McPherson came up with this inventive idea in 1824 after the British government imposed a timber tax on oak and squared pine that crippled the thriving timber trade between Britain and Lower Canada, depriving Lower Canada of its greatest source of wealth. McPherson's disposable boat was very much like a raft or a dragger made of squared timbers temporarily pegged together so that it could be sailed across the Atlantic Ocean and dismantled in Britain. Since there was no law against dismantling boats and using their timber for other purposes, this idea allowed Canadians to get around the new tax for several years before the British government got wise to the ploy.

The Atlantic region in general and Nova Scotia and New Brunswick in particular were hot beds of creativity at this time. Here were some of the best harbours in the world, especially Halifax. It is not surprising, then, that three of the country's most creative figures in transportation made their appearance in the Maritime Provinces: John Patch, one of the inventors of the screw propeller; Samuel Cunard, founder of Cunard Steamship Lines; and Robert Foulis, inventor of the fog horn.

John Patch was a resident of Yarmouth, Nova Scotia. He invented the screw propeller in 1833 and was experimenting in Yarmouth Harbour with many different types of screw propellers for powering boats a year later. Unfortunately, however, because Patch failed to register his invention, the first patent for a marine screw propeller was awarded to Francis Pettit-Smith, an Englishman, by the British government in 1836. This would not be the only time a Canadian was slow to act and was deprived of his or her claim to fame.

Patch was a fascinating individual. Son of a sea captain, his entire life was devoted to the sea, not only as a sailor and fisherman, but also as a shipwright. He experimented with many different designs for screw propellers, and finally developed one that was mounted on a 7.6-metre shaft secured beneath the water line at the stern of the boat, with a connecting windlass crank on deck which could be used to operate the gears. He was encouraged by his friend, Captain Silas Kelley, to apply for a patent in the United States, and Kelley even paid for Patch's travel costs to the U.S. But Patch was a poor businessman and was talked out of registering his patent by officials in Washington, thus opening the doors for Francis Pettit-Smith. The significance of Patch's work should not, however, be underestimated. It was one of the most significant technological breakthroughs of the time because it heralded the end of the age of sail and the beginning of modern ocean navigation. Interestingly, the screw propeller was eventually adapted for use in power turbines and propeller-driven aircraft, expanding its importance still further.

The Maritimes also produced the era's greatest shipping magnate: Samuel Cunard, who was born in Halifax in 1787. Capitalizing on a fortune amassed by his father through whaling, the timber trade, and the transportation of iron and coal, Samuel Cunard went on to found the largest steamship company in the world, capturing much of the overseas passenger and mail service between North America and Europe. He was also a major shareholder in the *Royal William,* the first vessel to cross the Atlantic Ocean by steam power in 1833 and constructed entirely in Canada. By the latter part of the nineteenth century, Cunard ocean liners had become famous throughout the world for their speed, comfort, luxury, and outstanding passenger service. The Cunard line eventually built some of the greatest ocean liners of the twentieth century, including the *Queen Mary*, the *Queen Elizabeth*, the *Queen Elizabeth 2*, and, more recently, the *Queen Mary 2*.

Robert Foulis rounds out this triumvirate of East Coast creative geniuses. Born in Glasgow, Scotland in 1796, he came to Canada in 1818 and settled in Saint John, New Brunswick. With a background in civil engineering and mechanics, he presented his design for a steam fog horn whistle to the Lighthouse Commissioners of New Brunswick in 1853. The first steam-powered fog horn in the world was installed at Partridge Island, New Brunswick in 1859. Foulis's invention did a great deal to improve maritime safety, since the fog horn emitted blasts of sound that could be heard for miles, warning vessels of impending danger. As one sea captain put it, "The man who invented that fog whistle should get to heaven if anyone does."

I mentioned earlier how in the nineteenth century numerous canals were built across Canada, tying important waterways together. The Lachine Canal, for example, was constructed between 1821 and 1825, making it possible to bypass the rapids of the St. Lawrence River upstream from Montreal; this was the first real canal built in Canada. Others followed in rapid succession, including the three Ottawa River canals and, in particular, the Rideau Canal. This latter canal is deemed one of the greatest early engineering feats in North America. Constructed in an incredibly short period of time between 1827 and 1832, largely to provide an alternative military route between Kingston and Montreal, it was overseen by Lt. Col John By, founder of Ottawa, and was 202 kilometres in length. It incorporated 47 locks to control water levels on the Rideau and Cataraqui rivers, and was driven through untamed wilderness and virgin forests at great expense to workers building it. It still functions today, and is enjoyed by countless boaters, canal enthusiasts, and tourists, especially at places like Merrickville, located 60 kilometres southwest of Ottawa and known as "the jewel of the Rideau."

Like the Rideau Canal, the Welland Canal was completed in the 1830s, making it possible to lift vessels over 100 metres from Lake Ontario to Lake Erie. The Welland Canal has been rebuilt several times since then to accommodate ever larger ships. Construction of the Trent Canal system also commenced in the 1830s. It followed a number of old Indigenous trails through the Kawartha lakes, and included the lift locks near Peterborough, the highest in the world from 1904 when they were constructed until quite recently.

Successes like these eventually led to the construction of the St. Lawrence Seaway, considered by many to be one of the greatest such developments in the world. The culmination of a series of events that began with the construction of the Lachine Canal and included the establishment of the International Joint Commission in 1909 and the building of the Seaway itself between 1951 and 1959, the St. Lawrence Seaway stands out as one of the largest and most daring engineering feats in the world. It is also one of the most ambitious ventures ever undertaken jointly by two countries, in this case, of course, Canada and the United States. While changing trade patterns have lessened the importance of the Seaway in recent years, this impressive 3,770-kilometre system still carries vast amounts of freight between the heartland of North America and the rest of the world.

With achievements like these, it should come as no surprise that Canadians have chalked up many creative successes in boat building, speed racing, and sailing over the years. The McKay brothers of Nova Scotia, for example, built some of the fastest clipper ships in the world, and Alexander Graham Bell and his colleague F. W. "Casey" Baldwin created one of the first hydrofoil boats in the world in 1908. Bell achieved another major marine milestone in 1919 when his HD-4 became the fastest boat in the world at that time, after reaching a speed of 70.86 miles per hour. Moreover, in 1921, 1922, and 1923, and again in 1931 and 1938, the famous schooner the *Bluenose* won the International Fisherman's Trophy, emblematic of sailing supremacy among fishing vessels on the North Atlantic. The success of the *Bluenose* led to the construction of the

Bluenose II, its replica, which was built at the Smith and Rhuland shipyards in Lunenburg, Nova Scotia in 1963 and continues to sail the high seas today.

As important as these creative achievements were for a country bounded on three sides by water and blessed with thousands of lakes and rivers, water transportation was not the only area where Canadians made their mark. When the focus of attention shifted from water to rail transportation in the middle and latter nineteenth century, Canadians were once again in the forefront.

Canada was ideally positioned to take advantage of the transition to rail. It was able to import a great deal of rail technology from Britain, as well as the expertise and people needed to apply this technology and make it operational. As a result, Canada shifted rather easily and quickly from the construction of canals and boats to the construction of railroads and trains. This shift made a great deal of sense for a country whose waterways were frozen over for much of the year and where an inadequate system of roads as yet existed. In consequence, many regional railroads were created in the eastern and central parts of the country during the middle decades of the nineteenth century, including the Champlain and St. Lawrence Railroad—the country's first railroad, which was opened in 1836—the St. Lawrence and Atlantic Railroad, the Grand Trunk Railroad, and several others.

Many creative successes in the railroad industry followed in the decades to come. As noted earlier, the sleeper car was invented by Samuel Sharp in 1857, the air-conditioned coach by Henry Ruttan in 1858, the locomotive braking system by W. A. Robinson in 1868, and the railway car brake by George B. Dorey in 1913. In 1869, a Toronto dentist named J. E. Elliott created the "rotary snowplough," which when refined by others did a great deal to facilitate transportation by rail during the winter months, especially through the Canadian Rockies and other mountainous areas. These achievements made it apparent that Canadians were not just "quick studies" when it came to adapting and applying rail technology from other parts of the world; they were also capable of manifesting a great deal of creativity in this area in their own right.

However, it was the construction of the Canadian Pacific Railway that is generally regarded as Canada's most creative achievement of the railroad era. The CPR was completed in 1885 and immortalized in Pierre Berton's two books, *The National Dream* and *The Last Spike*, which are concerned with the difficulties involved in creating a colossal "ribbon of steel" across the immensity of Canada. What was particularly creative about the CPR was not so much the construction of the railroad itself—railroad technology had been in existence for some time—but, rather, the ingenuity, determination, and courage that were needed to plan this incredible project and then drive it through some of the most difficult terrain in the world.

The impetus for creating the CPR was provided by the desire to thwart American expansion west and north of the Great Lakes, strengthen Canada as a country following its establishment through the passage of the British North America Act in 1867, and fulfill a promise made by the Canadian government to British Columbia. Built largely with British, Canadian, and American capital and expertise and Chinese immigrant labour, the CPR stands out as one of the greatest engineering and organizational feats in transportation history. By the time Donald Alexander Smith hammered in the last spike at Craigellachie in Eagle Pass, British Columbia in 1885, Canada had an east-west rail transportation axis that rivaled and complemented its already established water transportation axis.

It was at about this time that another Canadian, John Joseph Wright, created the first practical "street railroad." Born in Yarmouth, England in 1848, "J. J."—as he was called in Canada—came to Toronto and worked at the Toronto *Globe* for a time as a proofreader. He then moved to Philadelphia, where he developed a coal-fuel electric generator for that city that eventually became the standard power source for street lights in a number of North American cities. Returning to Toronto, he established Canada's first commercial power generating station, providing power to multiple customers and helping to pave the way for the growth of the electrical power industry.

He created the first practical street railroad or "electric streetcar" in collaboration with a fellow innovator named Vanderpol. In 1883, the two devised a system of poles and overhead wires that made trolley systems powered by underground rails obsolete. (Such systems were prone to short circuits during rain and snow storms.) The new system, which was showcased at the Canadian National Exhibition in Toronto in 1884, was adopted by Windsor, Ontario in 1886, St. Catharines in 1887, Toronto in 1889, and was quickly embraced by many other cities.

By the early twentieth century, pressure was building in Canada to establish another transcontinental rail line, largely because of the expansion of agriculture and industry throughout Canada and the flood of immigrants into the West. While the CPR was built mainly from scratch, this new line—later to be known as the Canadian National Railways, or CNR—was cobbled together through amalgamations of a number of existing private rail lines (many of them insolvent), such as the Grand Trunk, the Grand Trunk Pacific, the Intercolonial, the Canadian Northern, and the National Transcontinental, as well as construction of new track where required. Unlike the CPR, which followed the southern and more difficult route through the Rocky Mountains at Kicking Horse Pass, the CNR's transcontinental line followed the northern and easier route through Yellowhead Pass. The line was eventually completed, but not without a great deal of scandal, controversy, and claims of financial, political, and administrative mismanagement.

Just as transportation by water gave way to transportation by rail, so transportation by rail gave way to transportation by air. This began to happen early in the twentieth century, and once again, Canada and Canadians were in the forefront of international developments.

In 1909, J. A. Douglas McCurdy piloted the first powered flight in the British Empire, when he flew the *Silver Dart* at Baddeck in Cape Breton. He worked closely on this initiative with Alexander Graham Bell and Bell's wife Mabel, who was also very involved in the early stages of aviation through the creation of her Aerial Experiment Association at Baddeck, where the Bells had their summer residence and research facilities. McCurdy was also the first person in the world to fly an airplane out of sight of land, in this case off the coast of Florida. Interestingly, Canadians were back in the news in this area a century later when Todd Reichert flew a human-powered ornithopter called the *Snowbird*—an aircraft with bird-like wings—over 145 metres.

But the most important creative contribution by a Canadian to air transportation was undoubtedly the invention of the variable pitch propeller by Wallace R. Turnbull. The invention dates from around 1916, but wasn't patented until 1922 and successfully tested at the Camp Borden air base until 1927. Just as the invention of the screw propeller by John Patch transformed water transportation, so the invention of the variable pitch propeller by Turnbull transformed air transportation. By changing the angle or pitch of the propeller blades, the variable pitch propeller made it possible for aircraft to achieve maximum efficiency at all speeds. Turnbull's device, which was controlled by a small electric motor, enabled airplanes to take off more easily, climb higher and faster, and improve their fuel efficiency. It also made it possible for airplanes to carry economically viable payloads and a sufficient number of passengers to make commercial aviation feasible.

Turnbull was a fascinating person. Born in Rothesay, New Brunswick in 1870, he graduated from Cornell University in Ithaca, New York in engineering and did post-graduate work in Berlin and Heidelberg. Like many of Canada's creative geniuses, he worked in other parts of the world during important stages of his career, most notably in England during World War I, where in 1916 he developed the first working model for the variable pitch propeller, as well as in Harrison, New Jersey, where he worked in Thomas Edison's lamp factory. But the bulk of his life was spent working in a barn adjacent to his property in Rothesay on his twin passions: propulsion and aerodynamics. He built Canada's first wind tunnel in his workshop, and delved deeply into bomb sights, torpedo screens, hydroplanes, and, toward the end of his life, a project to harness the power of the tides of the Bay of Fundy. Despite being so busy with his research, he found time to play an excellent game of tennis, and won the mixed doubles championship with a partner in the all-Canadian final in 1910.

In light of creative contributions like Turnbull's, it is not surprising that Canadians created the first commercial jetliner in North America—and the second in the world by less than two weeks—in 1949. It was the C-102 or Avro Jetliner, designed by Dr. James Floyd and his team. Canada also holds the record for building what was for a time the fastest airplane in the world. This was the Avro Arrow, or CF-105. It was developed (as the C-102 had been) by A. V. Roe Canada, but was cancelled by the Diefenbaker government in 1959 amid great controversy due to pressure from the United States.

The Arrow was by no means the beginning—or the end—of the story of Canadian creativity in the aviation industry. Canadians have made important contributions in many other ways, including the creation of the Norseman Bush Plane by Bob Noorduyn in 1935. This helped to facilitate exploration, discovery, and search-and-rescue operations in the Far North. Moreover, Canadians have been pioneers in the development of aircraft capable of taking off and landing on very short runways, or what are called "STOL" (short take-off and landing) aircraft. The first true STOL airplane, *The Beaver*, was built at DeHavilland Aircraft of Canada in 1948. It was followed by many other STOL aircraft, including the *Turbo-Beaver*, *Otter*, *Twin Otter*, *Caribou,* and *Buffalo*. A variety of small aircraft ideally suited for short-haul flights, including the *Dash-7* and *Dash-8*, were also designed and built at DeHavilland Aircraft in Toronto. These contributions to aviation in remote areas complement the many devices that Canadians have created to facilitate transportation on land over very rough terrain, including the *Giraffe*, a wheeled vehicle raised and lowered by hydraulic power, the *Ridgewater*, a remarkable device capable of carrying heavy loads over treacherous terrains, and the *Rat* and *Jiger*, vehicles that travel equally well over land, water, snow, muskeg, and swampland.

Although Canada has recorded many firsts in transportation, perhaps its most creative achievement in this area is the snowmobile, or "skidoo," a vehicle perfectly suited for a country that is blanketed with "the white stuff" for a significant part of the year.

The person who invented these innovative vehicles, Joseph-Armand Bombardier, was born in Valcourt, Quebec in 1907. He dreamed in his youth of creating vehicles that could glide over the snow. Needless to say, Canadians had been utilizing vehicles that could glide over snow for a very long time, but these were sleighs and toboggans. But Bombardier dreamt of something different: he dreamt of *motorized vehicles* that could travel over the snow. His dreams were no doubt inspired by the huge snowfalls and snowdrifts that Quebeckers experienced during the winter months—snowfalls and snowdrifts so deep and relentless that many roads were blocked or closed, cutting off communities for a significant part of the year.

Bombardier was committed to inventing a vehicle that could come to grips with this challenge. He got his wish in 1922 when, at the age of 15, he took the motor out of an old Ford car his father had given him, and attached it to the frame of a four-passenger sleigh. He then installed a huge wooden airplane propeller on the drive shaft and produced the first power-driven mechanical vehicle capable of travelling over the snow.

Quite coincidentally, it was about this same time that another Quebecker, Arthur Sicard, who was born in Saint-Leonard-de-Port-Maurice, Quebec in 1876, invented the snow blower. This was in 1925. His invention consisted of three parts: a four-wheel-drive truck chassis and truck motor; a "snow scooping" section; and a snow blower with two adjustable chutes and a separate motor. Using this contraption, a driver could throw snow over 90 feet, and it worked equally well with hard, soft, and packed snow. Like Bombardier's snowmobile, Sicard's snow blower played an important part in helping Canadians cope with winter.

But back to Bombardier. Like many inventors and creators, Bombardier spent the bulk of his life perfecting his first invention and creating others like it. In so doing, he set in motion a chain of events that had a profound effect on the country and the world. He was granted a patent for his snowmobile in 1937 and immediately posted a sign above his garage—*L'Auto-Neige Bombardier*—where he started manufacturing snowmobiles commercially. This venture proved very successful. During World War II, he built several other mechanized snow vehicles, including the *Kaki B-1* and the *Armoured Track*, which was dubbed "The Penguin" by the armed forces because of its ability to travel over the snow. Immediately after World War II, his famous B-12 snowmobile sold worldwide. Then, in 1953, he produced his famous *MUSKEG*, an all-purpose vehicle with wheels and tracks on each side that was very popular with the Royal Canadian Mounted Police.

In 1959, Bombardier created the *Ski-Doo*. (The original name was Ski-Dog, but a promotional brochure called it the Ski-Doo by mistake—and the name stuck. In fact, the term became so popular that, while "Ski-Doo" is a trade name for snowmobiles produced by Bombardier, the generic name "skidoo" soon came to be applied to all snowmobiles, including those made by other companies.)

The Ski-Doo took Canada and the world by storm. Not only did it sell well across the country, adding a whole new dimension to fun in the snow, but it also resulted in the creation of a whole new industry. The Ski-Doo sold equally well in other northern countries that experienced winter conditions similar to those in Canada, most notably Sweden, Denmark, Norway, Greenland, Iceland, and Russia. By the year 2000, more than two million skidoos were being sold every year throughout the world, and Bombardier's company became one of the globe's largest manufacturers of transportation equipment in general, and recreational transportation equipment in particular. In 2003, that division of the company that manufactured Ski-Doos and other recreational equipment was spun off from the parent company as a separate firm, Bombardier Recreational Products, or, as it is now called, BRP Inc. It is still headquartered in Valcourt, Quebec. Bombardier itself still plays a major role in the global transportation industry, through its manufacture of subway cars, airplanes, buses, and railway cars, particularly after it acquired several large rail equipment manufacturers in Germany and elsewhere.

BRIDGES, CAUSEWAYS, AND CARTOGRAPHY

Of course, more than just vehicles are needed to move goods and people across Canada. Given the country's vast numbers of lakes and rivers, it was also necessary to construct many bridges and causeways to link important land masses and transportation arteries.

Most of the early bridges in Canada were made of logs hewn from the country's forests. In 1828, Colonel John By incorporated a 60-metre wooden arch in the Union Bridge spanning the Ottawa River near the Chaudière Falls. This was the first such link between Upper and Lower Canada, hence the name. Several decades later, in 1860, the Victoria Bridge was constructed across the St. Lawrence River at Montreal as part of the Grand Trunk Railroad system from Montreal to Toronto. But surely one of the most inventive achievements of those early years was the creation of an "ice bridge" across the St. Lawrence River from Hochelega to Longueuil (Montreal) during the winter months in 1880–81 and again in 1881–82. It even carried a small, standard-gauge train from January to March.

Such feats provided the impetus for the construction of a number of other well-known bridges, including the Quebec bridge that was designed to carry the National Transcontinental Railway across the St. Lawrence. It was intended to be the longest steel cantilever bridge in the world when construction began in 1906. Unfortunately, it collapsed in 1907 with considerable loss of life, and had to be rebuilt in 1919. Ten years later, the Jacques Cartier bridge was constructed at Montreal.

Following this, a number of well-known suspension bridges were constructed in different parts of the country. Especially important in this regard were the Lions Gate Bridge linking Vancouver to the North Shore municipalities, which was completed in 1938 and at that time was the longest suspension bridge in the British Commonwealth; the Angus L. Macdonald suspension bridge connecting Halifax and Dartmouth, opened in 1955; and the Rainbow Bridge crossing the Niagara River at Niagara Falls. But the most inventive and quite possibly the greatest engineering feat of all was the completion in 1997 of the Confederation Bridge linking Prince Edward Island to mainland Canada. The longest bridge in the world across waters with a winter ice cover, this two-lane toll bridge on the Trans-Canada Highway spans a distance of some 13 kilometres. It rests on 62 piers, and crosses the Northumberland Strait from Borden-Carleton, P.E.I. to Cape Jourimain, New Brunswick. It is a perfect complement to another remarkable engineering feat, the Canso Causeway linking Cape Breton to mainland Nova Scotia, which incorporates a swing bridge and which was completed in 1955.

In addition to remarkable feats of transportation infrastructure, Canadians have also demonstrated a great deal of creativity in the related fields of mapmaking and cartography. The Indigenous peoples produced the first maps of what is now Canada, often in the form of various types of pictographs and petroglyphs that also provided information about vital aspects of cultural life as well as migrations from one part of the country to another. The European practice of mapmaking in North American dates back to Samuel de Champlain, who created the first detailed maps of eastern Canada and the northern United States in 1616, combining his talents and knowledge of this area with those of Henry Hudson, a fellow explorer and mapmaker who worked farther south. But the most effective mapmakers in the early years were the explorers Peter Pond and especially David Thompson. Pond mapped much of the north and the west of the country, and Thompson, an outstanding mapmaker and surveyor as well as a great explorer, created the country's first comprehensive map by mapping over 3.9 million square kilometres from Hudson Bay to the Pacific Ocean. Perhaps this is why the Indigenous peoples called him *Koo-koo-sint,* or "The Man Who Looks at Stars."

In the years to follow, others followed in Thompson's footsteps, making many original contributions to mapmaking and cartography. Samuel Holland, who was appointed Surveyor-General of Canada and travelled to Canada from Great Britain following the signing of the Treaty of Paris in 1763, is generally credited with setting the stage for Canadians to become world leaders in this field. *The Atlas of Canada* became only the second national atlas in the world to be published (Finland was first) when it was issued by the Department of the Interior in 1906. Canadians have made major contributions to undersea mapping, such as determining the depth of water and the nature of coastlines and shorelines. Sir Edward Sabine was involved in creating the first apparatus for detecting the changing magnetic fields of the earth in such far-flung locations as Madras, India, Melbourne, Australia, the island of St. Helena, and at home in Toronto; and numerous contributions were made to mapmaking by Sir William Logan, founder and first director of the geological surveys on which the country's mining industry has depended so heavily.

This leadership continued throughout the twentieth century. In 1945 Dr. Les Howlett of the National Research Council developed a camera calibrator that set the standard for cameras used in aerial photography. Others, such as J. M. (Monty) Bridgman, T. J. Blachut, Stanley Collins, Douglas N. Kendall, and Gilbert L. Hobrough, developed various techniques and devices used in mapping the lands, forests, and mines of Canada. But the greatest creative contribution in the twentieth century probably came from U. V. Helava. He set the mapmaking community on fire by creating the analytical plotter that made it possible to take photographs from orbiting satellites, and in doing so, maintained Canada's tradition as a world leader in cartography. Most recently, Robert Zlot, a Canadian working in close conjunction with researchers at Australia's Commonwealth Scientific and Industrial Research Organization (CSIRO) in Brisbane, created the *zebedee*. This is a hand-held scanning device that makes it possible for an operator to walk through various sites and environments, indoor and outdoor, and map them in three dimensions rather than two.

With so many "firsts"—others we haven't mentioned include the radar profile recorder, stereo-orthophotography mapping, and the Gestalt photo mapper—it is hardly surprising that more than 60 percent of mapmaking technology used throughout the world today is based on Canadian inventions. It is a remarkable achievement, especially given the relatively small size of the country's population.

COMMUNICATION BY CABLE, TELEGRAPH, TELEPHONE, AND NEWSPAPERS

Canada can also lay claim to many creative accomplishments in communications. Canadians have been at the cutting edge of this field over the last two centuries, from undersea cables to mobile phone technology. These breakthroughs, including those made in collaboration with people in other countries or by Canadians working elsewhere, had the effect of creating whole new industries or transforming old ones. As J. J. Brown pointed out many years ago in his book *The Inventors: Great Ideas in Canadian Enterprise*: "Wherever we pick up a phone, open a picture magazine, switch on the radio or send a telegram, we are in debt to a Canadian inventor. All these modern means of communications, each of which changed our world, would not have been possible without the inventive genius of men like Bell, Desbarats, Gisborne, Creed, Stevenson and Rogers."

As far back as 1852, Frederick N. Gisborne, who came to Canada from England, was responsible for laying the first undersea telegraph cable in North America, when a cable impervious to salt-water corrosion was successfully run from Cape Tormentine, New Brunswick to Carleton, Prince Edward Island. Later, in 1858, Gisborne and his co-workers participated in laying the first transoceanic cable, across the Atlantic Ocean from Trinity Bay in Newfoundland to Valentia in Ireland. On August 16, 1858, the first telegraph message was transmitted across the Atlantic; it read, "Europe and America are united by telegraph. Glory to God in the Highest, on earth peace, good will towards men." Canadians also played a major role in laying the first marine cable across the Pacific Ocean, from Vancouver to Brisbane, Australia, in 1902.

Of course, by this time the telephone had become a reality. It was the perfect device for Canada and Canadians because it provided voice communication over long distances at a time when most people still lived in rural areas and were separated by long distances from friends and family living in other parts of the country.

The telephone was invented by Alexander Graham Bell. While Canadians were quick to claim Bell as their own and the telephone as a Canadian invention, this was disputed by Americans, who pointed out that Bell had undertaken much of his research in the United States. The dispute was settled by Bell himself —ever the diplomat in the best Canadian sense— when he declared that the telephone was "conceived" in Brantford, Ontario, in 1874, and "born" in Boston, Massachusetts, in 1875. The first long-distance telephone call took place from Mount Pleasant, Ontario to Brantford on August 3, 1876, and this was followed by a much longer call from Brantford to Paris, Ontario, a week later on August 10. Interestingly, the latter call was carried out using power from a battery located in Toronto, some 70 miles away.

Driving advances in communications was the need to transmit ideas and information from one end of the country to the other. Some of the most important developments came in the newsprint and newspaper industries, yet another area where such Canadians as Georges-Édouard Desbarats and William Leggo were at the cutting edge. Desbarats was at the Queen's Printer in Ottawa for a time, but resigned to found the *Canadian Illustrated News* in 1869. It was the first periodical in the world to use halftone photographs rather than engravings, a technique Desbarats evolved in conjunction with William Leggo, his engraver. Capitalizing on this achievement, Desbarats and Leggo moved to New York in 1873, where they founded the *New York Daily Graphic*, the first daily newspaper in the world to use photographic illustrations.

These were not the only contributions Canadians made to the development of newspapers. Far from it! Towards the end of the nineteenth century, Frederick Creed of Mill Village, Nova Scotia dramatically speeded up the transmission of Morse Code through the invention of the "Morse

Keyboard Perforator." Creed went on to invent two other devices, a transmitter-translator and printer, that served as the basis for the Creed High Speed Automatic Printing Telegraph System. When fully operational, this system could transmit and print information in a fraction of the time required by other systems. It was used to transmit the contents of entire newspapers from London, England to major centres in Europe and other parts of the world.

In the 1920s, William Stephenson of Winnipeg created the wireless photo transmitter, which made it possible to transmit pictures by radio waves or over telephone lines. It was immediately snatched up by newspapers throughout the world, including the *Daily Mail* in London, England, which published the world's first "wirephoto." Incidentally, Stephenson went on to become a famous spy and played a masterful role in coordinating British, American, and Canadian intelligence during the Second World War. He did so in the usual unassuming Canadian way, as suggested by the very title of one of the books about him—*The Quiet Canadian*. Ian Fleming wrote the foreword to the book, and it has been suggested that Stephenson served as the prototype for Fleming's famous James Bond character. As it turns out, Fleming (as well as the first five directors of the CIA) was at the top secret "Camp X" established by Stephenson and others on Lake Ontario at the Whitby-Oshawa border to train American, British, and Canadian spies during World War II. Nothing remains of the camp today but a flag pole.

Two other Canadians who played enormously important roles in the world of newspapers were William Maxwell Aitkin, Lord Beaverbrook, and Roy Herbert Thomson, the first Baron Thomson of Fleet.

Aitken was born the son of a Presbyterian minister in Maple, Ontario in 1879, and made a huge fortune in stock trading and the cement industry. He moved to England before the First World War and began building a newspaper empire with the acquisition of the *Daily Express*, which he eventually made the most popular newspaper in the world, with a circulation of 3½ million copies. He played an active role in the British government during both the First and Second World Wars, and was also the author of several books, including *Canadians at Flanders* and *Politicians and the Press*. Later in life, Beaverbrook became a major benefactor of many institutions in New Brunswick and other parts of Canada, especially the University of New Brunswick and Fredericton's Beaverbrook Art Gallery, which has one of the finest collections of paintings in Canada today.

Like Lord Beaverbrook, Roy Herbert Thomson became a giant of the newspaper industry, though he got his start in radio. Son of a barber, he started radio station CFCH in North Bay in 1931, and from this modest beginning went on to acquire newspapers and radio stations throughout the world, as well as magazines and printing companies. His crowning achievement was the purchase of *The Scotsman* in Edinburgh and *The Times* and *Sunday Times* in London. Following in Thomson's footsteps were others who became prominent in England and elsewhere as newspaper magnates, including Conrad Black and, most notably, Thomson's own son Kenneth, who parlayed his father's newspaper business into one of the greatest communications empires in the world.

As important as newspapers were and remain—despite the fact that in recent years many of them have fallen on hard times—the twentieth century saw the advent of communication technologies capable of transmitting information in even faster and more efficient ways. Here again, Canadians were at the forefront of developments.

COMMUNICATION BY RADIO, FILM, SATELLITES, AND MOBILE TECHNOLOGY

A new way of communicating across the oceans was inaugurated in 1901, when at Signal Hill, Newfoundland, Guglielmo Marconi received the first transatlantic wireless signal, transmitted from Poldhu near Cornwall, England. It was at about the same time that Reginald Aubrey Fessenden, who some believe was one of Canada's most creative individuals, was involved in experiments that were designed to transmit voices and music over long distances.

Born in East Bolton, Quebec in 1866, Fessenden went to New York City in 1886 and eventually ended up working with Thomas Edison at his laboratory in West Orange, New Jersey. While he never received the credit he deserved for his numerous accomplishments, many contend his experiments played a key role in the development of radio and later television. In fact, radio broadcasting began with Fessenden on December 23, 1900. He was working at his research facility on Cobb Island in the Potomac River when he hooked up a microphone to Morse Code equipment in his laboratory and observed that it was snowing. What made this seemingly casual observation so significant was the fact that Fessenden's assistant in Arlington, Virginia was able to hear his words clearly, despite being many miles away. Experiments like these led to Fessenden's being described as the "father of radio."

It didn't take long for radio to take off. Another major Canadian contribution came when Edward Samuel (Ted) Rogers invented the world's first commercial alternating-current radio tube, which led to the development of the "batteryless radio" in 1925.

Historical precedents like these help to explain why Canadians have made many seminal contributions to communications since the time of Bell, Fessenden, and Rogers. They also help to explain why Canada has one of the largest public broadcasting systems in the world in the Canadian Broadcasting Corporation, and one of the oldest and most creative public film agencies in the world in the National Film Board.

Public broadcasting in Canada dates from 1932, when the Canadian Radio Broadcasting Commission (CRBC) was established following intense lobbying on the part of the Canadian Broadcasting League, the passage of the Radio Act of 1927, and the report of the Royal Commission on Radio Broadcasting—the Aird Commission—in 1929. The CRBC was reorganized as the Canadian Broadcasting Corporation (CBC) in 1936. Established by the federal government as a Crown corporation, the CBC was tasked with developing "a national broadcasting service for all Canadians in both official languages that would be primarily Canadian in content and character." The decision to create it was historic. For one thing, it indicated that the federal government intended to combat the penetration of American broadcasting into Canada by encouraging domestic activity rather than impeding foreign activity. In addition, it demonstrated a preference for dealing with complex administrative problems in the field of broadcasting and communications largely by creating autonomous agencies at arm's length from government and the political process, rather than through direct involvement and control. With few exceptions, this course of action has been followed by successive federal governments ever since.

No sooner was the CBC created than it assumed a prominent role in the life of the country. There were two fundamental reasons for this. The first was the need to connect the country from coast to coast in a purely physical sense. This necessitated the creation of a vast network of capital facilities from one end of the country to the other and into the Far North. Doing so was a highly creative achievement in its own right, given the colossal size of the country. The second was the need to create hundreds of programs of interest to Canadians, in order to provide the country and its citizenry with news and entertainment in both official languages. By responding effectively to these two challenges, the CBC acted as an incredible stimulus to Canadian creativity at a crucial time in Canada's development.

In drama, the CBC's *Stage* and *Wednesday Night* series, for which special stock companies of actors, writers, and directors had to be assembled, produced everything from specially commissioned Canadian plays to the works of Shakespeare, Molière, Ibsen, Tolstoy, Shaw, and others. These ambitious undertakings helped propel many Canadian artists toward eventual national and international prominence, including Lorne Greene, Christopher Plummer, Barry Morse, William Hutt, John Drainie, W. O. Mitchell, Mazo de la Roche, Robertson Davies, Len Peterson, Lister Sinclair, and many others. In music, many symphonic, choral, and chamber concerts were presented, as were numerous recitals, prom concerts, and programs like *Singing Stars of Tomorrow* that featured such well-known Canadian singers as Maureen Forrester, Jon Vickers, Lois Marshall, Giles Lamontagne, Mary Morrison, and Marie José Forgues. The CBC Orchestra and the CBC Opera Company (the forerunner of the Canadian Opera Company) were also established to perform musical works. Programs like *The Happy Gang*, *La Famille Plouffe*, *Opportunity Knocks*, *Canadian Theatre of the Air*, *Hockey Night in Canada*, and many others also attracted wide followings. Small wonder the CBC is recognized as an icon throughout the country, particularly among older generations of Canadians who are aware of the longstanding role it has played in the development of Canadian culture.

If the CBC was originally created to be "the ears of Canada," the National Film Board (NFB) was created to be "the eyes of Canada." At least this was the opinion of the Board's founding director, John Grierson, who contended that the NFB "will, through the national use of cinema, see Canada and see it whole." When the NFB was created in 1939 to provide Canadians with information about the Second World War and Canada's involvement in it, few would have predicted that it would go on to become one of the largest and most respected public film agencies in the world. With its mandate to "produce, distribute and promote the production and distribution of films designed to interpret Canada to Canadians and to other nations," the NFB would make many creative contributions to the war effort and the art of film-making, including *cinema verité*, documentaries, animation, multi-screen and split-screen viewing, and the training of thousands of French and English film-makers, directors, and technicians. Who would have guessed that in time millions of people around the world would watch NFB films every year? Indeed, by the end of the Second World War, the NFB was the largest documentary filmmaker in the world, with some 800 employees strategically located in offices in London, Washington, New York, Chicago, Mexico City, and Sydney, and more than 500 films to its credit.

Major Canadian accomplishments in communications are not limited to broadcasting and film, or to the CBC and the NFB. In 1965, Pierre Péladeau created Québecor, Inc. It was focused initially on newspaper publishing, with *Le Journal de Montréal* launched in 1964 and *Le Journal de Québec* in 1967, with community newspapers, magazines, books, and other printing endeavours being added to the mix. In 1987, Péladeau acquired the paper company Donohue, giving Quebecor a stake in virtually every stage of the print production process through a strategy known as "vertical integration." Already the largest commercial printer in Canada and the second-largest in North America, in 1999 Quebecor merged with World Color to create Québecor World Inc., the largest commercial printer in the world. At its peak, Québecor provided its clients with a vast array of communications devices, products, and services, ranging all the way from commercial printing, cable television, and Internet access to newspaper, magazine and book publishing, television broadcasting, Internet portals, and the distribution and retailing of CDs, videos, DVDs, and books. It maintained numerous plants throughout the world and operated in some 17 countries. While Québecor continues as a major player in Canada, the printing operation, Québecor World, encountered financial difficulties and in 2010 was taken over by Quad/Graphics of Wisconsin.

Canadians have also played a seminal role in the use of satellites and wireless technology. Players in this sector have included the federal government, RCA Canada, SPAR Aerospace Ltd., COM DEV Ltd., MacDonald, Dettwiler and Associates, and many others.

In 1962, Canada's first satellite, *Alouette*, was launched by NASA to study the ionosphere. In 1969, the federal government created Telesat Canada to operate the country's domestic commercial satellite system. Canada was, in fact, the first country to employ satellites for long-distance domestic (as opposed to intercontinental) communications, beginning when NASA launched the country's first geostationary domestic communications satellite, the *Anik A-1*, in 1972.

In the late 1970's, Telidon was developed by the federal government's Communications Research Centre Canada. This long-distance technology combined specific aspects of television, the telephone, and the computer, creating an entirely new medium of communications and information processing. Television provided the capacity to display letters and images on screens; the telephone contributed the capacity to communicate over long distances; and the computer provided the capacity to utilize, store, and retrieve information rapidly and inexpensively. Unfortunately, Telidon was not commercially successful, but it did point the way toward other innovations that we now take for granted in today's "wired world."

Mention must also be made here of the *Canadarm*, officially known as the Shuttle Remote Manipulator System, which made its debut in 1981. Used by astronauts aboard NASA's space shuttle to manipulate large objects in space, the *Canadarm* immediately gave Canada and Canadians an outstanding international reputation in robotics and space technology. With copper wiring for nerves, graphite fibre for bones, and electric motors for muscles, the *Canadarm* acts in very much the same way as the human arm, with two rotating joints at the "shoulder," one at the "elbow," and three at the "wrist." Built by a group of companies with SPAR Aerospace taking the lead, the *Canadarm* was used in numerous space shuttle missions. Though weighing less than 480 kilograms, it can move objects weighing as much as 266,000 kilograms in the microgravity of space. Although the space shuttle has been retired and the *Canadarm* along with it, a second *Canadarm* is now installed on the International Space Station.

The *Canadarm* is but one example of Canadian creativity in space technology. More recently, Canadians played a major role in using *lidar,* a three-dimensional mapping and surveying technology, to study the climates of other planets. Scientists from York University contributed to the Canadian-supplied meteorological station on NASA's Phoenix Mars Lander, which made important observations about the nature of the water cycle on Mars.

Then there is Chris Hadfield, and the highly creative contributions he has made to space exploration. Born in Sarnia, Ontario in 1959, Hadfield became interested in flying at a very early age, and decided he wanted to be an astronaut when he watched the Apollo 11 moon landing on television when he was just nine years old. After serving in the Canadian armed forces, including an exchange program with the U.S. Air Force, Hadfield was accepted into the Canadian Space Agency's astronaut program in 1992. After acquiring a great deal of experience—including walking in space and helping to install the *Canadarm 2* aboard the space station—he was appointed commander of the International Space Station as part of Expedition 35 in 2013. In this capacity, he was responsible for a crew of five astronauts and gained international prominence and a global following when he depicted what it is like to live (and sing!) in space. His humour, imagination, and vitality rekindled interest in space travel among millions of people around the world, especially young people.

Canada has also made remarkable contributions to the field of mobile communications technology. Most noteworthy was the creation in 1999 of the BlackBerry—for a time the most popular wireless device in the world—by Mike Lazaridis and Douglas Fregin, who had teamed up to create the firm Research in Motion (RIM), established in Waterloo in 1984. RIM grew exponentially, with sales of its BlackBerry smartphones running into the billions of dollars. The BlackBerry was viewed as being "as Canadian as maple syrup, the moose, and hockey," as one author put it. Unfortunately, RIM fell on hard times, due largely to stiff competition from companies like Apple and its own failure to deliver new products on time and keep its customers happy. However, the company (now, like the device itself, named BlackBerry) appears to be making something of a comeback.

Finally, it was a Canadian—James Gosling—who developed the Java programming language, which is now the standard language used in many computer systems around the world. Gosling did his work on Java while working at Sun Microsystems in the United States in 1994.

Canadians have embraced new wireless and computer technologies with enthusiasm. According to the Canadian Wireless Telecommunications Association, Canadians employ more than 17 million wireless devices and send nearly three million text messages a day.

SPANNING TIME AS ESSENTIAL AS SPANNING SPACE

If spanning space is of vital importance to the country and its citizenry, so is spanning time. For Canadians must be able to travel backward and forward in time, as well as move people, products, ideas, resources, information, and messages in space, if the transportation and communications requirements of the country and its citizens are to be effectively met.

Like the ability to span space, the ability to span time—and especially the creative contributions Canadians have made in this regard—should not be undervalued. By "spanning time," we don't mean, of course, the ability to travel *physically* into the past or the future, in the fashion of H.G. Wells' famous Time Traveller. But the ability to span time *mentally* is needed to maintain contact with the past, thereby providing Canadians with a sense of identity, belonging, and history; and it is needed to function effectively in the future, and prepare properly for that future. If, as the distinguished futurist John McHale once observed, "people survive, uniquely, by their capacity to act in the present on the basis of past experience considered in terms of future consequences," then it only makes sense to develop a country's ability to span time as well as space. Marshall McLuhan was getting at the same idea when he declared that we see the future through a rear view mirror, thus emphasizing the fundamental importance of being able to look backward as well as forward in time in order to prepare properly for the years ahead, as well as to create a continuous bond between the past, present, and future.

Just as it is no coincidence that some of the world's greatest thinkers about communications have been Canadian, neither is it coincidence that one of the greatest thinkers about the subject of time was also Canadian. This was Sir Sandford Fleming, much of whose interest in time was sparked by problems he encountered living in a country as vast as Canada. As every Canadian is told in school, Fleming played a crucial role in the creation and adoption of what is called *international (or universal) standard time*. This made it possible to address the many problems associated with the keeping of time that were becoming increasingly troublesome as the nineteenth century wore on.

Until standard time was adopted, every city and town had its own *local time*, which was based on when the sun reached the highest point in the sky at that locality each day. If you were in Toronto, it might be noon right now, but in cities or towns to the west of Toronto, the sun would not yet be as high in the sky, and it might still be only 11:45 a.m.

This was fine so long as transportation between different centres was slow and there were no means of instantaneous communications. But after the advent of the telegraph and the building of transcontinental railway systems, the system of local time gave rise to a great deal of confusion. If a railway printed a timetable, for instance, and that timetable said a particular train would be leaving at 12 noon, did that mean 12 noon Toronto time or 12 noon Montreal time or 12 noon Detroit time? And which it was certainly mattered, because noon came at different times in each city, depending on how far east or west it was. With every city having its own local time, the schedules and timetables were difficult to figure out, and it was easy for both the railways and their passengers to make mistakes.

Fleming first set his mind to the creation of an international standard time system in 1876, when he had been held up in an Irish train station for more than 12 hours because of a typographical error that confused 5:35 a.m. and 5:35 p.m. This event caused him to think seriously about time and how it might be kept more effectively. He spent the next few years of his life studying the many different time systems in use, before making his case for an international system acceptable to all countries.

Eventually Fleming suggested that instead of each city having its own local time, a series of *time zones* spanning the globe should be created—24 of them in all. Within these wide geographical zones, all clocks would be set to the same time of day, regardless of the sun's actual position in the sky at that particular locality. It would no longer be necessary to remember that while it might be 12 noon where you were, in a city a little way down the road to the west it was only (say) 11:48 a.m. (Of course, people still had to remember the differences between various time zones—that when it was noon in Toronto, it was only 11 a.m. in Winnipeg, 10 a.m. in Calgary, and 9 a.m. in Vancouver.)

In order to get various countries to agree on a system of standard time—this was essential, since the 24 time zones spanned the globe—Fleming convened the International Prime Meridian Conference in Washington, D.C., in 1884. There, representatives of some 25 major countries agreed to adopt Fleming's system of international standard time.

Fleming made many other contributions to Canada. He was a skilled engineer and surveyor as well as an outstanding inventor and scientist, and played a key role in the construction of the transcontinental railway. While his proposal to take the Yellowhead route through the Rocky Mountains was not adopted, it is generally agreed that the Canadian Pacific Railway could not have been built without Fleming's boundless energy, enthusiasm, and ingenuity.

Even after Fleming's international standard time system was accepted, the sheer size of Canada continued to pose problems. As Canadians know only too well, many difficulties can ensue when on one side of the country it's morning while in another part it's already afternoon. The biggest challenge in this regard is probably that experienced by Elections Canada, which has the difficult task of determining how to hold federal elections so that returns in one part of the country do not influence voting patterns in other parts of the country where the polls are still open. Great strides have been made in resolving this issue in recent years.

Let's turn now from time zones to the challenges associated with the country's system of "collective memory." Every country needs an effective system to provide citizens with access to the information they need and want about the past, regardless of where they live, what they do for a living, or what their specific socio-economic circumstances are. We are talking here, of course, about Canada's system of libraries, museums, art galleries, archives, and other heritage institutions. While advances in this area have tended to follow those in Europe and elsewhere and are not as distinctive as those made by Canadians in other areas of transportation and communications, there are still some worth noting.

In many ways, libraries are the most important component in this system, since they provide Canadians with access to the information and ideas needed to link the country together in an historical sense. It is not surprising, then, that libraries were among the first heritage institutions to be created in Canada.

The earliest libraries were private, and belonged to prominent families and wealthy European immigrants. The most illustrious example of this was the library created by Marc Lescarbot, a well-known Parisian scholar and lawyer who came to Canada in 1606 and settled in Port-Royal, Nova Scotia. While he only lived in Canada for slightly more than a year, he built up an impressive collection of books, articles, and other documents during this time. He also had his play, *Théâtre de Neptune*, presented at Port Royal in 1606; this performance is now generally acknowledged as the first theatrical production in North America. He maintained a keen interest in Acadian development all his life, and wrote a book, *Histoire de le Nouvelle-France*, when he returned to Paris in 1607. It made a strong case for the systematic development of the country's natural resources, rather than seeking quick profits through commerce and finance.

With initiatives like this, it did not take long for many other types of libraries to appear in different parts of the country. In the seventeenth and eighteenth centuries, many religious organizations, fur-trading companies, forts, and cities created libraries, including the Jesuits in Quebec and the Hudson's Bay Company at York Factory, Fort Chipewyan, Niagara Falls, and Quebec City. The first university library was created at King's College, Nova Scotia in 1789, although it was not until the nineteenth century that libraries began to appear with increasingly regularity throughout the country.

Many of these libraries were highly specialized in nature and belonged to professional associations, schools, and community groups. The first school libraries, for example, were created in 1850 by Joseph Howe in Nova Scotia and Egerton Ryerson in Ontario. The first public libraries were also created about this time, with Saint John, Guelph, and Toronto being the first cities in the country to create *free* public libraries. Prior to this time, most libraries required some form of subscription fee or nominal payment. Travelling libraries also made their debut. Originally created in Scotland in 1817, they made a great deal of sense in Canada as a result of the country's great size and the dispersed nature of its population.

By the middle of the nineteenth century, a solid foundation had been laid for the country's present system of public, private, and professional libraries. It is a system that has grown rapidly since that time, thanks in part to the valuable role played by the Carnegie Foundation in the development of libraries in Canada and the United States in the early and middle decades of the twentieth century, and is now one of the most effective, well-developed, and innovative library systems in the world. In Toronto, for example, the city's network of 100 branch libraries loans out more than 32 million books, videos, and other materials a year, making it the busiest and most frequently used library system in the world on a per capita basis. Not only are its holdings and services available in many different languages—imperative in a city and country that has one of the most ethnically diverse populations in the world—but in recent years it also has become an essential community resource. It provides a great deal of valuable information on the historical development of Toronto and other key institutions and resources in the city, and helps orient numerous newcomers and immigrants to the city. And what is true for Toronto and its many libraries is equally true for other Canadian communities and their libraries.

Speaking generally, museums, art galleries, and archives originated later than libraries. The first museum in Canada, for instance, was created at Niagara Falls in 1831. It was followed shortly thereafter by a museum at Niagara-on-the-Lake. In New Brunswick, one of the country's most creative talents, Dr. Abraham Gesner, inventor of kerosene, founded a museum in Saint John in 1842. Nova Scotia followed suit by founding the first provincial museum in Halifax in 1868. This was followed by provincial museums in British Columbia, Ontario, and Quebec in 1886. By this time, the museum and gallery boom was well under way in Canada. Many communities and cities built museums and art galleries in the decades following Confederation. In Toronto, the Art Museum of Toronto was established in 1900 and the Royal Ontario Museum in 1914. The National Gallery of Canada was also a reality by this time. And while Quebec had appointed an archivist as far back as 1724, most of Canada's archives were not established until the late 1800s or early 1900s. It was in 1904, for instance, that Arthur C. Doughty was appointed Dominion Archivist. He spent the next 30 years of his life building up an impressive national archival system, including the Public Archives of Canada, which had actually been established as part of the Department of Agriculture but only transformed into an independent entity in 1912.

The patchwork nature of these developments can be attributed to the fact that different levels of government tended to create libraries, museums, art galleries, archives, and other heritage and custodial institutions on their own initiative, without a great deal of consultation, cooperation, or the development of a national plan. This situation was complicated by the British North America Act, which made it difficult to ascertain who was actually responsible for the creation, funding, administration, and control of heritage institutions in general and libraries, art galleries, museums, and archives in particular. Unlike defence, foreign affairs, natural resources, education, and other areas for which the Act assigned specific responsibility to the federal, provincial, or municipal governments, virtually nothing was said about heritage institutions and governmental responsibility for them.

Nevertheless, pressure was building to develop an effective heritage system for the country as a whole. This pressure resulted from the need to conserve and protect the rapidly expanding cornucopia of books, artefacts, monuments, historical records, historic sites, manuscripts, artistic masterpieces, films, photographs, and paintings. If nothing were done, the country risked losing a valuable part of its cultural heritage.

The federal government was the first to respond in a concerted and systematic way. It established the Library of Parliament, Dominion Archives, National Gallery of Art, Canadian Motion Picture Bureau, and Historic Sites and Monuments Board between the late 1880s and early 1930s. These institutions complemented the federal government's involvement in other related matters, such as the organization of exhibitions, trade fairs, tours by artists and arts organizations, acquisition of artistic works, financial support for multicultural festivals (for instance, the New Canadian Folk Song and Handicraft Festival, which occurred in Winnipeg in 1928), and numerous commissions to create monuments, plaques, coins, and other heritage items.

Prime Ministers Wilfrid Laurier and Mackenzie King, as well as Governors General and diplomatic figures such as the Earl of Dufferin, Lord Bessborough, Lord Stanley, the Marquis of Lorne, and Lord Grey, played a prominent role in these developments. They founded several key Canadian artistic and academic institutions, such as the Royal Canadian Academy of

Arts, the Royal Society of Canada, and the Dominion Drama Festival; created awards and trophies for national achievements in sports and athletic endeavours, such as the Stanley Cup and the Grey Cup; and, in general, recognized the crucial importance of the country's cultural heritage for national unity, identity, and survival.

Unfortunately, the country had to wait another four decades before the federal government took another major step forward in this direction. This occurred in 1970 when Secretary of State Gérard Pelletier announced the creation of a national cultural policy. It was predicated on five key principles: pluralism; democratization; decentralization; federal-provincial relations; and international cooperation. The initial announcement was followed by the establishment of specific policies for film, publishing, and museums. All of these policies were designed to increase access to Canadian culture and heritage. For example, the national museums policy announced in 1972 included a program of associate museums tied to the national museums in Ottawa; strengthening of the National Museums Corporation to coordinate the work of all the national museums and the National Gallery of Art; creation of a number of exhibition centres across the country, particularly in more remote areas; the use of "museum mobiles" and other means to bring exhibitions to communities not served by museums and art galleries; creation of a major funding program for museums; and the establishment of the Canadian Conservation Institute (CCI) and the Canadian Heritage Information Network (CHIN). This latter institution provides detailed information about the country's heritage to citizens, community groups, and specialized institutions, regardless of where they are situated in the country.

As a result of these and other developments Canada now has one of the most advanced, sophisticated, and effective systems of collective memory in the world. This system has been enriched by many initiatives at the provincial and municipal level in recent years, as well as by numerous individuals and institutions in the private sector. In each of the various heritage areas, non-governmental organizations like the Canadian Library Association, the Canadian Museums Association, the Canadian Historical Association, and others are active, working to ensure that Canadians are able to "span time" as well as "span space."

Of course, spanning time not only requires the ability to maintain intimate connections with the past, but also the ability to prepare properly for the future. Interestingly, Canada and Canadians have played a seminal role in this area as well, both in domestic and international terms. Not only was Marshall McLuhan one of the world's leading futurists, predicting the importance of the mass media (and social media!) long before this was obvious to others, but Canada has produced many other outstanding futurists, including Arthur Cordell, Ran Ide, Ruben Nelson, Alan Tough, Frank Feather, John Kettle, Don Tapscott, and others.

Canada also hosted the First Global Conference on the Future, sponsored by the World Future Society, in Toronto in 1980. For the first time, outstanding futurists from many different fields were brought to a single location. Included in this group were Alvin Toffler, Isaac Asimov, Willis Harman, Robert Theobald, Hazel Henderson, Lester Brown, Elizabeth Mann Borgese, Herman Kahn, Ervin Laszlo, Hugues de Jouvenel, and others. Their discussions and presentations spanned the gamut of possibilities, from the need for a global rather than national perspective to effect world transformation and change, to the necessity of developing new forms of thinking about the economy, education, communications, values, and personal, social, and religious development. Not only did this conference put Canada on the map as far as futures studies were concerned, but it did a great deal to make Canadians more aware of the importance of planning for the future.

With these efforts to glimpse what the future may hold, we conclude our examination of how Canadians have worked over the centuries to span both space and time, in the process exhibiting vast creativity in virtually every domain of transportation and communications. Without such efforts, it is quite possible that Canada would not even exist as a country today.

CHAPTER FOUR

Resources, Industry, Science, and Technology

It is a well-known fact that Canadian development over the centuries has relied heavily on the country's natural resources. In earlier times, fish, fur, timber, and wheat were most important. More recently, ores and minerals, hydroelectricity, natural gas, and oil have been important.

Each resource has given rise to a distinct phase in Canadian history, sparked the growth of one or two major industries, resulted in the export of the country's natural wealth to other parts of the world, and unleashed a great deal of creativity.

The Indigenous peoples saw the natural resources of the country largely in terms of survival. Fish, berries, fruit, and vegetables were there to eat, animal skins (and especially fur) were there to protect them from the elements, and wood, minerals, ice, and snow were there to provide the materials needed to construct homes, create agricultural implements, and fashion the vehicles needed to traverse the country.

Needless to say, Europeans also saw natural resources in these terms. However, they also saw them in another important way—as commodities that could be developed, exploited, and exported for profit. For the most part, the countries from which they came and colonial masters they served weren't much interested in survival and settlement in the northern half of the North American continent. They were far more interested in exploiting the region's natural wealth and exporting it to other parts of the world.

THE FISHING INDUSTRY AND THE FUR TRADE

Fish was the first natural resource to be exploited by the Europeans in a systematic and sustained manner. This was especially true of cod, which could be kept for months in dried and salted form and transported over long distances without too much difficulty. As early as the sixteenth century, English, French, Spanish, Portuguese, and Basque fishermen were busy fishing off the coast of Newfoundland for cod and other marine delicacies. By the end of that century, England and France—the two main rivals in the North American fishing industry—were engaged in a fierce battle to capitalize on the profuse fish stocks in and around the Grand Banks. The English preferred the "dry method" of curing fish, which saw semi-permanent fishing stations established on the southeast coast of Newfoundland and the fish loaded onto wharfs, split, cleaned, lightly salted, and dried on huge "flakes" or tables. The French, by contrast, preferred the "green method," with the fish processed and cured right on the ships. Doing so enabled the French to get their fish to market sooner than the English. Placentia, in Newfoundland, served as the headquarters for the French fishery in North America until in 1713 Newfoundland and Nova Scotia were lost to France through the Treaty of Utrecht.

In the centuries to follow, a substantial fishing industry flourished on both Canada's east and, later, west coast. With this came the establishment of many fishing villages, the construction of numerous schooners, fishing fleets, and processing plants, the harvesting of large volumes of cod, halibut, salmon, sole, haddock, and the like, and the export of millions of dollars' worth of fish to other parts of the world. A major boost to the development of the fishing industry occurred during the American Revolution and the Napoleonic Wars, when British dependence on Atlantic fish and lumber increased exponentially. This led to what many consider a "golden age" in development along the east coast of Canada, since fish was in abundant supply and most trade in the Atlantic region was conducted in wooden boats.

Strange as it may sound, the fishing industry along the east coast of the country also gave rise to the fur trade—the next great resource to be exploited in Canada. The establishment of permanent fishing villages along the east coast spurred trade in furs, largely because the fishing villages needed an additional source of revenue if they were to be sustained in a cold climate and punishing geography. The Europeans quickly learned that the Indigenous peoples were very skilled at catching and skinning animals, and were anxious to trade furs for knives, kettles, axes, blankets, and trinkets, especially after they discovered that the Europeans had an insatiable demand for fur. When the demand for wide-brimmed fur hats and coats skyrocketed in Europe in the seventeenth century, fur traders, merchants, and the Indigenous peoples moved quickly to fill this need and capitalize on a "once-in-a-lifetime" opportunity. This was particularly true for the export of beaver pelts, which made the best hats because the fur was soft and had a wonderful matting quality, especially if acquired in the winter when it was at its thickest and finest.

France was the first country to recognize the incredible gains to be had from the fur trade. Short-term monopolies were granted to authorities along the St. Lawrence River in exchange for promises to send settlers and colonists there. The colonies established by Samuel de Champlain and especially Jean Talon, who became Intendant of New France from 1665 to 1672, depended heavily on the fur trade. Indeed, Talon was the first person to recognize Canada's enormous potential for exporting furs and other natural resources, as well as for engaging in international trade. He exhibited an incredible amount of creative ingenuity during his residency, largely by converting a small fur-trading and missionary outpost into a large, prosperous, highly productive royal province. He did so by taking advantage of the fur, timber, and minerals in the area, encouraging commercial farming and agriculture, promoting shipbuilding and fishing, and exporting products such as wood, wool, hemp, hides, barley, hops, and tar to France, the West Indies, and other destinations.

What happened next was nothing short of astonishing. Unlike the fishing industry, which was focused outward and confined largely to the east and later west coasts, the fur trade was focused inward and extended eventually from one end of the country to the other and into the far north. And just as the French and the English were engaged in a fierce battle to establish control over land and resources in the northern half of the North American continent, so they were engaged in a fierce battle to control the fur trade. Indeed, the fur trade became the battleground where the titanic struggle between these two great European powers was played out in earnest in the new land.

Between 1650 and 1750, both France and England created huge fur-trading empires in what eventually became Canada. Despite countless difficulties, the French moved progressively across the southern and central parts of the country, establishing forts, garrisons, and trading posts whenever and wherever possible and desirable. They preferred to go to the Indigenous peoples to get their furs, and to "follow the fur across the country." In contrast, the English preferred to let the Indigenous peoples come to them, largely by encouraging traders to bring furs to the Hudson's Bay Company outpost at York Factory on Hudson Bay. While this system was not without its difficulties—especially in the later decades of the fur trade, when competition between these two great fur-trading nations became incredibly cutthroat and intense—it had the advantage of reducing the high overhead cost of acquiring furs, since the Indigenous peoples absorbed most of the cost involved in trapping the animals and transporting their fur to York Factory and other distribution centres. This system was further enhanced by the creation of the "York boat," named after the post at York Factory. This ingenious device made it possible to transport large volumes of furs south and east from Hudson Bay, despite the difficulties involved in portaging these boats between the region's numerous lakes and rivers.

By the time of the English conquest of New France in 1759–60, these two great competing systems dominated the commercial fur trade in the northern half of North America. The St. Lawrence–Great Lakes or "French system" was based in Montreal, extended to the upper reaches of the Mississippi River and its northern tributaries, as well as to the Prairies and the southern part of the Canadian Shield. The Rupert's Land or "English system" covered the whole region draining into Hudson Bay and James Bay. After the conquest, Anglo-Americans, English, and Highland Scots replaced the French merchants in Montreal and established the North West Company. Competition between this company and the Hudson's Bay Company was fierce, with the North West Company initially demonstrating a remarkable capacity for reducing the high cost of acquiring fur and gaining a foothold in British and continental markets. What is most significant about this situation is the tremendous amount of creative energy that went into establishing and managing these two great fur-producing and revenue-generating empires, with their string of forts, garrisons, and collection and distribution centres strategically located across the country.

Eventually, the Hudson's Bay Company was compelled to abandon its practice of waiting for the Indigenous peoples and fur traders to bring their furs to York Factory. The Company set in motion a plan to establish a series of forts, garrisons, and trading posts of its own across the Northwest and into the Far North in places like Fort Churchill in Saskatchewan, Fort Edmonton in Alberta, and Fort Langley and Fort Rupert in British Columbia. It also became much more aggressive in its pursuit of fur. This caused a decline in the North West Company's fortunes and, ultimately, its demise and absorption into the Hudson's Bay Company. Matters came to a head in the years after 1810 when the Hudson's Bay Company was totally reorganized, hired most of the best administrators of the North West

Company, and was run by Governor George Simpson. Under Simpson's skillful, creative, and ruthless direction—he wasn't called "the little emperor" for nothing—the Hudson's Bay Company generated huge profits, fought off competition from American and Russian companies in the Far North and West, established a monopoly over the entire fur trade, and eventually played a key role in negotiations to determine the actual boundaries between Canada and the U.S.

It is not difficult to see what is going on here. In the process of chasing that furry little animal the beaver across the country, first the French and later the English and Scots created a system of forts, garrisons, and trading posts from coast to coast and into the Far North that played a crucial role in the creation of Canada as a country. Harold Innis, Canada's great economic historian, called out the fur trade as *the* defining factor in the country's economic development:

> Canada emerged as a political entity with boundaries largely determined by the fur trade. These boundaries included a vast north temperate land area extending from the Atlantic to the Pacific. *The present Dominion emerged not in spite of geography but because of it. The significance of the fur trade consisted in its determination of the geographic framework.* Later economic developments in Canada were profoundly influenced by this background.

While fish and fur continued to generate badly needed revenue throughout the nineteenth century (and especially the century's first half), it was apparent by this time that other sources of wealth were desperately needed. Fortunately, timber provided this source. It came just in time. Major changes in transportation and communications were beginning that would make the harnessing of the country's natural wealth commercially viable.

TIMBER, PULP AND PAPER, AND MANUFACTURING

Just as there was a huge demand for fish and fur in Europe in the sixteenth, seventeenth, and eighteenth centuries, so there was a huge demand for timber in the nineteenth century. Unlike the fishing industry and fur trade, however, the timber trade required much larger investments of capital and significantly more workers. It also had a much more profound effect on the natural environment. On the one hand, it necessitated the creation of many towns and villages, the construction of numerous railroads and canals, the opening up of countless roads and ports, and a great deal more settlement. On the other hand, it blighted the rural landscape. Logging was pursued with reckless abandon and little thought for the future. In little more than a moment of historical time, the ancient forests of North America were destroyed.

What fuelled the development of the timber trade was the demand for masts for the ships of Britain's Royal Navy, which was rapidly becoming the largest and most powerful navy in the world. Not only was Britain locked in a fierce battle with Spain, France, Portugal, and Holland for supremacy on the high seas, but it was heavily committed in North America and the West Indies, and going through the Industrial Revolution. While Britain still had a good supply of certain types of timber, it was deficient in pine, which made the best ships' masts and was accessible in large quantities along the North American seaboard. Britain turned to North America for wood after the supply from the Baltic countries proved erratic, insufficient, and complicated by various political and transportation problems. This caused a huge surge in the demand for North American wood, especially shingles, barrel staves, box shooks, and spoolwood for the textile industry. By 1810, the timber trade accounted for more than 70 percent of British North America's exports.

Most of the timber sent to Britain was of the "square timber" variety. This required felling trees, cutting four flat sides with a broad axe, and sending the wood to Britain before any further cutting or sawing was done. While this satisfied Britain's demand for wood, it was extremely inefficient. A great deal of wood was not used and instead was left on the forest floor to rot. The timber resources of the country were also exploited far more rapidly and ruthlessly than would have been the case had other, more efficient methods of cutting, processing, and transporting lumber been used. This explains why the centres of timber activity in Canada soon shifted from Nova Scotia, New Brunswick, and the Saint John River valley to the St. Lawrence valley and major waterways further west in Ontario and Quebec. Put simply, the East Coast was running out of timber.

While the timber trade was initially dependent on lakes and rivers to transport lumber, the construction of railroads stimulated this trade in the middle and latter parts of the nineteenth century. By this time, areas in Ontario and Quebec far removed from rivers and lakes were being exploited for their timber. Moreover, British Columbia was rapidly becoming one of the largest suppliers of timber in the country, primarily after 1850, when the Fraser River gold rush had run its course. Not only were there huge trees in British Columbia—Douglas fir, red cedar, Sitka spruce, hemlock, balsam, and so forth—but the construction of the Canadian Pacific Railway in the 1880s reduced the cost of transporting British Columbian timber to markets in eastern Canada and other parts of the world. British Columbia soon became one of the largest, most profitable timber-producing areas in the world.

Changes in the transportation of timber and the location of the timber trade were matched by changes in methods of organization, financing, and administration. Prior to the beginning of the nineteenth century, timber was supplied largely by farmers and small-scale operators. Not a great deal of capital was required, and farmers could work the land in the summer and turn to logging in the winter. But when the timber trade moved into more remote areas, it came to be dominated by large, well-capitalized firms able to employ large numbers of loggers, build efficient saw mills, and operate their own transportation systems (including railways). Many of these firms got a further boost when a dramatic expansion took place in the pulp and paper industry. In time, Canada's pulp and paper industry was among the largest in the world, and pulp and paper the country's most profitable export.

Many creative developments were required to make the pulp and paper industry a success. Prior to Confederation, a number of paper mills were operating in Upper and Lower Canada, as well as in the Maritimes. At that time paper was made from rags. However, as the demand for paper soared and the supply of rags began to dry up, the search was on for ways of making paper from other materials. As often happens, necessity proved the mother of invention. In the 1830s, Charles Fenerty of Sackville, Nova Scotia began experimenting with alternative ways of making paper. Since his father owned several saw mills and he had access to the nearby Holland paper mill, Fenerty learned a great deal about the process of making paper from a very early age.

Observing that the vegetable fiber in paper was derived from the cotton and linen in rags, Fenerty believed that paper could also be made from wood fiber. The most finely ground wood was the fuzzy, almost lint-like residue that was produced when a wooden saw frame rubbed against wooden sides. Fenerty carefully collected and worked this fine wood residue by hand, using all the standard techniques of wetting, bleaching, molding, flattening, and shaping that were required to make paper. This enabled him to manufacture a small quantity of "pulp-wood paper." It is

Fenerty's method on which the paper-making industries depend today. Unfortunately, he, like John Patch and many other Canadian creators, did not patent his invention. As a result, Friedrich Keller, a German from Saxony, was awarded the first patent for making paper from wood. This does not alter the fact that it was Fenerty, a Canadian, who is generally regarded as the first person in the world to make paper from wood.

This is by no means the end of the story of creative contributions by Canadians to the pulp and paper industry. In 1864, John Thomson of Napanee, Ontario created the first chemical wood-pulp process. Then, in 1866, Alex Buntin built the first commercial mechanical pulp mill in North America at Valleyfield, Quebec. By the time of Confederation a year later, Canada already had one of the largest paper-making industries in the world. The centre of economic gravity for this industry soon shifted from the Maritimes to Upper and Lower Canada as a result of numerous developments, such as the huge influx of immigrants into the St. Lawrence Lowlands, the creation of many small businesses and family firms, the construction of canals and some of the country's first railways, and growing economic uncertainty in the Maritimes. Canada was in the early throes of industrialization, and while agriculture remained the foundation of the Canadian economy, more people were moving to the country's towns and cities, especially rapidly growing industrial centres like Quebec City, Montreal, Toronto, and Vancouver.

Quebec City prospered greatly from the steady expansion of the timber trade and became the most important lumber port and shipbuilding centre in the land. Montreal and Toronto were also rapidly expanding. Montreal had more than 500 industrial establishments employing more than 1,300 workers by the early 1840s, and Toronto had some 30,000 inhabitants by this time as well as a rapidly growing number of commercial establishments. Typical industries included shipbuilding, furniture-making, match-making, brewing, distilling, textiles, leather work, and so forth.

The result was a boom in commerce and industry in the middle part of the nineteenth century, particularly in Ontario. Two of the most successful entrepreneurs of the era were William McMaster and William Eli Sanford.

McMaster was a dry goods merchant on Yonge Street in Toronto whose company was rated by the Dun credit agency (later Dun and Bradstreet) as "the largest dry goods concern in Canada West" (as Ontario was called at the time). Later, he became the founder of the Bank of Commerce. Not to be outdone, William Eli Sanford became known as "the Wool King of Canada" because of the huge fortune he amassed in the wool trade. Sanford specialized in ready-made clothes, which were manufactured at his company in Hamilton. It grew to be the largest such company in the country, due largely to its moderate pricing and attention to quality control and details. The production of musical instruments also thrived during this time, especially in Ontario and Quebec, where Heintzman, Weber, and Mason and Risch became prominent piano and musical instrument makers.

It was also at this time that Canada in general, and Ontario and Quebec in particular, became one of the largest and most creative manufacturers of cheese and dairy products in the world, taking advantage of a tradition that can be traced back to the earliest French settlers and the production of Îsle d'Orléans cheese in Quebec. While farmers had long produced many varieties of cheese for local consumption, the development of faster transportation technologies made it possible to export cheese and other dairy products to other parts of the country and around the world. When the Reciprocity Treaty, reducing tariffs on trade between the United States and the British North American colonies, was terminated by the Americans in 1866, the price of cheese shot up dramatically. Coupled with a decline in the price of wheat, this caused many Canadian farmers to turn to the production of cheese and other dairy products. What resulted was a "cheese mania" so pronounced and intense that by the end of the nineteenth century, more than 2,300 cheese factories were operating in Canada, the vast majority in Ontario. While overproduction led to numerous bankruptcies, the country's cheese exports nevertheless shot up astronomically, making cheese the second most valuable export after timber. Many towns in Ontario and Quebec, as well as some of Quebec's best-known monasteries, became famous for their cheeses. Moreover, one of the biggest cheeses in the world was created in Perth, Ontario. "The Canadian Mite" weighed over ten tons, and was displayed at the World Exposition in Chicago in 1893.

MINERALS, MINING, AND THE PETROCHEMICAL INDUSTRY

Despite the importance of agriculture and the beginning of industrialization, Canada's economy was still dependent on timber and pulp and paper in the years after Confederation. There was, however, a growing awareness that the country possessed an abundant supply of mineral resources, as well as the creative capacity to take financial advantage of them. As J. J. Brown put it in *The Inventors*:

> Canada possesses one of the world's great treasure houses of raw materials and Canadian inventors have, accordingly, been pioneers in the techniques of mining, chemicals, metallurgy, and paper making. The first commercial oil well, the first oil pipeline, the first commercial acetylene, the first wood pulp mill in North America all resulted from the work of Canadians.

Interest in the country's mineral wealth—the fourth major natural resource to be exploited commercially, after fish, fur, and timber—can be traced back to the middle of the nineteenth century. In 1842, the first Geological Survey of Canada was conducted, and then, in the 1850s, came the Fraser River gold rush. The Geological Survey confirmed that "the Province of Canada" (as what would later become the provinces of Ontario and Quebec were known from 1841 to 1867) had one of the largest and most diversified endowments of mineral resources of any region in the world. In turn, the Fraser gold rush sparked the excitement needed to stimulate interest in exploiting British North America's mineral wealth.

As the Geological Survey revealed, the mineral wealth of the country is centred largely in and around the Canadian Shield, that vast geological formation underlying the central and northern parts of the country. It is one of the richest ore-bearing areas in the world, with enormous deposits of metals such as copper, zinc, lead, gold, silver, nickel, iron, cobalt, platinum, magnesium, titanium, and uranium. In addition, the Interior Plains, encompassing most of the Prairies, boasts vast supplies of petroleum, coal, potash, and salt. And just west of the Plains is the Cordilleran region, which covers most of British Columbia, the Yukon, Nunavut, and the North West Territories. It contains extensive mineral deposits as well, especially coal, natural gas, and petroleum. Finally, and also of importance, the continental shelves off the East, West, and Arctic coasts of Canada harbour huge deposits of petroleum and natural gas.

It is doubtful if the exploitation of the mineral wealth of the country—and the industrial development that ensued——would have been possible without contributions from two of Canada's most inventive individuals. The first was Abraham Gesner, and the second Thomas L. "Carbide" Willson. Both played a crucial role in showing how the country's natural resources could be used to commercial, industrial, and financial advantage.

Gesner was born at Cornwallis, Nova Scotia in 1797. Son of United Empire Loyalists, he was keenly interested in geology from an early age. He studied and mapped the geology of his native province between 1827 and 1837, and set out his findings in a remarkable book called *Remarks on the Geology and Mineralogy of Nova Scotia*. He also worked for several years as official geologist of New Brunswick before focusing his attention on the creation of a better source of indoor illumination. Up to this time, light had been produced by burning various substances, including both animal and vegetable oils, wax, and wood. The problem was that light from these sources was feeble and smoky. What Gesner did was produce a far superior source of light, through the invention of kerosene in 1846, as well as the process whereby kerosene could be produced commercially from petroleum. Burned in lamps, kerosene gives rise to a beautiful bright yellow light.

Not only did Gesner's invention revolutionize indoor lighting, but it contributed to the development of the petrochemical industry, one of today's largest and most lucrative industries. Petroleum, of course, is used not only as a fuel, but in producing many substances that play a key role in modern civilization, including plastics, fertilizers, detergents, paints, textiles, and so forth. But Gesner's contribution does not end here. He also played a seminal role in the creation of the North American Gas Light Company, which eventually became part of Standard Oil of New Jersey—the forerunner of Exxon Mobil, which controls Canada's Imperial Oil Ltd. (best known for its Esso gas stations—"Esso," of course, meaning "SO," which is short for Standard Oil). Many of the techniques that Gesner developed were documented in his book, *A Practical Treatise on Coal, Petroleum, and Other Distilled Oils,* which was deemed to be "the source" in the petrochemical industry for many years.

In 1854, Charles N. Tripp of Woodstock, Ontario created the first oil company in North America, the International Mining and Manufacturing Company. This company was later taken over by James Miller Williams, who drilled the first commercial oil well in North America at Oil Springs, Ontario in 1858.

Williams was a fascinating individual who, like many of Canada's creative talents, was born in another part of the world but came to Canada at a very early age. He was born in Camden, New Jersey shortly after the War of 1812. From British stock and strongly attached to Britain and British values and traditions, Williams emigrated to British North America at the age of 22. Having been trained as a carriage maker, he moved in 1846 to Hamilton, where he established the Hamilton Coach Factory with H. G. Cooper that same year. It was extremely successful, largely because it manufactured railroad cars for the new Great Western Railway that ran from Toronto through Hamilton and London on its way to Detroit. Believing that petroleum was the fuel of the future, Williams acquired lands in Enniskillen, west of London, where Indigenous peoples had gathered tar that they used to waterproof their canoes. Williams struck oil in 1858 in the village of Black Creek, whose name was immediately changed to Oil Springs. He went on to build a highly successful business refining and shipping oil through the Canadian Oil Company he founded. He is identified in U.S. geological records in Washington, D.C., as "the discoverer of petroleum and the pioneer in its refinement and preparation for illuminating and lubricating purposes." Just how important this achievement was for Canada and the world is revealed in an article by Murray White on the "Oil Industry's Birthplace":

> Oil Springs today is a unique perch from which to view the oil industry's impact on modern society—without it, there wouldn't be one.
>
> The discovery of oil here, and its first commercial application as lamp oil in 1858 by James Miller Williams, seed[ed] a global revolution: A cheap, plentiful energy source had been found, and in the century that followed, it would enable the rapid growth of the industrial era.
>
> Oil allowed for the engineering of combustion engines, which would replace steam power as powerful, efficient drivers of transportation, from trains to ships to, eventually, cars and planes.
>
> With it came complete social transformation: geography disappeared as means of transportation got faster and faster. Global travel and commerce became quick, efficient, cheap. Urban centres dwindled as cars transported more and more people into suburbs. The automotive industry created empires. With it, oil wealth, and its pursuit, proliferated.

Williams' creative achievements were merely the first in a long line in the petrochemical industry in Canada. In 1862, the first of numerous "oil gushers" occurred in the southwestern Ontario town of Petrolia, which went on to achieve international fame in the 1860s when the first oil pipeline in North America was laid from Petrolia to Sarnia. It is claimed by locals that the "jerker rod system" was also invented at Petrolia. This made it possible to distribute power to many widely dispersed oil wells by using a series of linked poles that were made to oscillate by a single power source.

Canada has never looked back as far as the petrochemical industry is concerned. Later developments included the federal government's creation in 1942 of Polymer Corporation (which played a key role in the production of synthetic rubber); the discovery of oil at the Leduc field in Alberta in 1947; and the opening up of the Athabasca oil sands in northern Alberta in the mid-twentieth century. Such developments helped propel Canada into the front lines of major industrial powers in the world in the years after the Second World War.

What Gesner did for kerosene and Williams for the petrochemical industry, Thomas "Carbide" Willson did for calcium carbide and acetylene. Willson was born in Woodstock, Ontario in 1861. While calcium carbide and acetylene were both already known, Willson invented and patented a process whereby calcium carbide could be produced inexpensively by heating coal, lime, and tar to very high temperatures, and acetylene could be produced equally cost-effectively by adding water to calcium carbide. Willson's discoveries eventually gave rise to two huge companies: Union Carbide in the United States, and the Shawinigan Chemical Company in Canada. Willson was also involved in the development of the oxyacetylene torch between 1895 and 1904. The torch could reach temperatures of 6,000 degrees Fahrenheit, hot enough to weld even metals with high melting points, and consequently facilitating key developments in the shipbuilding and automotive industries. Interestingly, Willson also played a pioneering role in the development of hydroelectric power in Quebec.

By this time, two other Canadians, Henry Woodward and Matthew Evans had patented the first incandescent electric light bulb. This occurred in 1874. Thomas Edison later bought out their patent, and went on to develop the first practical light bulb suitable for everyday use. It is possible to claim, however, that Canadians played an important role in "lighting up the world" through the achievements of Gesner, Woodward, and Evans.

As we have seen, Canada was well on its way to becoming one of the largest producers of mineral wealth in the world by the end of the nineteenth century. Canadians capitalized on discoveries of specific minerals, including gold in British Columbia in the mid-1850s and in Quebec in the 1860s; phosphate in various parts of the country in the 1870s; asbestos in the Eastern Townships of Quebec in 1877; nickel in Sudbury, Ontario in 1883; coal and iron in Newfoundland in 1893; copper and gold in

Rossland, British Columbia in 1889; and lead and zinc in Kimberley, B.C. at about this same time. This was capped off by the Klondike gold rush in the Yukon in 1896, one of the most spectacular gold rushes the world has ever known and immortalized in Pierre Berton's book *Klondike*.

While the wealth generated by natural resources yielded numerous benefits, it was becoming apparent that too much dependence on natural resources—no matter how lucrative in the short run—was not advisable for the Canadian economy in the long run. It was necessary to create a more diversified economy, one that could capitalize on the country's natural wealth while simultaneously building a strong financial, industrial, and manufacturing base, as well as a robust domestic market for Canadian products.

While the need to diversify the economy had been recognized since Confederation—in fact, it was one of the driving forces *behind* Confederation—the real impetus to do so did not occur until Prime Minister John A. Macdonald introduced his National Policy in 1879. The new policy was designed to raise tariffs on manufactured goods from abroad to a high level, generate commercial and industrial activity, and promote immigration and settlement in the West. These goals were buttressed by strong federal government support of many manufacturing ventures and possibilities. As Tom Easterbrook and Hugh Aitken point out in their book *Canadian Economic History*:

> It was only in the culminating years of this programme that capital, man-power and enterprise could be attracted in sufficient volume to complete the process of building the strong and unified economy which had been visualized at Confederation. . . . Gold and base-metal mining, the production of pulp and paper, and the development of the country's power resources were to spearhead Canada's progress to the advanced state of development she occupies today. . . . In the half-century following Confederation, the federal government had become committed to the achievement and maintenance of a national unity based on wheat, railways, tariffs, on iron and coal, and on the continuance of close relations with Europe.

Mining and resource extraction continued to play a vital role in Canada's economic development in the years following Confederation and the introduction of the National Policy. The mineral bonanza was accompanied by major developments in the mining, metallurgical, geological, and engineering industries. In the second half of the nineteenth century, many universities and professional institutions created engineering schools to teach courses and undertake research in mining, metallurgy, and mechanical and civil engineering, including King's College in Fredericton in 1854, McGill University in Montreal in 1871, the School of Practical Science in Toronto in 1873, the École Polytechnique in Montreal in 1873, and the Royal Military College in Kingston in 1876. In addition, many "mining towns" sprang up, including Labrador City in Newfoundland and Labrador, Amherst and Glace Bay in Nova Scotia, Schefferville, Chibougamau, Rouyn-Noranda, and Murdockville in Quebec, Cobalt, Sudbury, Copper Cliffs, Kirkland Lake, Timmins, and Elliot Lake in Ontario, Flin Flon and Thompson in Manitoba, Esterhazy in Saskatchewan, Grande Cache in Alberta, Kimberley, Trail, Kitimat, Barkerville, and Gold River in British Columbia, Yellowknife in the North West Territories, and Whitehorse in the Yukon.

Many of these towns, the mining equivalents of mill towns like Bathurst, New Brunswick or Chicoutimi, Quebec—not to mention "cheese towns" like Warkworth, Balderson, and Perth in Ontario!—depended on a single resource or product, with hundreds if not thousands of people employed by the industry in question. Such towns became a characteristic feature of Canada and Canadian culture in the latter part of the nineteenth and early part of the twentieth century. (The sociologist Rex Lucas even published a study of what he considered this distinctively Canadian settlement pattern; it was entitled *Minetown Milltown Railtown*.) As economic times changed, however, many of these towns fell on hard times. While some have gone on to "reinvent themselves" in recent years—for example, Chemainus, B.C., which after logging ran its course turned to tourism and created Canada's largest outdoor gallery with painted murals on buildings depicting the community's early years—others have not been so fortunate. Indeed, many are threatened with becoming "ghost towns" if they are not successful in finding suitable alternatives to dependency on a single resource or product.

As Canadians harvested their country's natural wealth, companies large and small sprang up in different parts of the country. The fisheries spawned the fish processing industry; timber created a need for saw mills, pulp and paper mills, and the lumber industry as a whole; and farming led to the modern agricultural industry. Backward and forward linkages were at work in all these areas.

With industrial development came the need for reliable and cost-effective sources of power. As a result, Canadians turned their attention to the development of another resource the country possessed in abundance—hydroelectric power in particular. As J. J. Brown noted, "the art of making electric power out of running water changed the face of Canada."

HYDROELECTRIC POWER AND RAPID INDUSTRIALIZATION

The first person to utilize hydroelectric power in Canada was probably John R. Barber, who used it to drive the wheels of his factory in Georgetown, Ontario in 1888. Following this, the use of electric power escalated rapidly, particularly in Ontario with its easy access to Niagara Falls and other major waterways. It is not surprising that two of North America's (and possibly the world's) greatest and most creative pioneers in the development of hydroelectric power—Sir Adam Beck and Thomas H. Hogg—were both Canadian.

Beck, an engineer and politician, was born in Baden, Canada West (now Ontario), in 1857. He was fascinated with hydroelectricity, and created the Hydro-Electric Power Commission (later Ontario Hydro) in 1910. In order to do this, Beck had to engage in numerous battles with private companies that wanted to capitalize on Ontario's rapid industrial growth. Believing that hydroelectricity was the birthright of all citizens and should be provided at the cost of production, Beck was successful in creating what was at the time the largest publicly owned power authority in the world, thus providing cheap power to industry and to individual consumers, as well as furnishing an excellent model for infrastructure development and public administration.

Another pioneer of hydroelectric power in North America was Thomas Ahearn. Born in Le Breton Flats, the timber district of Ottawa, in 1855, Ahearn graduated from Ottawa College, now the University of Ottawa. Following this, he worked for the Montreal Telegraph Company in Montreal and the Western Union Telegraph Company in New York for a time, before returning to Ottawa to become chief operator of the Montreal Telegraph Company. He also worked for the Bell Telephone Company for a number of years. But his real passion was hydroelectric power. In 1881, he and Warren Sopher, an American working at Dominion Telegraph, resigned from their jobs to form Ahearn and Sopher Electrical Contractors, which became the Canadian representative of the Westinghouse Electric Manufacturing Company of Chicago.

Another firm, the Ottawa Electric Light Company, which Ahearn founded in 1885, was contracted to install 165 arc street lamps in Ottawa, the first time that electricity was used to light up that city. Then, in 1891, he and Sopher convinced the city to establish the Ottawa Electric Railway to manufacture street cars and operate a street railway system in Ottawa. He promptly invented and patented electric heaters to warm the cars, as well as a rotating brush cleaner to clear the tracks during the winter months. His companies quickly set the standard for other companies across Canada. Interestingly, the Ottawa Electric Railway operated successfully in Ottawa for 58 years, eventually becoming OC Transpo, which still provides public transportation in Ottawa.

Nevertheless, Ahearn's real "claim to fame" is the invention of the electric oven. Yet another Canadian invention destined to have a profound effect on the country and the world, this valuable device was created and refined in collaboration with Sopher between 1882 and 1892. On August 29, 1892, Ahearn and Sopher produced the first meal cooked entirely by electricity at the Windsor Hotel in Ottawa. It was dubbed the "Electric Dinner" because everything on the menu was cooked using electricity.

Ahearn went on to play an important role in the development of Ottawa in many other ways. The hydroelectric company he founded became known as Ottawa Hydro, and Ahearn invented water heaters that are still rented as part of the overall service. He chaired the Ottawa Improvement Commission, which eventually became the National Capital Commission, as well as financing the construction of the Champlain Bridge across the Ottawa River. Between 1891 and 1921, Ahearn patented no fewer than 11 inventions, including the electric flat-iron, the electric heater, the electric warming bottle, and various types of sound-reproducing equipment. He also built telegraph lines that later became the North American Telegraph System. Because of these impressive achievements, he was appointed by Prime Minister William Lyon Mackenzie King to organize the special events on Parliament Hill for the Diamond Jubilee of Confederation. The occasion was broadcast on the country's first coast-to-coast radio program in 1927. Ahearn was named to the Privy Council in 1928. While not as well-known as, say, Alexander Graham Bell, Ahearn certainly deserves a prominent place among the country's most creative people.

These were not the only areas where Canada was making its mark through the harnessing of hydroelectric power. There are probably no greater feats in this area than the construction of the hydroelectric power stations at Churchill Falls in Labrador and James Bay in Quebec. Indeed, the construction of the hydroelectric power station at Churchill Falls has been called one of the greatest engineering feats of the twentieth century of any kind. Constructed between 1968 and 1972—in itself a remarkably short span of time, given the magnitude of the project—it involved the creation of a system of 68 dykes to dam up an area the size of New Brunswick, as well as construction of the world's largest powerhouse, which is more than ten football fields in length and some nine stories high. The rushing water drops through more than one thousand feet to drive what was the biggest electric generator in the world when it was installed.

Construction of Quebec's James Bay hydroelectric system proved an even more remarkable engineering feat. Located on the east side of James Bay, the project was announced by Quebec premier Robert Bourassa in 1971 and took several decades to complete. The project sparked a great deal of resistance among Indigenous groups in the area and raised major environmental concerns. Nonetheless, it went forward, becoming the largest hydroelectric project in the world up to that time. The James Bay project includes numerous power stations as well as the largest single underground power station in the world, as well as a series of huge reservoirs about half the size of Lake Ontario. In all, the James Bay project can generate enough power to satisfy about 20 percent of Canada's hydroelectric requirements. It rivals, if not surpasses, the later Three Gorges Dam in China, a project that has also generated a great deal of resistance and controversy.

In the years after World War II, Canada remained a world leader in resource extraction, with several new technologies being developed. L. M. Pidgeon developed the "Pidgeon process" to crystallize magnesium and cast it as ingots. Inco (the International Nickel Company of Canada) created a new "flash smelting technology" in the late 1940s. Using pure oxygen, technicians were able to spontaneously ignite sulphide concentrates, thereby combining the roasting and smelting requirements in a single operation. In the late 1960s, Noranda developed a highly creative continuous copper-making process using a single furnace known as the "Noranda reactor."

These developments were complemented by the completion of the St. Lawrence Seaway. By the 1960s, Canada was exporting millions of tons of iron ore from Northern Quebec and Labrador to steel plants in Pittsburgh. The signing of the Canada-U.S. Auto Pact in 1965 provided a major boost to the production of steel and the overall Canadian economy. Production of car parts, nominal in 1960, expanded greatly, as accessories production flourished and exports multiplied. A great Canadian success story in this field was Magna International, founded by Frank Stronach, now one of the largest and most successful manufacturers of automobile parts in the world.

The export of minerals also expanded rapidly during this period, due primarily to the discovery of asbestos in Quebec, lead in British Columbia, nickel in Manitoba, copper in New Brunswick, uranium in Saskatchewan, barite in Nova Scotia, and fluorspar in Newfoundland. At mid-century, Canada was also the second largest producer of aluminum in the world, producing some 15 percent of the world's total.

Interestingly, many minerals in Canada are named after places where they were first discovered. Thus, *madocite* was named after a marble quarry near Madoc, Ontario, *sudburyite* was named after Sudbury, Ontario, and *carletonite* was named after Carleton University, where this mineral was first identified. Other minerals are named after the Canadians who discovered them, such as *sabinaite,* named after Ann Phyllis Sabina, a geologist; *sperryite*, named after Francis Lewis Sperry, chief geologist at the Jeffery Mine in Asbestos, Quebec; and *howlite*, named after Henry Howe, a chemist and author of *The Mineralogy of Nova Scotia*.

Minerals were not the only natural resource to stimulate Canadian creativity during the course of the twentieth century. The pulp, paper, and newsprint industries continued to play a dynamic role. Canada progressed from having five pulp and paper mills in 1881 to becoming the largest producer of pulp and paper in the world by the beginning of the First World War. By 1929, the country's pulp and paper plants were producing more than three million tons of paper a year, well over 50 percent of the world's total. The demand for paper in general, and newsprint in particular, grew rapidly as a result of the increasing circulation of newspapers across Canada and the United States. Huge plants were established by the *Chicago Tribune* at Thorold, Ontario and in Baie Comeau, Quebec, to ensure a continuous supply of newsprint. Canadians continued to make creative contributions to these industries, including the development of the stronger kraft paper, as well as "black liquor,"a by-product of the kraft process that is used as a source of energy in paper mills. The Riordon Company specialized in boiling shredded wood in sulphite and then breaking it down under steam pressure, creating various types of bleaching processes and techniques, and developing products like rayon.

AGRICULTURAL IMPLEMENTS, AUTOMATION, AND INDUSTRIAL PRODUCTS

The creation of agricultural implements is another area where Canadians have demonstrated a high degree of creativity, something which is not surprising in view of the fact that agriculture has played a crucial role in Canadian development over the centuries.

We begin with the Reverend Patrick Bell, a Scot, who came to Canada in 1833 and settled near Fergus, Ontario. While there, he developed a reaper—a machine for harvesting grain and pulse crops—which incorporated a conveyor belt made of canvas that carried the cut grain out of the machine and formed it into sheaves.

Like Patrick Bell, John Fisher was also a creative person. This blacksmith from Hamilton developed a threshing machine between 1833 and 1837 with financing from New York. Then, in 1847, Daniel Massey established the Newcastle Foundry and Machine Manufactory, and in 1857 Alanson Harris, a sawmill operator in Brant County, created a foundry in Beamsville, Ontario and started manufacturing farm equipment. These two companies would eventually merge to become Massey-Harris Company Limited, Canada's largest manufacturer of farm implements and machinery for many years.

An important step forward in cultivating the relatively arid Prairies came with the invention in 1935 of the "Noble blade" by Charles Noble, a blacksmith from Nobleford, Alberta. By changing the shape of the blade and the frame, Noble created a cultivator that was capable of loosening soil and destroying weeds without damaging the surface of the soil. Even more important was the invention of the self-propelled combine harvester by Thomas Carroll at Massey-Harris in the late 1930s. This unique device transformed farming in Canada by making it possible to cut, thrash, clean, and deliver grain in one operation

Canadians have made creative contributions in other areas of manufacturing, too. One of the most important was the creative contribution made by Eric Leaver to automation.

Leaver was born in England in 1915, came to Saskatchewan at an early age, and established himself as a major inventor of automatic landing systems for aircraft in the 1930s. After World War II, Leaver founded Electronic Associates Ltd. in association with Research Enterprise Ltd. and started creating robotic machine tools as well as a functional "hand-arm machine." In 1946, he created a system known as the Automatic Machine Control by Recorded Operation, or "AMCRO." He wrote about this system and its implications for industrial production in an article published in the November 1946 issue of *Fortune* magazine entitled "The Automatic Factory." In this article, Leaver became the first person to visualize what a fully automated system of production would look like. In conjunction with G. R. Mounce, a Canadian engineer, Leaver established a small plant in Toronto that produced the first production tool that could be programmed to mimic the actions of a human worker. This was a forerunner of the automated systems used in so many factories today.

Although AMCRO was patented in 1949, Leaver and Mounce lacked the capital to develop their system in Canada. As a result, it was taken over by American licensees. Nevertheless, Leaver and Mounce did go on to produce many other electronic devices, including a portable Geiger counter for uranium prospectors, radar altimeters for aerial surveys, and automatic process controls for industry, most notably pulp and paper mills and mines.

Nor does the list of Canadian innovations end here. While few Canadians are aware of it, the automatic lubricating cap, the caulking gun, the Robertson screwdriver and screw, Plexiglass, the paint roller, green garbage bags, the electronic wheelchair, the Ardox spiral nail, the alkaline battery, biodegradable plastics, safety paint, the gas mask, the fathometer, the interchangeable head screwdriver, and stainless steel sinks were all invented by Canadians, or Canadians played a seminal role in their development.

The automatic lubricating cap was invented by Elijah McCoy in 1872 and patented in the U.S. in 1920. McCoy was born in Colchester, Ontario, the son of black slaves who fled from the United States along the Underground Railway. He and his family returned to the U.S. while he was still a boy. McCoy's inventions included a lawn sprinkler, a folding ironing board, and rubber-heeled shoes. The automatic lubricating cap revolutionized mechanized production, and gave rise to the phrase "the Real McCoy," which is still in use today.

In 1894, Theodore Witte invented the caulking gun. He claims to have thought of this ingenious device for insulating windows and filling gaps by watching his baker decorate a cake. Anyone who has used a caulking gun and decorated a cake will instantly realize the connection, since in both cases the filling is squeezed out through a small hole at the end of a tube.

In 1908, Peter Robertson invented the Robertson screwdriver and screw. According to legend, Robertson was using a slot-head screwdriver one day when the screwdriver slipped out of the slot-head and slashed his hand. Thinking there must be a better way to do things, he created a new type of screwdriver and screw. With their square-shaped tips and slight taper, such screws quickly became essential in the construction industry, so much so that Robertson called them "the biggest little invention of the twentieth century so far." He may well have been right, especially after the Fisher Body Company, famous for constructing Model T cars for the Ford Motor Company, decided to use his invention in its production processes.

In 1928, a chemistry graduate from McGill University, Dr. William Chalmers, played a key role in the development of Plexiglas—polymerized methyl methacrylate—or acrylic. It was instantly popular because it had many different uses, none more important than the production of shatter-proof plastic lenses, which are now a standard feature in workshops and construction sites around the world.

The paint roller, an invention that many say revolutionized the home renovation industry, was also created by a Canadian. It was invented by Norman Breakey in 1940, although Breakey, like many other Canadian inventors, did not have the funds to capitalize on his invention or ward off imitations by other inventors and disagreements with other patent contenders. Green garbage bags were also invented by Canadians, in this case Harry Wasylyk and Larry Hansen in 1950. Other notable inventions include the invention of the electric wheelchair in 1952 by George Klein, as well as Allan B. Dove's invention of the Ardox spiral nail, which was patented by Stelco in 1954. Unlike most nails in use at the time, the Ardox nail had an irregular rather than a smooth finish, allowing it to maintain its grip more effectively when nailed into wood.

And this is not all. The long-lasting alkaline battery was invented by Lewis Urry in the late 1950s; biodegradable plastics were invented by Dr. James Guillet in 1971 and patented in 1973; safety paint was invented by Neil Harpham in 1974; and the interchangeable head screwdriver was invented by the George H. Cluthe Manufacturing Company in 2001. Like the Robertson screwdriver and screw, this timely device plays an important role in the construction industry because many different types of screwdriver tips can be stored in the cap. Finally, John Fairfield Thompson, a metallurgist who joined Inco in 1906, is credited with playing a major role in the creation of stainless steel sinks, which are now commonplace.

THE NATIONAL RESEARCH COUNCIL, SCIENTIFIC RESEARCH, NOBEL LAUREATES

Canada would not be the country it is today without the National Research Council. This highly innovative institution can trace its origins back to the establishment of an eleven-member Honorary Advisory Council on Scientific and Industrial Research in 1916. Since its establishment in 1925, the NRC has played a major role in scientific and industrial research, in both the public and private sectors. As Roy Mayer, who has done so much to document and popularize the achievements of the NRC, points out in his book *Scientific Canadian:*

> For the better part of a century, hundreds of high-calibre scientists, engineers and technicians gravitated to one place in Canada: the National Research Council. These people were intellectual adventurers, and from all places in Canada they came: rural parts, hamlets, towns, and cities. They also came from countries all over the world, perhaps to escape political insurgency and its horrors or because Canada offered a better life and career opportunities. All were very different people, but they were of one mind—to become initiators of innovations that might someday be great ones.
>
> They were the exceptional ones, who had, even when young, shown particular adeptness in their chosen fields of space, aeronautics, medicine, genetics, communications, chemistry, electronics, arts and entertainment, food, energy, machinery, electricity, building construction, public security, information systems, and many other essential fields. Either for a few years or often for their entire working lives these dedicated people conceptualized and developed innovative solutions to problems facing society.

The contributions of the NRC are legendary, not only in Canada but also in other parts of the world. Many innovations that are well known today, such as the Canadarm, the Crash Position Indicator, the Flight Recorder Playback Centre (the familiar "black box" of airline crash investigations), ultrasound, virtual museums, the laser scanner, cleaning with microbes, fuel cells, and energy-efficient homes, to name but a few, can trace their origins in whole or part to the NRC.

A good example is the electronic music synthesizer, created by Hugh Le Caine. Le Caine was born in Thunder Bay, Ontario and designed an electronic free-reed organ in 1937. Following this, in the mid-1940s he built the "Electronic Sackbut," now generally recognized as one of the world's first music synthesizers. After his instruments proved successful in a number of public demonstrations, he transferred his activities to the NRC in 1954 to work full-time on them. Over the next two decades, he built more than 22 new instruments. He also collaborated in the development of highly innovative electronic music studios at the University of Toronto and McGill University.

Many world famous researchers and scientists like Le Caine have worked at the NRC over the years. So have some of the country's Nobel Prize-winners. There is, unfortunately, room to mention only a few of them here.

Of course, the NRC did not yet exist when Ernest Rutherford won Canada's first Nobel Prize in 1908 for chemistry. Like many of the country's creative talents, Rutherford was born in another part of the world—in his case, New Zealand. He studied in England for several years before coming to McGill University in 1898 as a professor of physics, where he studied the structure of the atom and the principles of radioactivity.

Perhaps Rutherford set a precedent, as Canadians have won several Nobel prizes in chemistry, more than in any other field. One of the most prominent of these prize-winners was Gerhard Herzberg. He was born in Germany in 1904, and came to Canada during the Second World War. In 1945, he was appointed a research professor at the University of Saskatchewan, and became a Canadian citizen shortly thereafter. He was made Director of Pure Physics at the NRC in 1955, and spent much of the rest of his life there helping other scientists get established and undertake research, largely in the fields of electromagnetic radiation and spectroscopy. In the late fifties, Herzberg became famous throughout the world for the pioneering work he did on "free radicals," molecules that are chemically very active. He received his Nobel Prize in 1971 for his work in this area. Due to Herzberg, the NRC became a world leader in the field of spectroscopy.

It didn't take long for Herzberg's dedication, commitment, and creativity to rub off. A number of well-known scientists followed in his footsteps, most notably Henry Taub and John C. Polanyi, who also won Nobel prizes in chemistry.

Saskatchewan was a real hotbed for scientific creativity and research in the middle part of the twentieth century. Not only did Herzberg work there for a time, but so did Henry Taub, who was also born there. Born in Saskatoon in 1915, Taub received his B.A. and M.A. in science from the

University of Saskatchewan in 1935 and 1937 respectively. Following this, he went to the University of California at Berkeley where he remained for the rest of his life, primarily because Canada lacked the research facilities he needed to undertake his work in Canada. He received a Nobel Prize in 1983 for his pioneering work on electron transfer reactions.

Being born somewhat later, Polanyi was able to spend the bulk of his career in Canada, although he was actually born in Berlin in 1929. Upon completing his Ph.D. in chemistry in 1952, Polanyi did post-graduate work at the NRC from 1952 to 1954, and was appointed a professor of chemistry at the University of Toronto in 1956, where he stayed for the remainder of his academic career. He was awarded the Nobel Prize in chemistry in 1986 for his pioneering work on a new field called “reaction dynamics.” This involved intensive studies of what are called “chemical lasers,” molecules that get so energized when they undergo a chemical reaction that they give off infrared radiation. If enough of them do so in a controlled manner, a laser beam is produced, or what Polanyi called “chemical luminescence” or a “molecular dance.” The importance of this work should not be underestimated in view of the pivotal role lasers now play in many areas of life.

More recently, Canadians have won Nobel prizes in physics and medicine. The 2009 prize in physics was won by Willard Boyle. Boyle was born in Amherst, Nova Scotia in 1924, flew Spitfires for the Royal Canadian Navy during World War II, and undertook most of his research in the United States rather than in Canada. Along with fellow prize-winners George Smith of the United States and Charles Kao of China, Boyle played a key role in opening the door to digital cameras through the development of the imaging semiconductor circuit, or “CCD sensor.” He also played an important role in the use of fibre optics and lasers in communications. The Royal Swedish Academy of Sciences, which awards the Nobel prizes, called the three aforementioned individuals “masters of light” whose scientific research and accomplishments have “helped to shape the foundations of today’s networked societies.”

The 2011 Nobel Prize in medicine was won by Ralph Steinman, who was born in Canada and graduated from McGill University. He then went to Harvard Medical School where he became extremely interested in the immune system. Following a residency at Massachusetts General Hospital, he joined the laboratory of cellular physiology and immunology at the Rockefeller University in New York in 1970. While he was there, he discovered a new class of immune cells, called dendritic cells, that lay at the core of the whole immune process, although the importance of his discovery was not generally recognized until a decade later. His winning of the Nobel Prize was tinged with tragedy, however. Steinman died of pancreatic cancer just three days before the Nobel Prize was to be awarded to him.

Most recently, Arthur McDonald was awarded the Nobel Prize in physics. McDonald and his co-winner, Takaaki Kajita of Japan, were recognized for their work in helping to explain the complex character of the mysterious subatomic particles called neutrinos. By confirming that neutrinos actually have mass—it was long thought they did not—McDonald and Kajita caused scientists to rethink (in the words of the Royal Swedish Academy) their understanding of the "fundamental constituents of the universe."

Finally, although he did not receive a Nobel Prize, any list of eminent Canadian scientists would be incomplete without mentioning Eli Franklin Burton and his creative team. Burton was born in Green River, Ontario in 1879 and obtained an undergraduate degree from the University of Toronto and a Master's degree from Cambridge University. He then returned to the University of Toronto where he completed his Ph.D. in 1910 and became a full professor in 1924. Eventually, he was appointed Director of the McLennan Physics Laboratory at the University of Toronto and conducted most of his pioneering research there. Working in close cooperation with three graduate students—James Hillier, Albert Prebus, and Cecil Hall—Burton was involved in the development and successful testing of the first practical *transmission electron microscope*. The significance of this invention should not be underestimated. Microscopes using visible light had first been used by Anton van Leeuwenhoek in the seventeenth century, but despite all the refinements made since then, the nature of light waves themselves limited the amount of magnification that could be achieved. The initial invention of the electron microscope by Ernst Ruska in Germany in 1931, and then the work of Burton, Hillier, Prebus, and Hall in the late 1930s, totally transformed this situation, making it possible for scientists to see objects in incredible detail that had only appeared as fuzzy shadows through optical microscopes. Transmission electronic microscopes use focused beams of electrons to magnify objects by up to two million times. Scientists were able to study objects too tiny to previously be seen in detail, allowing for vital advances in medicine and biology. The transmission electron microscope has also been used in industry, magnifying such substances as wood fibres, asphalt, textiles, plastics, dyes, inks, paints, and metal surfaces.

With the transmission electron microscope, we come to the end of our discussion of Canadian achievements in science, technology, and industry. There are, of course, many other accomplishments that we haven't had room to discuss in this chapter, but the ones that have been included confirm the fact of Canadian creativity in these fields—a creativity that has played a vital role in providing Canadians with a high standard of living and quality of life.

CHAPTER FIVE

Education, Politics, and Political Milestones

Education and politics have always been closely associated in Canada. There is a reason for this. As Egerton Ryerson, one of Canada's greatest and most innovative educators, once observed, wise governments make education a high priority because educated people are extremely loyal to, and supportive of, good government and enlightened political policies and processes.

The challenge of building an effective educational system in Canada has been long and arduous. Difficult transportation, communication, and geographical problems had to be overcome, as well as many religious, linguistic, ethnic, and cultural challenges. While all countries grapple with such problems, few nations are as geographically large, culturally diverse, and linguistically divided as Canada. Perhaps only Russia, China, and to some degree the United States have had to confront a similar set of challenges.

BUILDING AN EFFECTIVE EDUCATIONAL SYSTEM

Religion lay at the heart of virtually all attempts to build an effective educational system in Canada in the seventeenth through early twentieth centuries. While far too little is known about the religious and educational practices of the Indigenous peoples, especially during their early years in the Americas, it is clear that there must have been an intimate connection between learning and spirituality among these peoples, as such a link is still conspicuous today in their lives, cultures, and educational practices.

Religion was also intimately connected to the educational activities and efforts of the first French colonists. As early as 1616, eight years after New France was founded, four Récollect priests accompanying Samuel de Champlain were involved in many matters related to education. Not long after this, the Jesuit order arrived in New France and established the first elementary and secondary schools.

Women played a central role in forging the close connection between religion and education in New France. The Ursuline order opened a school for girls in 1642, and the Congregation of Notre Dame, founded in Montreal in 1659, became the first organization of educators indigenous to Canada. These developments set the stage for the centuries to follow. Every parish had its own school taught by a brother, sister, or priest. Since the vast majority of the parishioners were Roman Catholic, a strong bond was created between education and the Catholic Church—a bond that proved exceedingly difficult to break when the time came to do so.

The same pattern repeated itself in other parts of the country. A variety of religious institutions were involved in education, but the Roman Catholic Church and the Church of England played the dominant role. Many "missionary-teachers" were sent out by the Church of England to Newfoundland and the Maritime provinces in the early years, under the auspices of an organization known as the Society for the Propagation of the Gospel in Foreign Parts, or the S.P.G. An S.P.G. missionary established the first school in what is now English-speaking Canada at Bonavista, Newfoundland in 1726. Roman Catholic priests quickly followed suit, and by 1800, Anglicans, Roman Catholics, and Methodists were all involved in building schools and establishing churches in Newfoundland and the Maritimes, usually on a highly competitive basis. In the early years of the nineteenth century, these religious groups were joined by a number of philanthropic organizations, such as the Society for Improving the Condition of the Poor. This was the first indication that the intimate connection between religion and education was about to be challenged.

That challenge occurred first in the Atlantic region. In 1836, the Newfoundland Legislative Assembly authorized government grants to schools. While these grants were given to schools with religious affiliations—a practice that became well established in Canada in the years to follow—the move signaled that the state intended to play a role in education. In New Brunswick and Nova Scotia, the arrival of large numbers of United Empire Loyalists, who were largely Episcopalians, stimulated efforts to eliminate the preferential treatment given to the Church of England and set in motion a movement to create "free schools." This was followed by another creative development of crucial importance to the development of the educational system in Canada, namely the use of local taxes to pay for schools. In 1852, Prince Edward Island became the first jurisdiction in Canada to establish free "common schools"—schools supported entirely by taxation under the Free Education Act. By the time of Confederation, Nova Scotia and New Brunswick were also using local taxes to pay for schools, and all three Maritime provinces had a provincial educational administration directed by a professional educator.

Concerted attempts were also made around this time to unify approaches to education. In 1841, for instance, following the amalgamation of Lower and Upper Canada into one province, efforts were made to bring together all elements of the population—French and English, Protestant and Catholic—in a single integrated school system. It was a valiant effort, but proved to be a resounding failure in the end. Instead, the Common School Act stipulated that members of a religious minority in any local school district had the right to establish their own school board, open their own common schools, and receive a share of provincial school grants. This became the legal basis for the dual system of Protestant and Roman Catholic school commissions that developed in Canada East and persisted in Quebec after Confederation, and also served as the justification for the development of "separate schools" in Canada West (later Ontario). While many thought this guarantee of educational autonomy for a religious minority was a concession to Roman Catholics, principally in Quebec, it was actually incorporated into the Common School Act in response to concerted pressure by the Protestant minority in Montreal to establish its own schools.

As education became more specialized, outstanding educators emerged to champion the educational cause. In Canada East, Dr. Jean-Baptiste Meilleur, a strong advocate of "dual education," became superintendent of education. He was succeeded by Pierre-Joseph Chauveau, who became the first Quebec minister of education as well as the first premier of Quebec. In Canada West, Egerton Ryerson, son of a Methodist minister and United Empire Loyalist, was made superintendent of education. He followed on the heels of another powerful and highly creative and successful educator, namely John Strachan, an Anglican bishop, member of the Family Compact, founder of district grammar schools in what later became Ontario, and a pioneer in the development of what ultimately became the University of Toronto.

Ryerson is credited with creating one of the most progressive systems of common schools in North America, one that was on par with the best Europe had to offer. (It should be added, however, that he has been criticized in recent years for the role he played in the development of residential schools for the Indigenous population.) Ryerson walked a fine line between "completely separate schools" on the one hand and "a totally integrated school system" on the other. He realized it was imperative that the provincial Department of Education maintain control over curriculum (except for religious education), textbooks, teacher training, and teacher certification in the separate schools, while at the same time allowing separate schools to control their own finances and gradually increase their share of local taxation and provincial grants. By and large, this type of system has been maintained in Ontario ever since, despite criticisms leveled at it from time to time.

By Confederation, the pattern for educational development in Canada had been set, particularly with respect to constitutional authority over education and its relationship with religion, religious institutions, and minority groups. Constitutionally, education was to be a provincial responsibility. Roman Catholics and Protestants were guaranteed denominational schools supported by provincial governments where the numbers warranted it and they constituted a minority. If any province refused to recognize this guarantee, the BNA Act made it possible for the federal government to intervene and enforce it. This provision profoundly affected the development of educational institutions and systems in the west, especially Manitoba, Saskatchewan, and Alberta, where the question of whether there would be separate schools or a single integrated system was played out in earnest.

Meanwhile, another problem was brewing on the educational front that required a creative response. This was the problem of preserving the languages and heritages of ethnic minorities and communities other than the English and French. Many of the immigrants who came to Canada after Confederation were from countries other than England and France. Like the English and French, they wanted their own languages and heritages preserved and protected, and the country's emerging elementary and secondary schools became the focus of this desire. In the West, strong pressures were exerted to teach Polish and Ukrainian in school in areas where these ethnic groups were concentrated. In Toronto and Montreal, similar efforts were made to teach Hebrew and preserve Jewish customs, traditions, and culture where numbers warranted. As these developments illustrate, multiculturalism is anything but a new phenomenon in Canada. It is deeply rooted in the country's history and culture.

Like the development of Canada's elementary and secondary schools, the development of the country's post-secondary educational institutions was long and complex. In the technical and vocational sense, it can be traced back to 1688 when Bishop Laval created L'Ecole des Arts et Metiers to teach agriculture and train artisans in New France. Technical and vocational training evolved rapidly in Canada, particularly in the nineteenth century when "normal schools" to train teachers and trade schools to train nurses and labourers were created. They are the forerunners of today's junior and community colleges, which were established after World War II. The names of these institutions vary from province to province. In Ontario, for example, they are called "colleges of applied arts and technology," whereas in Quebec they are called "general and vocational colleges" or, in French, *Collèges d'enseignement général and professionel* or, as they are popularly known, "CEGEPs." Regardless of what they are called, however, they are a fundamental part of higher education in Canada today, and increasingly so as in recent years many agreements have been negotiated between universities and colleges to provide both theoretical training and practical experience through the provision of joint degrees.

The history of Canada's universities also dates back to the years before Confederation. Two of the oldest universities in Canada are Laval University and the University of New Brunswick. They trace their origins back several centuries and each claims to be the oldest university in Canada, although they did not receive their charters until long after they were founded. The University of King's College in Halifax also claims to be the oldest university in the country. It was established as far back as 1789.

But far more important than the question of which university is the oldest is the role played by religious institutions and authorities in the development of the country's universities. By and large, this role was predicated on one of two models, both essentially imported from Europe. (It might be argued, therefore, that rather less creativity went into the development of Canada's educational system than in other areas of the country's cultural life.) On the one hand, there was the "French model," in the tradition of the system of "*collèges classiques*" that existed in France prior to the French Revolution. On the other hand, there was the "British and American model," following in the footsteps of the great universities of Britain, such as Oxford, Cambridge, and Edinburgh, as well as universities and liberal arts colleges in the United States.

Regardless of which model was preferred, religious institutions and authorities were actively involved in the development of many universities. In English-speaking Canada, the Anglican Church played a seminal role in the development of many universities, with teaching appointments and student enrolment often restricted to members of the Anglican Church. This provoked strong reactions from other religious groups, and ultimately led to fundamental changes in administration and control. For instance, in Ontario, the provincial university—for which Bishop Strachan received a Royal Charter in 1827—changed its name from King's College to the University of Toronto in 1850. In New Brunswick, another Anglican stronghold, King's College in Fredericton passed from control of the Church of England and was renamed the University of New Brunswick in 1859. In fact, the only "King's College" in Canada to retain its original name and affiliation with the Church of England is the aforementioned University of King's College, originally established in Windsor, Nova Scotia in 1789, but now in Halifax.

The Anglican Church was responsible for the creation of many other universities in the country, including Bishop's in Lennoxville, Quebec, Trinity in Toronto, and Huron College, the founding college of the University of Western Ontario in London. But Baptists, Methodists, Presbyterians, and Roman Catholics were all getting into the act in the latter decades of the nineteenth century. Baptists created Acadia in Wolfville and McMaster, first in Toronto and then in Hamilton; Methodists created Mount Allison in Sackville and Victoria College in Coburg, which moved later to Toronto; Presbyterians created Queen's University in Kingston; and Roman Catholics created Mount Saint Vincent and Saint Mary's in Halifax, St. Francis Xavier in Antigonish, Nova Scotia, St. Michael's College in Toronto, Assumption College in Windsor, and the University of Ottawa, which was in fact created by the Oblates and not the Jesuits as is often assumed.

While most of these universities have now become non-denominational in order to qualify for grants and governmental support, some have amalgamated with other degree-granting institutions in order to expand their operations and facilities even while they maintain certain theological activities. The University of Toronto for many years was composed of several religiously based colleges, including Victoria College, St. Michael's College, and Trinity, which were all affiliated with religious institutions, in addition to University College, which was non-denominational. It would, however, be a mistake to assume that all universities in Canada had or have ties with religious institutions. Many, including Dalhousie, McGill, the University of British Columbia, Memorial University, the University of Prince Edward Island, and major universities in Manitoba, Saskatchewan, and Alberta, were created and developed without any strong religious involvement.

Mention should be made here of the fact that Canada also has a number of highly specialized post-secondary educational institutions that are well-known throughout the country and the world. Included in this roster are the Ontario Institute for Studies in Education (OISE), which specializes in advanced educational studies and pedagogical research; the Royal Military College (RMC), Royal Roads, and the Collège Royal de St. Jean, which specialize in training personnel for the armed forces; and the Technical University of Nova Scotia and the University of Ontario Institute of Technology, which specialize in technological training at an advanced level. In combination with the other degree-granting institutions across the country—well over a hundred in all—they round out a post-secondary educational system that is as complex and diversified as it is distinctive and unique.

In the process of building the country's educational system, Canadians have manifested a certain degree of creativity, although, as noted earlier, not to the same extent as in some other areas of Canadian life, because of the tendency to duplicate models from France, Great Britain, and the United States. What creativity has been exercised has stemmed largely from the huge size of the country and the highly diversified, diffuse nature of the population. Especially important in this regard are distance, correspondence, and adult education, as well as the use of audio-visual and digital technologies; heritage and language education, which has been developed far more fully over the last 40 years as a result of Canada's official designation as a "bilingual, multicultural country"; and education for people with special needs.

A few examples should suffice to expose the nature and extent of this creativity. For many years, railroad cars were used in Northern Ontario to educate people in isolated areas. These cars were outfitted with classrooms, pulled onto sidings, and remained in remote communities for weeks at a time, much as "museum-mobiles" did decades later. Moreover, a number of universities have distinguished themselves in distance and correspondence education and become leaders in the field, such as Athabasca University, an open university which instructs by means of self-study, Ryerson University, which now ranks high in terms of the number of distant education students, the Université du Québec, and the University of Waterloo, which has a long-established distance education program. This latter institution has also become internationally famous for cooperative education—programs that combine academic training in the classroom and practical experience on the job—as well as for applying various types of audio-visual equipment and computer technology to education.

The Toronto District School Board is equally renowned for its use of audio-visual equipment and computer technology, in part because Toronto was one of the first cities in the world to make coaxial cable installations available to households that requested them. This made it possible to deliver specially designed television programs by cable to any classroom in the city, as well as to homes where children were not able to attend school. Toronto was also the first city in Canada—and the second in North America—to make kindergarten an integral part of the public school system. This occurred in 1883; two years later, Ontario became the first state or province in North America to authorize kindergartens in all elementary schools. Toronto was also one of the first municipalities in the world to establish a permanent program for convalescing students in collaboration with the Hospital for Sick Children.

To this list of innovators should be added Mount Allison University, which was the first university in Canada to combat sexual discrimination in education by granting a degree to a woman—Grace Annie Lockhart—in 1875. Canada also played a key role in the development of education for people with special needs and physical disabilities. In 1857, for instance, Halifax created the first School for the Deaf, and in 1871, two schools were built for the blind, in Fredericton and Brantford respectively.

Canada is also well known throughout the world for highly creative work in adult education. This can be traced back to the latter part of the nineteenth century, when extramural and extension courses were offered by Queen's University, night classes were provided by the YMCA, many farmers' institutes were established with educational and training mandates, and Adelaide Hoodless founded the first Women's Institute in Stoney Creek, Ontario, in 1897. Predicated on helping women obtain formal education while simultaneously carrying out numerous household responsibilities, the Women's Institute organized rural women across Canada and enabled them to speak with a unified voice for educational reform. Hoodless was a highly innovative trailblazer who was involved in many other areas. She was elected national president of the Young Women's Christian Association in Canada in 1895, helped to found the National Council of Women and the Victorian Order of Nurses in Canada (working in close conjunction with Lady Aberdeen), and was treasurer of the National Council of Women from 1893 to 1901.

Another significant development in adult education occurred when Frontier College was established in 1899. Founded by Alfred Fitzpatrick, a Presbyterian minister, working together with Queen's University in Kingston, it was one of the first colleges in the world to concern itself with adult education in remote areas. Other creative contributions to the development of adult education by Canadians include those of Roby Kidd, who, in concert with many others, including Walter Pitman and Ian Morrison, was instrumental in founding and developing the Canadian Association for Adult Education. Kidd also worked closely with UNESCO and other international organizations in this area, and was largely responsible for the International Association for Adult Education establishing its headquarters in Canada.

Canada now has one of the most complex and highly diversified educational systems in the world. It is a system that functions effectively on the whole, despite the usual problems of funding, teacher training, teacher certification, governmental involvement in educational matters, and so forth. The biggest problem is the lack of uniformity across the country, particularly in terms of curriculum offerings and academic standards. This often results in demands for unification of the educational system and the establishment of national standards, goals, objectives, and guidelines. While some of these concerns, such as the development of a pan-Canadian curriculum and national standards in certain subjects, have been addressed by the Council of Ministers of Education, fundamental differences in approach across the country continue to affect educational development in Canada.

SOME RELEVANT POLITICAL AND MILITARY ACHIEVEMENTS

Like the country's educational system, the country's political system has a long, distinctive, and complex history. It can also be traced back to the Indigenous peoples, and the creation of "confederacies" to provide effective government, governance, and leadership for the communities and societies they served.

The best-known examples of this are the Huron Confederacy and the Iroquois Confederacy. The Huron Confederacy was created in central Ontario in the area around Georgian Bay and Lake Huron. It brought together four major bands and twenty autonomous villages through the establishment of a governing council chosen by clan mothers that provided procedures and policies for solving disputes and collaborating on matters of mutual interest and concern. Even better known was the Iroquois Confederacy, which straddled eastern Ontario and upper New York State. It resulted from the creation of the Five Nations League and a Grand Council composed of 50 federal or national chiefs. Most matters were settled peacefully through discussion, debate, compromise, concession, and the passing of the peace pipe. It is seen by some as a model for political and governmental decision-making—a model said to have been used to advantage when the Constitution of the United States was drawn up.

Despite the influence of the Indigenous peoples, in the end Canada's political system was shaped most of all by France and Great Britain. In fact, it is probably fair to say that Canada's political system is largely a product of British and French antecedents.

While the French were active in North America from the earliest days of exploration and settlement, the decision by Louis XIV to revoke the charter given to the Company of the Hundred Associates and make New France a royal province in 1663 had a fundamental bearing on virtually everything that followed. Giving New France the same status as a province in France did more than anything else to establish a permanent and powerful French-speaking colony in North America, and gave rise to expectations about how that colony would be governed (and treated politically and culturally) that have persisted to this day.

The colony was governed by a sovereign (or superior) council appointed by the Crown. Its governor held overall responsibility, as well as being specifically responsible for military and external affairs. An intendant was responsible for internal affairs and administration, and a bishop oversaw the affairs of the Church in the colony. From the 1660s to the 1680s, these three posts were held by the powerful triumvirate of Frontenac, Talon, and Laval respectively. New France grew rapidly after being made a royal province, and had a population in excess of 60,000 by the time it was transferred to Britain following the battle of the Plains of Abraham.

The question then facing Britain was how to deal with New France, which had a significant population, strong culture, and distinctive way of life. The question was answered initially by the Royal Proclamation of 1763, which prescribed boundaries, government, laws, and regulations for British holdings throughout North America. It was assumed that the French would be assimilated into the British system of government and overall way of life.

It was not long, however, before it became apparent that this approach was not working. Not only was the culture of New France too strongly entrenched to be swept aside, but the British required the support of the French colonists in dealing with the ambitious and rapidly expanding English-speaking colonies along the eastern seaboard—the famous Thirteen Colonies that would soon break away from Britain in the American Revolution. As a result, the British passed the Quebec Act of 1774. It proved to be a highly creative response to an exceedingly difficult and complex problem. Not only did it recognize that homogeneity was not an option, but also it signaled the beginning of "duality" between the French and English in Canada. It did so by placing much more emphasis on integration and understanding of cultural differences than on assimilation and oppression, thereby enabling the French to preserve many of their cherished legal and civic procedures and overall way of life. It also extended the boundaries of New France south and west to the Ohio Valley, despite the fact that this would exclude settlers from the English colonies.

In specific terms, the Act recognized the seigneurial system, retained French civil law, accepted the power and authority of the Roman Catholic Church, allowed the Church to collect tithes, and in fact gave the Roman Catholic Church in New France more rights than were accorded to religious sects in Britain. It also appointed a legislative council comprised of French and English members directed by a governor, thereby preventing the English minority from controlling the French colony (something which otherwise might have happened, because Catholics were not allowed to vote or hold office). This did more than anything to permanently sanction the French presence in what became Canada.

The Quebec Act caused a great deal of resentment and discontent despite its creative character. English colonists felt that the French had been given too much power over their own affairs by the British government, and the large amount of land granted to Quebec was also deemed unacceptable. The Quebec Act was one of the list of "Intolerable Acts" that led to the American Revolution and subsequently the establishment of the United States as an independent country.

Nevertheless, the Quebec Act did a great deal to shape the political future of Canada by recognizing the dual character of British North America and the distinctiveness of the French-speaking population. This made respect for cultural differences, rather than subservience to a single, dominant English culture, the cornerstone of Canada's rapidly evolving political system.

While the British government did this for strategic rather than idealistic reasons—it didn't want to be waging a war with the French colonists at the same time that it was waging one with the Thirteen Colonies—the decision had a profound impact. Not only did it secure the existence of French Canada and subsequently Quebec as a distinctive entity in Canada—a "distinct nation" as it is referred to today, following official recognition by the federal government—but also it gave rise, somewhat ironically in retrospect, to an equally distinct loyalist English Canada, as well as the creation of an overall framework within which relations between these two major linguistic and cultural groups would be conducted. In so doing, it opened the doors for Canada to eventually become a bilingual, multicultural country, with two official languages and many diverse cultures.

Just as France was forced to give up much of its empire in North America after 1759, so Britain was forced to do likewise after 1782 because of its defeat in the American War of Independence. Subsequently, the Canada Act of 1791 created the British colonies of Upper Canada, now Ontario, and Lower Canada, now Quebec. It was about this time that approximately 60,000 United Empire Loyalists—refugees from the United States who remained loyal to Great Britain—flowed into various parts of British North America, most notably Upper and Lower Canada, New Brunswick, and other areas of the Maritimes. Like the French, they were destined to play a crucial role in the development of Canada's political system and institutions in the centuries to follow.

If the Quebec Act had a profound impact on the development of Canada and its political institutions and system, so did the War of 1812. This is especially true of the battles at Queenston Heights in 1812 and Chrysler's Farm and Chateauguay in 1813. Had the War of 1812 not been won, it is quite likely that Canada would be part of the United States today.

As it was, the War of 1812—what some call Canada's "war of independence"—gave Canadian troops (as well as British regulars) a sense of confidence that they could turn back the American invaders. This was especially true of the battle General Isaac Brock and his troops waged—and won—against the Americans at Queenston Heights in 1812. The victory was due to some well-trained, highly disciplined soldiers as well as some very good luck, rather than any overall military superiority on the part of the Canadian and British troops. But in retrospect it paved the way for a number of important future political developments that eventually led to the establishment of the longest undefended border in the world between the two countries.

There is another reason why the War of 1812 was a major political and military achievement. It was a war of defense and survival rather than rebellion and aggression. In consequence, it did a great deal to shape the conviction that Canadians are prepared to fight whenever they are required to do so, but they do not initiate fights, battles, or wars unless this is absolutely necessary. This has had a major effect on Canada's political evolution, including the creation of the Canadian Constitution and its commitment to "peace, order, and good government," as well as the way Canadians approached the First and Second World Wars and later foreign policy positions such as the decision not to participate in the U.S.-led invasion of Iraq.

This is not to say that Canadians have not had rebellions of their own, or that rebellions have not played an important part in the country's political development. For instance, the Rebellion of 1837, which occurred in Upper and Lower Canada, led to the creation of the Durham Report—the *Report on the Affairs of British North America*—written by Lord Durham in 1839 following his investigation of the rebellion's causes. Durham criticized the defective constitutional arrangements that were in place in British North America at that time. In Upper Canada, a small, petty, and corrupt Tory clique—the so-called "Family Compact"—controlled the province's government. In Lower Canada, two nations were "warring in the bosom of a single state," as Durham put it. His solution was the union of Upper and Lower Canada, and the implementation of what was called "responsible government"—that is, a system in which the people's representatives in the legislature would have far more say in the colony's government. The British government accepted the recommendations contained in Durham's report, including a limited form of responsible government, although this was not officially granted until 1848. As a result, the Durham Report is generally recognized as a major milestone in the country's political development that eventually led to the establishment of Canada as an independent country.

The period between the writing of the Durham Report in 1839 and the acceptance of a limited form of responsible government in 1848 was a tedious one. As John Ralston Saul pointed out in his book *Reflections of a Siamese Twin: Canada at the End of the Twentieth Century,* it was only after an informal agreement was reached between Robert Baldwin and L. H. Lafontaine—sealed by "a simple handshake," as Saul put it—that responsible government became a reality in Canada. For this is when Robert Baldwin was able to become a rallying figure, rebuilding the post-rebellion Reform opposition and forging an alliance with Lafontaine and his Lower Canadian liberals. For his part, Lafontaine did a great deal to protect the interests of Quebec in his quest to establish responsible government in Canada. He also insisted on speaking French in the Assembly, eventually causing the British Government to repeal the Act of Union clause that prohibited the official use of French. For these reasons, Lafontaine is considered by some to be "the first real prime minister Canada ever had."

The next major milestone in Canada's development was the British North America Act of 1867, which united Quebec, Ontario, New Brunswick, and Nova Scotia to form the Dominion of Canada. The creation of Canada was the result of a great deal of creative ingenuity and visionary zeal on the part of the Fathers of Confederation. Also playing a part was the British government's desire to reduce its colonial obligations in North America, and perhaps most importantly of all, a strong desire on the part of Canadians as well as the British to counter the perpetual threat of Canada's annexation by the United States. There was a real danger that if the various British provinces in the northern part of the continent did not amalgamate to become a single, independent country linked to Great Britain, they would be gobbled up by the United States, which at the time was being swept by the "manifest destiny" movement. As Sir John A. Macdonald, who would become Canada's first prime minister, put it in a speech in Halifax in 1864, "Nothing could be more distasteful to me than to become what is called a citizen of the United States, though I admire the enterprise and intelligence which characterizes people of that country."

The underlying reasons for creating the Dominion of Canada strongly influenced the character of the British North America Act (or the BNA Act, as it is often called). Since both Britain and the Fathers of Confederation were anxious to create a country capable of defending itself against aggression and preventing possible annexation by the United States, they wanted to ensure a strong central (federal) government. While they wanted to make sure that "peace, order, and good government" prevailed, they were equally anxious to ensure that squabbling among the provinces would not handicap the federal government's ability to act decisively in the event of external threats or internal problems. As Macdonald said in 1865, two years before the passage of the BNA Act, "We thereby . . . make the Confederation one people and one government . . . with the local governments and legislatures subordinate to the General Government and Legislature."

The federal government was given authority over defense, external relations, criminal law, money and banking, trade, transportation, citizenship, Indian affairs, and any other matters not specifically set out in the Act. The provincial governments were given jurisdiction over education, civil law—including property and civil rights—health and welfare, natural resources, and local (municipal) government. The two levels of government were given joint authority and jurisdiction over agriculture, immigration, and most sources of revenue.

It is within this overall framework that the various arrangements and battles among the federal, provincial, and municipal governments have played out ever since, profoundly affecting the political evolution of the country. In some cases, the federal government has had the upper hand and taken the lead, such as in the latter part of the nineteenth century, when the government in Ottawa used its control over tariffs to encourage the development of industry in the east and a combination of land and money grants to private companies to build the two major railways promised at the time of Confederation. In other cases, the provincial governments have taken the lead, such as in the middle part of the twentieth century, when they were extremely active in building numerous dams and highways and expanding schools and health care services. Municipal governments remained largely in the background and played a tertiary or subordinate role, largely because they were made the responsibility of the provinces by the BNA Act and have never had a strong revenue-generating capacity. In fact, it is only recently that municipal governments have made a strong case for playing a much more active role in the political life of the country. Most Canadians now live in towns and cities, and municipal problems have grown rapidly in recent years, threatening to escalate out of control if municipalities' revenue-generating ability is not increased.

While Canada came into existence at the time of Confederation, it "came of age" during the First World War. Canada played a key role in the overall war effort from 1914 to 1918, and a crucial role in the later stages of the war, particularly at Vimy Ridge. On Easter Day—April 9, 1917—the Canadian Corps of four divisions was assigned its first independent mission. It was to capture Vimy Ridge, after other allied forces had failed to take this strategically located ridge held by the Germans. The Canadian Corps succeeded brilliantly after a powerful offensive. They sustained this momentum by spearheading the final Allied campaign from August 4 to November 11, 1918. As a result, this period has been called "Canada's hundred days" or "Canada's finest hour."

These events constitute one of those rare "defining moments" in Canadian history that have acquired greater political and military significance ever since. The reason for this is not difficult to determine. Canada was finally recognized internationally as a country in its own right—a country with strong historical and emotional ties to Britain and France, but nevertheless separate from Britain and capable of acting on its own. For although Canada was given power over its external affairs when the BNA Act was passed in 1867, everybody knew that Britain still "called the shots" and exercised a great deal of control over Canada's foreign policy. It was only after the First World War that Canada was finally recognized throughout the world as a sovereign country and independent political entity. Not only did it sign the Versailles Peace Treaty on its own, but it also became an independent member of the League of Nations in spite of strong objections from the United States. In 1932, the Statute of Westminster formally recognized the equality of Canada (and the other dominions) with Great Britain within the British Commonwealth of Nations. Canada had taken the lead among the self-governing dominions in advocating for the Statute, and with its passage, although the English monarch remained Canada's monarch so long as Canada wished that to be the case, any other involvement of the British government in Canadian affairs (unless requested by Canada itself) came to an end.

It was around this time that a number of highly creative female "political trailblazers" made their appearance on the scene. Most prominent among these, all of whom lived and worked in Alberta for some time, were Emily Murphy, Canada's first female judge and the first woman appointed to the bench in the British Empire; Louise McKinney, the first woman to sit in the Alberta legislature in 1917, as well as the first female elected official in the British Empire; Irene Parlby, who emigrated to Alberta from

London, England in 1896 and was elected to the Alberta legislature in 1921; Nellie McClung, who was also elected to the Alberta legislature in 1921 and was a well-known social and political activist as well as an outstanding orator and author; and Henrietta Muir Edwards, who was instrumental in founding the forerunner of the YMCA in 1875 and helped to establish the National Council of Women in 1893. The creative contributions of these "famous five" women were so substantial that a statue commemorating their contributions stands outside the East Block of Parliament in Ottawa. They were also made honorary senators quite recently.

Mention should also be made here of John Humphrey and Lester B. Pearson, who were also highly creative political trailblazers. Humphrey played a key role in the drafting of the *Universal Declaration of Human Rights* in 1947 as director of the Human Rights Division of the United Nations Secretariat and a close collaborator with Eleanor Roosevelt on this important endeavour. Pearson was both a prominent public servant and diplomat, effective minister of external affairs, and one of Canada's most innovative prime ministers. He played a crucial role at the United Nations in working to resolve the Suez Crisis in the Middle East, and was awarded a Nobel peace prize for his contributions.

As was the case elsewhere in Europe and North America, labour unrest began percolating in Canada in the years after the First World War. It was brought on by numerous factors, including high unemployment rates, inflation, and the example of the Russian Revolution in 1917, and resulted in several major strikes across the country. The unrest manifested itself most vigorously in the Winnipeg General Strike in 1919. When negotiations broke down between labour and management in the building and metal trades, the Winnipeg Trades and Labor Council called a general strike, seeking collective bargaining rights, higher wages, and improved working conditions. Within hours of the breakdown in negotiations, an estimated 30,000 workers walked off the job. When workers in many other occupations joined the strike, the entire city was paralyzed. Factories were closed, retail trade ceased, and trains and other forms of transport ground to a halt. Moreover, when "sympathy strikes" were organized in other parts of Canada ranging from Amherst, Nova Scotia in the east to Victoria, British Columbia in the west, Canada had its first real taste of social and political unrest from coast to coast. But another three decades had to elapse before Canadian workers finally secured recognition for their unions as well as collective bargaining rights.

Not long after the Winnipeg strike came another event destined to have a profound effect on political life in Canada. This was the founding in Calgary in 1932 of the Co-operative Commonwealth Federation (CCF), which eventually became the New Democratic Party (NDP) in 1961. The CCF was founded as a political coalition of progressive socialist and labour forces anxious to bring about economic and social reforms. Its first leader was J.S. Woodsworth, who was actively involved in the Winnipeg General Strike and its aftermath and was arrested and jailed for this, despite the fact that he had been a Member of Parliament. At a follow-up meeting in Regina in 1933, the CCF adopted the Regina Manifesto, which included such objectives as creation of a mixed public-private economy through nationalization of key industries, as well as the creation of a welfare state with universal pensions, health and welfare insurance, children's allowances, unemployment insurance, and workers' compensation.

Many of these proposals paralleled developments taking place in Europe and especially Britain at this time, as politicians and governments scrambled during the Great Depression to develop democratic socialism as an alternative to Marxism, communism, and dictatorship by the State.

It was left to political reformers and creative talents like Stanley Knowles, David Lewis, and especially Tommy Douglas to pursue these policies and programs. The real breakthrough occurred when Douglas's CCF government was elected in Saskatchewan in 1944, the first socialist government to hold office in North America.

Interestingly, such developments were confined largely to Canada and did not take hold in the United States to any significant extent. As a result, Canada started to move in some very different political and social directions from the United States during the middle part of the twentieth century—a trend that still persists today. This led to Canadian initiatives such as universal health care, which has only recently taken root in the U.S. in a far more modest form, despite the fact that many Americans are compelled to pay huge bills for private health insurance and medical treatment. It also led to Canada's adopting other social policies and programs that were more progressive than those seen in United States. Without developments like the Winnipeg General Strike and the election of a socialist government in Canada, it is highly unlikely that Canada would have gone as far as it has over the last 60 years in adopting socially progressive legislation such as universal public health care, same-sex marriages, the banning of capital punishment, and the legalization of marijuana for medicinal and related purposes. These measures have increasingly differentiated Canada from the United States. Whereas Americans have preferred a more conservative approach to such matters, Canadians have taken a more contemporary and liberal position.

SOME MAJOR POLITICAL MILESTONES

One major political milestone was the Royal Commission on National Development in the Arts, Letters, and Social Sciences in Canada, or the Massey-Lévesque Commission as it is sometimes called. The commission was established by the federal government in 1949 and completed its work in 1951. It was created as a result of pressure that was rapidly building in the artistic, scientific, and academic communities to undertake a comprehensive assessment of the arts and sciences in Canada and make recommendations concerning their future development. For the first time in Canadian history, these areas were considered sufficiently important—and sufficiently differentiated from other areas, such as the economy—to warrant a full-scale assessment.

In general terms, the commission was charged with examining "the needs and desires of the citizens in relation to science, literature, art, music, drama, films, and broadcasting." More specifically, it was charged with making recommendations concerning broadcasting, higher education, the activities of government departments and agencies in these areas, international relations, and the work of voluntary organizations. In the course of its work, the commission found deficiencies in virtually all of these areas. It also revealed an appalling lack of Canadian content in every aspect of the country's artistic, humanistic, academic, and scientific life. This made it difficult to come to grips with the commission's two principal preoccupations: how to allocate public funds to worthwhile causes without stifling private initiative; and how to distribute financial assistance to these causes in a manner consistent with the federal structure of government and the regional diversity of the country.

In coming to grips with these concerns, the commission demonstrated a remarkable degree of foresight, vision, and creativity. Its 1951 report was predicated on the conviction that the arts, humanities, and sciences have a crucial role to play in maintaining a strong, united, and sovereign Canada. It was within this context that the commission made a series of recommendations that were destined to have a powerful effect on the political and cultural life of the country, even if a considerable amount of time was to elapse before some of the most important of these recommendations were implemented. Most importantly, the commission recommended the creation of a Canada Council for the Encouragement of the Arts, Letters, Humanities, and Social Sciences; promotion of Canada's artistic and academic interests abroad; and establishment of a major scholarship program. Other important recommendations included granting authority to the CBC to license private television stations, expanding federal agencies concerned with artistic, scientific, and academic matters, and encouraging the employment of domestic talent.

While reaction to the Massey-Lévesque Report was enthusiastic in most parts of Canada, it was mixed in Quebec. Some saw it as a spur to artistic and cultural development there, whereas others saw it as a threat to Quebec's ability to create artistic and cultural institutions and programs of its own choosing. As a result, the report divided the province's intellectuals into two main camps. The first group maintained that the soundest way to protect the cultural development of Québec was to let the federal government defend Canadian culture from the influences pouring in from the United States. The second group felt that Quebec must develop its own cultural institutions, parallel to these being established by Ottawa, and that the province should exercise exclusive jurisdiction in the field to avoid becoming a mere tributary of the central source.

This division of Quebec intellectuals into two camps had an important effect on the creation of Quebec's first separatist political party, L'Alliance laurentienne, which eventually led to the Parti Québécois in 1968.

While action on many of the recommendations of the Massey-Lévesque Report commenced shortly after the report was released, six years were to elapse before the principal recommendation—creation of the Canada Council—was carried out in 1957. And this only occurred, according to many, because two wealthy benefactors from the Maritime provinces died and left substantial bequests to the federal government that seemed ideal for this purpose.

The reason for the delay in the creation of the Canada Council is not difficult to discern. It was one thing for the federal government to accept responsibility for cultural agencies of its own creation—such as the CBC and the NFB—as well as for the preservation, protection, and conservation of the country's cultural heritage through museums, galleries, and other institutions. It was quite another matter, however, for the government to accept responsibility for supporting institutions and individuals *outside* government. Not only would this open up a whole new level of governmental involvement in the cultural life of the country, but it would establish a precedent that future governments would be expected to honour. Yet this was precisely what the federal government was being pressured to do.

In the end, the pressure proved to be too great. In 1956, Prime Minister Louis St. Laurent announced the decision to create the Canada Council at the National Conference on Higher Education in Ottawa. It was established the following year and given a mandate to "foster and promote the study and enjoyment of, and the production of, works in the arts, humanities and social sciences in Canada." This confirmed two things beyond a shadow of a doubt. First, public support for the arts, humanities, and social sciences is a legitimate political responsibility. Second, governments have no business making decisions about the specific allocation of funds for artistic and academic purposes. Funding should be as free as possible from political interference and government control. With few exceptions, successive governments in the country at every level have respected these two fundamental principles.

The creation of national signs, symbols, emblems, and anthems has also played a pivotal role in the political and cultural life of Canada, since such symbols provide the touchstones necessary to give Canadians a sense of identity and belonging. Over time, these signs and symbols become powerful tools for binding people together in space and time and enabling politicians and citizens to say "this is who we are." Two of the most important in this regard are the national anthem and the Canadian flag.

The country's national anthem, *O Canada*, was sung for the first time on June 24, 1880. The music was created by Calixa Lavallée, a well-respected Canadian composer, with lyrics by Sir Adolphe-Basile Routhier. The French lyrics for the anthem have remained the same ever since, although the English lyrics, which were originally written by Justice Robert Stanley Weir in 1908, have been changed several times and were revised by a special joint committee of the Senate and the House of Commons in 1968. The version sung across the country today was officially proclaimed the country's national anthem on July 1, 1980, although a desire continues to be expressed to make the wording more inclusive.

The history of the Canadian flag was far more contentious. Given the importance of flags, it is surprising that Canada did not have a flag of its own until February 15, 1965, when Queen Elizabeth proclaimed the current flag, which features a stylized red maple leaf on a white and red background, to be the country's official flag. Its adoption brought to an end a century of disagreement, countless different designs, and a heated "flag debate" in Parliament. Prior to that time, the most common flag flown in the country was the Union Jack, the official flag of Britain. It was flown over many government buildings, as well as over the large majority of Canadian embassies. It was also carried by numerous Canadian athletes during the Olympic Games, as well as by Canadian troops during the Second World War. Also popular was the Red Ensign, which featured the Union Jack and the Canadian coat of arms on a red background.

Following the upsurge of nationalism that took place in Canada after the First World War, many Canadians felt it was time for the country to have its own national flag. However, deciding on a design for the flag proved far more difficult than agreeing that the country should have a national flag in the first place. Between 1918 and 1963, numerous attempts were made to create a flag, but none succeeded. Then, in 1963, the Liberal government under Prime Minister Lester Pearson suggested a flag with three maple leaves on a white centre, with square bars on each side. While the NDP was more or less in agreement with this design, the Conservatives under John Diefenbaker objected strongly, favouring a version of the Red Ensign that would honour both British and French traditions in Canada.

A rancorous debate in the House of Commons in 1963 and 1964 was resolved when Pearson appointed a three-member committee to come up with a proposal for an official flag. The committee proposed a flag similar to that of the Royal Military College, except with a red maple leaf at its centre. Parliamentary debate ensued until closure was imposed and the proposal was voted on and adopted by Parliament in 1964. After a century of disagreement, Canada finally had a flag of its own. Like many creative achievements, the end result was simple, although the road to get there was long and complicated.

There were good reasons for selecting the maple leaf as the central symbol for the flag. Not only is the maple tree ubiquitous in Canada, but its foliage changes colour in the fall, often turning brilliant red. Many institutions have used the maple leaf as a symbol over the course of Canadian history. For example, the St. Jean-Baptiste Society made the maple leaf its emblem when it was created in 1834. Moreover, the maple leaf was referred to as "the chosen emblem of Canada" in an 1848 issue of the literary periodical called the *Maple Leaf.* In 1867, Alexander Muir composed the popular song "The Maple Leaf Forever," which was regarded by many as a kind of "national hymn." And the coats of arms granted to Quebec and

Ontario in 1868 both incorporated a sprig of three maple leaves in their design. Interestingly, the maple leaf also appears on the country's official coat of arms, which, incidentally, has a history of its own to rival that of the flag. Since Canada was not assigned armorial bearings at Confederation in 1867, it took considerable debate before a coat of arms was finally established. This occurred in 1921, when King George V assigned armorial bearings for the country—bearings that included, among other things, lions, flags, and shields symbolizing the English, French, Scotch, and Irish, as well as three maple leaves that were originally green but eventually red in order to signify a new nation with many different groups of people. A motto was added—*A Mari Usque ad Mare*, or "from sea to sea"—which was taken from the seventy-second Psalm to recognize the fact that the country stretched from the Atlantic to the Pacific to the Arctic Ocean.

Like the flag and the coat of arms, the beaver is another symbol of fundamental importance to Canada and Canadians. It has a long history as well. The beaver played a vital role in the early development of the Canadian economy. As far back as 1663, it was used as an emblem to symbolize the fiefdom given in the New World to Sir William Alexander by King James I, now known as Nova Scotia. Both the Hudson's Bay Company and Governor Frontenac used the beaver as a symbol, the Hudson's Bay Company in one of its armorial seals, and Frontenac as an emblem for the colony of New France. Although the use of the beaver as an emblem declined in the second half of the nineteenth century (just as the fur trade itself declined in importance), the animal's emblematic appeal returned when Sir Sandford Fleming used it in his design for Canada's first postage stamp. And, of course, it continues to appear on the reverse side of the country's five-cent piece.

For many people, both the beaver and maple leaf symbolize key elements in the country's culture. The maple leaf symbolizes the natural environment and its importance to Canadians. What could be more symbolic of the country than this? And the beaver symbolizes industry, effort, and commitment to a cause—qualities that many feel are as applicable to Canadians themselves as to the beaver.

If creation of the national anthem, the flag, the coat of arms, and official recognition of the beaver and the maple leaf were key milestones in the country's political history, so was the declaration of Canada as a bilingual, multicultural country in 1971. Setting the stage for this declaration was the Royal Commission on Bilingualism and Biculturalism, which studied the matter from 1963 to 1965, as well as the proclamation of the Official Languages Act in 1969.

When the Royal Commission on Bilingualism and Biculturalism was established, it proceeded on the assumption that Canada was essentially a *bilingual, bicultural* country with two major "founding peoples" and two principal languages and cultures, namely French and English. While the Indigenous peoples and Canadians not of English or French descent were prepared to accept that Canada was a bilingual country, they were not prepared to accept that Canada was a *bicultural* country. They believed that the Indigenous peoples and many other ethnic groups had made—and were making—valuable contributions to the development of the country that should be recognized in the official, public sense.

Recognition of this fact eventually caused the commission to replace its description of Canada as bilingual and bicultural with the characterization of Canada as bilingual but *multicultural*. The commission released its final report in a series of publications between 1965 and 1970, and Book IV, released in 1969, was devoted almost entirely to the contributions made by ethnic groups and communities other than the English and French.

The Official Languages Act was passed in the same year. It declared that French and English would be the two official languages of Canada. As a result, all federal institutions would be compelled to provide their services in English or French according to citizens' choice. The Act also created a Commissioner of Official Languages to oversee the Act and its implementation. The Act together with the work of the Bilingualism and Biculturalism Commission paved the way for Canada to be officially declared a bilingual, multicultural country in 1971, with "multiculturalism within a bilingual framework" as the official political policy of Canada:

> We believe that cultural pluralism is the very essence of Canadian identity. Every ethnic group has the right to preserve and develop its own culture and values within the Canadian context. To say that we have two official languages is not to say we have two official cultures, and no particular culture is more official than another. A policy of multiculturalism must be a policy for all Canadians.

The government went on to state that public support and encouragement would be provided to "the various cultures and ethnic groups that give structure and vitality to our society. They will be encouraged to share their cultural expression and values with other Canadians and so contribute to a richer life for us all."

The federal government has maintained and reinforced the policy of bilingualism and multiculturalism since it was officially declared in 1971. It has done so through a variety of measures, such as the appointment of a Minister of State for Multiculturalism and, later, a Ministry of Multiculturalism and Canadian Identity, rigorous enforcement of bilingualism in all federal institutions, confirmation of the official policy of bilingualism and multiculturalism in the Canadian Constitution and Charter of Rights and Freedoms of 1982, passage of the Canadian Multiculturalism Act in 1988, and so forth. While there has been resistance in some quarters, by and large the policy of multiculturalism within a bilingual framework has been embraced by all Canadian governments—municipal and provincial as well as federal—as well as by most other organizations, institutions, and the nation's individual citizens. While more people speak languages other than English and French today than in 1971, there is no doubt the policy continues to accurately describe the reality of Canadian life, with French and English as the two main languages and many different cultures in existence across the country. Indeed, Canadian society is becoming more multicultural all the time. The OMNI television system, which includes six stations across Canada, now broadcasts in more than 30 languages and is the largest producer of multicultural programming in the world. Moreover, there is a much greater commitment to multiculturalism, interculturalism, and pluralism in communities and schools, which celebrate such occasions as Black History Month and many different ethnic holidays and special events.

One final milestone should be discussed—the Constitution Act of 1982. It brought home the Canadian constitution, and guaranteed certain fundamental rights and freedoms for all Canadians.

No one was more responsible for this milestone than Pierre Elliott Trudeau. As prime minister at the time, he was the driving force behind the Constitution Act, which enabled patriation of the Canadian Constitution and passage of the Charter of Rights and Freedoms. As he said on April 17, 1982, "Today, at long last, Canada is acquiring full and complete national sovereignty. The Constitution of Canada has come home. The most fundamental law of the land will now be capable of being amended in Canada, without any further recourse to the Parliament of the United Kingdom." He went on to declare:

> I speak of a Canada where men and women of Aboriginal ancestry, of French and British heritage, of the diverse cultures of the world, demonstrate the will to share this land in peace, in justice, and with mutual respect. I speak of a Canada which is proud of, and strengthened, by its essential bilingual destiny, a Canada whose people believe in sharing and in mutual support, and not in building regional barriers. I speak of a country where every person is free to fulfill himself or herself to the utmost, unhindered by the arbitrary actions of governments.

Patriation of the Constitution and passage of the Charter of Rights and Freedoms were exceedingly difficult, and resulted in much debate, disagreement, compromise, and concession. Even then, the outcome left a lot to be desired, since René Lévesque, premier of Quebec at the time, refused to sign the accord because he felt he had been betrayed by the other provincial premiers and Quebec had been "abandoned at the very moment of crisis." As a result, there is still an element of incompleteness to Canada's constitutional situation.

In total, the Constitution Act is comprised of seven main sections. In addition to incorporating the BNA Act (now renamed the Constitution Act, 1867) and the Charter of Rights and Freedoms, it includes specific sections dealing with the rights of the Indigenous peoples of Canada, equalization and regional disparities, a constitutional conference, a procedure for amending the constitution, an amendment to the 1867 Act dealing with "non-renewable natural resources, forestry resources and electrical energy," as well as a general section dealing with the overall intentions, interpretation, and implementation of the Act.

The bulk of the Act has to do with ensuring that every Canadian is accorded and guaranteed certain basic rights and freedoms, including freedom of conscience, religion, thought, belief, opinion, expression, the press, peaceful assembly, and association. The Act spells out Canada's commitment to democratic, mobility, legal, and equality rights, as well as to the official languages of Canada and minority language rights in education. It is a comprehensive and ingenious document that goes much further than the constitution of virtually any other country in terms of enshrining the basic rights and freedoms of citizens—thus its historical significance as one of the most creative milestones in Canadian history. Very fitting in this regard, and yet another example of Canadian creativity, is the Human Rights Museum established recently in Winnipeg to recognize the achievements of Canadians in the area of human rights and freedoms. Canada is one of the first countries in the world—if not *the* first—to create such a museum.

To sum up: Even though Canadians have been less creative in the educational and political realms than in other areas of the country's cultural life—largely because they have tended to rely on models and practices imported from elsewhere in the world—a significant degree of creativity has nonetheless been manifested over many years. Let us now proceed to another area of Canadian cultural life, one where creativity has manifested itself in earnest—health, welfare, and well-being.

CHAPTER SIX

Health, Welfare, and Well-being

It is often said that Canadians are a caring, sharing, and compassionate people. Whether they are more caring, sharing, and compassionate than other people in the world is impossible to say. What can be said is that Canadians have exhibited these qualities from the outset of their history to the present day.

These characteristics are most evident in the health care and social security systems Canadians have built up over the years. These systems typify Canadian creativity in many ways, since they relate so fundamentally to the problems Canadians have been compelled to confront and overcome in order to help their fellow citizens and carve out a high standard of living for themselves.

As in other areas of Canadian life, the country's health care system can be traced back to the Indigenous peoples, who had developed an intimate knowledge of the healing properties of the flora and fauna of the country and were willing to share their knowledge with European settlers. Not only did the First Nations peoples possess many highly developed medical insights and capabilities—including the use of steam baths, sweat lodges, and massages to clean the body, clear the mind, and satisfy the soul—but they relied on numerous supernatural practices to ward off different types of illnesses and diseases. These practices were part and parcel of their religious beliefs and spiritual convictions, which ascribed mystical causes to many diseases that required magical cures, usually by shamans or medicine men. But the Indigenous peoples also knew a great deal about botanical remedies, and were familiar with the medicinal properties of most of the country's trees, plants, herbs, and berries, such as wintergreen, bloodroot, cranberries, blueberries, and many others. As Susanna Moodie wrote in her book *Roughing It in the Bush*:

> They [the Aboriginal peoples] are very skilful in their treatment of wounds and many diseases. Their knowledge of the medicinal qualities of their plants and herbs is very great. They make excellent poultices from the bark of the bass and slippery elm. . . . From the root of the black briony they obtain a fine salve for sores, and extract a rich yellow dye. The inner bark of the root of the sumach, roasted, and reduced to powder, is a good remedy for the ague, a tea-spoonful given between the hot and cold fit. They scrape the fine white powder from the large fungus that grows upon the bark of the pine, into whiskey, and take it for violent pains in the stomach. The taste of this powder strongly reminded me of quinine.

SMALLPOX, SCURVY, TYPHUS, AND OTHER DISEASES

Disease was a constant threat and perpetual concern to the Indigenous peoples and first Europeans. This is understandable in view of the fact that just one disease—smallpox—wiped out nearly the entire Indigenous population of North America when it was brought to the continent by Europeans in the seventeenth century. Smallpox was only one of a number of diseases that ran rampant in the early years of European settlement. Scurvy was another. For example, many of the men accompanying Jacques Cartier fell ill from scurvy, a potentially deadly disease that results from a deficiency of vitamin C, in the winter of 1535–36.

Fortunately, the Indigenous peoples had devised a creative cure for scurvy long before the arrival of the Europeans. Through their knowledge of native plants, they created a tea made from the bark and twigs of the white spruce and hemlock trees that was capable of curing scurvy. When it was fed to Cartier's men, they recovered quickly.

Typhus was another dreaded disease. Just as the Indigenous peoples devised a cure for scurvy, so an early European immigrant, Michel Sarrazin, devised a creative way of dealing with typhus. Sarrazin was one of the country's first medical doctors, as well as a celebrated naturalist and scientist. He was born in Nuits-sous-Beaune, France in 1659, and came to New France in 1685. Initially, he was appointed surgeon-major to the French troops in New France, but he went on to become the official physician of the Hôtel-Dieu in Quebec City in 1699. His fame resulted from helping thousands of colonists to recover from typhus, largely through his scientific knowledge of various plants and herbs and his emphasis on personal and collective hygiene. But his fame did not end there. He spent much of his time over the next 30 years documenting the flora and fauna of his adopted land and sending numerous specimens back to the Académie Royale des Sciences in France for analysis. He also played an important role in the development of the maple syrup industry in Canada, and was well known throughout the colonies for his comprehensive studies of the beaver and the muskrat.

As the French established themselves in Quebec, medical and health practices improved accordingly. Religious institutions, and particularly those whose members were women, played a dominant role. The first hospital created in North America was the aforementioned Hôtel Dieu in Quebec City, which was created in 1639 by three sisters from the order of Les Religieuses Hospitalières de la Miséricorde de Jésus. By the late 1660s, three other religious hospitals had been created, including a second Hôtel Dieu in Montreal. Numerous hospitals were established in other parts of the country in the years to follow. Most of them were charitable institutions, and were closely connected to religious orders and the Church. They relied heavily on donations from benevolent organizations and wealthy patrons (rather than government funding, as is the case today), and most patients paid little if anything for services.

Medical knowledge was still very much in its infancy in Canada in the seventeenth and eighteenth centuries. Little was known about the nature and causes of most illnesses and diseases, particularly about how they were transmitted from one person to another. Regrettably, many years were to pass before medical authorities established the link between hygiene, sanitation, health, and disease prevention.

Most of the people who practiced medicine in early Canada pursued other careers to make ends meet, attending to their medical interests on the side. All too many were charlatans or quacks. Little training was available.

Epidemics ran rampant, especially diphtheria, chickenpox, measles, cholera, typhus, and smallpox. Life expectancy was less than 40 years, and 50 percent of infants died before their first birthday. Nevertheless, some solid gains were made in specific medical practices as conditions improved in Europe and more medical expertise was imported into Canada.

THREE MEDICAL TRAILBLAZERS

Although women played a key role in health care from Indigenous times onward, Canada didn't get its first accredited female doctor until 1867. She was Emily Stowe. She taught school in Brantford and Mount Pleasant in Canada West, was a life-long champion of women's rights, and married

John Stowe in 1856. It is said that her husband's illness from tuberculosis caused her to want to become a doctor. Since no Canadian college would accept her, she enrolled in the New York Medical College for Women and set up a practice in Toronto shortly after she graduated in 1867, although she was not actually licensed until 1880. Her struggles to enter the medical profession caused her to create the Woman's Medical College in Toronto in 1883.

The challenges Stowe faced as a woman in nineteenth-century Canada led her to pursue a number of creative initiatives. In 1883, she founded the Toronto Women's Literary Club, which focused in general on the difficulties women were experiencing in the professions and in particular on the problem of gaining access to the necessary educational training and qualifications. It was the first real suffrage group in Canada. Building on this, Stowe became the principal founder and first president of the Dominion Women's Enfranchisement Association in 1889—a forerunner of the Women's Christian Temperance Union—as well as a driving force in the Young Women's Christian Association, the National Council of Women, and the Federated Women's Institutes of Canada. Interestingly, her daughter, Augusta Stowe Gullen, was the first woman to acquire a medical degree from a Canadian medical institution. Like her mother, she was a leading figure in the women's movement, and followed her mother as president of the Dominion Women's Enfranchisement Association in 1903.

Stowe and her daughter were not the only women to establish themselves as pioneers in the medical field. Elizabeth McMaster was another. She played a key role in the creation of what was the first hospital for sick children in North America, and only the second in the British Empire. Concerned about the fact that nearly half of all deaths recorded in 1875 were children under the age of ten, McMaster and a group of women rented an 11-room house on Avenue Road in downtown Toronto. Although at the beginning it contained only six iron cots, this hospital went on to become the world-renowned Hospital for Sick Children, or, as it is better known, "Sick Kids."

While few Canadians are aware of the fact, Pablum, one of the world's most popular baby foods, was created by Canadian doctors and medical specialists at Sick Kids, as we noted earlier. Pablum's popularity was predicated on its ease of preparation, as well as its ability to prevent rickets—a crippling childhood disease—by ensuring that children had enough vitamin D in their diets. It was the world's first precooked dry baby food, and could be mixed easily with water or milk to produce a smooth, nutritional, and digestible paste.

Due to the work of trailblazers like Stowe and McMaster, opportunities began to open up for women committed to pursuing medical careers in the latter part of the nineteenth century. In 1883, a medical program at Trinity College opened its doors. While it offered the requisite medical courses, it did not grant degrees. Nevertheless, after 1895, students at the Ontario Medical College for Women were able to take exams at a medical school of their choice and obtain a degree. Although medical training for women was provided by Dalhousie University, the University of Western Ontario, and the University of Manitoba in the late 1880s, a number of years were to pass before comparable training was provided by other academic institutions throughout the country.

Meanwhile, medical knowledge and training continued to evolve. For example, anaesthetics, which made surgery virtually painless and were originally discovered in the 1840s, were soon in use in Canadian hospitals. Canadian doctors and researchers played a creative role in the development of anaesthesiology in the century to follow, including innovative contributions from W. E. Brown and Harold Griffith. In addition, Archibald Malloch introduced antisepsis into Canada toward the end of the nineteenth century, and the Hospital for Sick Children introduced the use of x-rays following their discovery by the German physicist Wilhelm Röntgen.

It was around this time that a real medical giant—William Osler—made his appearance. He went on to become one of the country's and the world's most famous doctors, largely because of the creative approach he took to medicine. Especially noteworthy were his treatment of patients (including his bedside manner) and his way of training medical practitioners. He was eventually knighted by the British government for his prolific contributions to the medical field.

Osler was born in Bond Head, Ontario in 1849, educated at the Toronto Medical School and McGill University, and undertook two years of postgraduate studies in Europe. Following this, he taught medicine at McGill University for a time, was appointed professor of medicine at the University of Pennsylvania in 1884, and, five years later, became the first professor of medicine at Johns Hopkins Hospital and Medical School in Baltimore. While at Johns Hopkins, Osler was instrumental in creating a whole new approach to medical training. He eventually went to Oxford University where he became Regius Professor of Medicine.

Osler had a wide range of medical interests, and was particularly skilled in the diagnosis of heart, lung, and blood diseases. He played a role in the establishment of the Royal College of Physicians and Surgeons in Canada in 1929, and is often identified as "the father of Canadian medicine." His most important book, *The Principles and Practice of Medicine*, was published in 1892. It was used as a textbook in medical schools throughout the world for more than 40 years, and is still considered a classic today. Small wonder the name Osler is still associated today with advanced medical practices.

According to Charles G. Roland, another outstanding Canadian doctor, Osler was "one of the greatest medical masters the world has ever known"—not only extremely creative, but known for his compassion for others:

> His (Osler's) importance derives largely from five inter-related areas: his contributions to medical knowledge through clinical and pathological research; his activities as a gifted educator; his ability to stimulate and inspire students who later became leaders of the medical profession in North America; his love of books and his unselfish support of medical libraries; and—perhaps most important to students and practitioners today—his quite unconscious role as an exemplar of integrity, humanity, kindliness, and professional honesty.

While Osler became one of the best-known doctors in the world, he was not the only Canadian to contribute to the advance of medical knowledge in the later nineteenth and early twentieth century. Much of this had to do with the intense rivalry between Montreal and Toronto, two of the greatest medical centres in the world at the time.

NOT ONLY IN HOCKEY

The intense rivalry in hockey between Montreal and Toronto is well known. The Montreal Canadiens and the Toronto Maple Leafs have been competing for decades, and dominated the National Hockey League (NHL) when it was made up of only six teams. This competition is best captured in Roch Carrier's famous story "The Hockey Sweater." It is about a young boy from Quebec whose mother orders a Canadiens hockey sweater from the Eaton's mail-order catalogue only to be sent a Toronto Maple Leafs jersey. The boy is compelled to wear this jersey to the local rink where he is utterly humiliated by his teammates. Could there be anything worse for a young boy from Quebec than to have to wear a Toronto Maple Leafs sweater?

But Toronto and Montreal were rivals not just in hockey but in many other areas, including medicine. Not only were both places creative hotbeds of medical research in the first half of the twentieth century, but both were developing rapidly as major urban centres. Medical researchers were pouring into these two metropolises at a remarkable rate, attracted by the growing number of hospitals, medical facilities, and research laboratories.

Montreal has always had the edge in hockey. Not only did the game first become popular in Montreal, but the city was the home of the Montreal Maroons and other teams prior to the Canadiens' founding in 1909. But Montreal also has a long and distinctive tradition in medicine, one dating back to 1664 and the creation of the Hôtel Dieu. By the beginning of the nineteenth century, a group of medical specialists had established Montreal General Hospital, created a medical faculty at McGill University—the first of its kind in the country—and gained control of the medical licensing board of Quebec. Medical standards improved rapidly after this, as various controls were established to ensure that patients received the best care available.

Among the outstanding doctors and highly creative medical specialists in Montreal at this time was Maude Elizabeth Seymour Abbott, a resident of Quebec who was unable to gain admission to McGill because she was a woman. So she attended Bishop's College in Lennoxville, Quebec to receive her medical training. Following this, she followed a suggestion made by William Osler to undertake research into congenital heart disease, acquiring malformed hearts at autopsies and examining them in detail. She published her findings in a series of brilliant papers, dramatically improving life expectancy for infants with congenital heart disease and becoming one of the first doctors in the world to deal effectively with so-called "blue babies." She quickly became world-famous, and served as permanent secretary of the International Association of Medical Museums and editor of its journal from 1907 to 1938.

The city boasted many other creative medical pioneers at this time, most notably Wilder Penfield, Gordon Murray, and Hans Selye. Penfield was born in the United States in 1891. He trained in Europe and the United States under William Osler, and graduated from Johns Hopkins University. He came to Canada in the late 1920s to set up the Montreal

Neurological Institute, which rapidly became known throughout the world for its work on diseases of the nervous system.

As a neurosurgeon, Penfield was interested in the human brain, and particularly how the brain functions under normal and abnormal conditions and affects other parts of the body. He became extremely interested in epilepsy, and undertook detailed studies of how the brain operates in terms of speech, motor skills, memory, sensory experience, and so forth. He is generally credited with focusing attention on the different skills, abilities, and characteristics of the right and left hemispheres of the brain. Penfield believed that how the two hemispheres interact was the key to understanding human beings. He turned his attention later in life to writing and public service, serving as the first president of the Vanier Institute of the Family. He actively promoted second-language training as a way to improve brain function, and wrote a number of books, including *The Mystery of the Mind* and *No Man Alone*.

Penfield's work was expanded upon by other doctors and researchers at the Institute. Brenda Milner, who came to Montreal from Manchester, England, served as director of neuropsychology at the Institute in the 1980s, and continued to work there until she was well into her nineties. She has often been called "the founder of neuropsychology" for the pioneering work she did on brain development, memory loss and retention, and neuroplasticity. Milner's work paved the way for a new generation of doctors to do important work in this rapidly expanding field, including Norman Doidge, a Canadian doctor who has written several popular books on neuroplasticity, including *The Brain That Changes Itself* and *The Brain's Way of Healing*.

Like Penfield, Gordon Murray was a surgeon and researcher who focused on a particular part of the body. In his case, it was the kidneys, and especially kidney transplants and the possibility of creating artificial kidneys. First, however, Murray had to solve two key problems. The first was to find a suitable anticoagulant, and the second to find a viable kidney membrane. He solved the first problem in 1935, when he became the first person to develop a way of effectively using the anticoagulant drug heparin. He solved the second problem in 1946, when he successfully performed the first artificial kidney operation on a patient in North America. He went on to pioneer many other difficult surgical procedures related to the kidneys, the heart, and other internal organs. He also developed the parallel plate dialyzer and the dialyzer pump, two devices of critical importance in the treatment of various types of kidney disease.

Hans Selye was also a world-famous medical pioneer. He specialized in, and popularized, research on "biological stress," particularly in humans. He was educated in Prague, Paris, and Rome, joined the staff of McGill University in 1932, became the first director of the Institute of Experimental Medicine and Surgery at the University of Montreal in 1945, and stayed there until he retired in 1976. He contended that stress plays a fundamental role in the development of all diseases, and identified three major phases in the stress process: alarm, resistance, and exhaustion. Inability to deal with stress results in various "diseases of adaptation," including high blood pressure, gastric and duodenal ulcers, and mental disorders. Selye was a prolific author, whose books included *The Stress of Life*, *Stress Without Distress*, and *The Stress of My Life*. Many thought Selye should have received a Nobel Prize for his achievements, but he was probably too provocative and controversial to be given the award.

If Montreal was a hotbed of creative medical research in the first half of the twentieth century, so was Toronto. And just as the Toronto Maple Leafs stormed back to win several Stanley Cups after the Cup finals had been dominated by the Montreal Canadiens for many years, so Toronto's medical pioneers gave Montreal a real run for its money.

Particularly important was the research undertaken by Frederick G. Banting, Charles H. Best, John J. R. Macleod, and J. Bertram Collip. In 1921–22, they discovered insulin, the hormone created in the pancreas that breaks down sugar. When insulin is not produced in sufficient quantities, the result is diabetes, which afflicts millions of people throughout the world. Through experiments initially on dogs and later cattle, Banting, Best, Macleod, and Collip found an economical way of extracting insulin that could then be injected into people suffering from diabetes. This achievement immediately catapulted the group into the forefront of international attention. As representatives of the team, Banting and Macleod were awarded the Nobel Prize for their achievements in 1923, the first "born in Canada" scientists to be accorded this prestigious honour.

While each of these medical pioneers had their own particular unique characteristics, the group is probably best epitomized by Banting. He was the youngest of six children from a middle-class family. Persevering through high school with only mediocre results, he failed his first year of arts at the University of Toronto but then went on to graduate from medicine in 1916 with better-than-average grades. An article in a medical journal inspired Banting to suggest a research project aimed at understanding the production of insulin in the body. When he received support for this proposal in 1921, he immediately set to work under the direction of J. J. R. Macleod, with valuable assistance provided by Charles Best and J. B. Collip. While the first experiments were crude and unsuccessful, Banting and the group persevered. A year later, they discovered insulin. An interesting footnote to the discovery is the fact that Banting was so enraged when he received the Nobel Prize and his chief co-worker Charles Best did not, that he decided to give half of his share of the award to Best. Talk about sharing in the best Canadian sense!

MAINTAINING CANADA'S CREATIVE MEDICAL TRADITION

About the same time that Toronto and Montreal were competing vigorously in the field of medicine, a number of Canada's doctors were heading to China. They were sent there by various religious, governmental, and non-governmental organizations to help the Chinese, who were suffering greatly because of one of the worst famines ever to hit the Middle Kingdom, as well as from the disruptions caused by civil war and the Japanese invasion of Manchuria and China in the later 1930s.

One of these doctors was Robert McClure. Son of medical missionaries in China, McClure went to Henan in 1923, where he served as a surgeon, educator, and pioneer in the development of the Hwaiking rural medical system. He was field director of the International Red Cross when war broke out with Japan, and led the Friends Ambulance Unit in China from 1941 to 1946. Later, McClure provided medical advice to the Palestinian refugees in Gaza, and then went to India, where he was appointed superintendent of the Ratlam Hospital. McClure also served as moderator of the United Church of Canada, and continued to provide medical expertise in Borneo and Peru until he was well into his eighties. An outspoken individual, McClure's heroic self-sacrifices on behalf of the distressed people of the world made him well-known as a great humanitarian.

Like McClure, Norman Bethune was a medical doctor, surgeon, inventor, activist, and humanitarian who spent the bulk of his life helping others, especially in Spain and China. Prior to this, he studied medicine at the University of Toronto, then became a teacher at Frontier College and a stretcher-bearer during the First World War. After a number of years in the Royal Navy, he contracted pulmonary tuberculosis and devoted the next few years of his life to helping tuberculosis victims and conducting thoracic studies and surgeries in Montreal. He invented many medical procedures and surgical instruments while he was there, and wrote numerous papers describing his creative thoracic techniques.

After a visit to the Soviet Union in 1935, Bethune joined the Communist Party and immediately took up the cause, first in the civil war in Spain—where he created the first mobile blood transfusion service in the world—and later in China during the Sino-Japanese war. He laboured intensively in China on behalf of the Chinese people in general and the Chinese Communist Party in particular, not only as a surgeon and inventor but also as an activist and teacher. Following his death in 1938 from an accidental cut he incurred while performing an operation, he was immortalized by Mao Zedong in a famous essay—*In Memory of Norman Bethune*—which called on all communists to emulate Bethune's virtues of internationalism, humanitarianism, and dedication to helping others. Bethune's legacy did a great deal to create the strong bond that has existed between China and Canada over the last 70 years—a bond that has yielded fruitful results for both countries, not only in health care but also in the arts, humanities, and physical and social sciences.

McClure and Bethune were not the only Canadian doctors to have a "China connection." Another was Harold Johns, who was born in a Buddhist temple near Chengdu, China in 1915, where his father was a missionary involved in teaching mathematics at West China University. After the family returned to Canada in 1927, Johns went to university, receiving a bachelor's degree in physics from McMaster University in 1936 and a Ph.D. from the University of Toronto in 1939. Like a number of other famous Canadian inventors and scientists mentioned earlier, Johns also spent a considerable amount of time at the University of Saskatchewan, where he taught from 1945 to 1956. He became especially interested in biophysics and the potential that radioactive cobalt possessed to treat cancer.

What fascinated Johns about cobalt was its ability to generate far more powerful radiation than radium, which was used extensively to treat cancer at that time, as well as the ways its radiation could be focused on a single point in the body to bombard a tumour. After years of research, Johns invented the "cobalt-60 bomb," a device which was installed in the University Hospital in Saskatoon and at Victoria Hospital in London, Ontario in 1951, with the assistance of Atomic Energy of Canada. This invention helped usher in the age of modern nuclear medicine. By using radiation to treat deep tumours in the body, the remission rate for cervical cancer, for example, increased from 25 percent to 75 percent after the development of the cobalt bomb. The new technique drastically reduced the amount of time required for cancer treatments, from an hour to roughly five minutes. In 1953, Johns published *The Physics of Radiology*, and in 1956, became head of the Physics Division at the Canadian Cancer Institute and professor of medical biophysics at the University of Toronto.

Other creative contributions to medical research were made by Wilfred Bigelow, who was born in Brandon, Manitoba to parents who were both involved in the medical profession. His father, Wilfred Abram Bigelow, founded the first private medical clinic in Canada, and his mother, Grace Ann Gordon, was a nurse. Their son Wilfred, working in close conjunction with John Callaghan and John Hopps, created the artificial pacemaker. Bigelow is often deemed the father of biomedical engineering in Canada because of his achievements in this area. The pacemaker uses electrical impulses to maintain a regular heart beat when it is inserted into the body. Pacemakers are implanted in more than half a million people each year.

Following his graduation from the University of Toronto in 1938, Bigelow served as a captain in the Royal Canadian Medical Army Corps during the Second World War and conducted many surgical procedures and operations on the battlefield during this time. He became a member of the surgical team at the Toronto General Hospital in 1947 after spending a year at Johns Hopkins Medical School, and joined the Department of Surgery at the University of Toronto in 1948. Apart from his work on pacemakers, he was also well-known for the pioneering role he played in the early 1950s in open-heart surgery and especially the use of hypothermia, a technique that reduces the temperature in the body in order to decrease the amount of oxygen required during surgery. Much of the knowledge and expertise he acquired in these areas was spelled out in his book *Cold Hearts*. It proved helpful in spurring a great deal of research into heart disease in Canada by doctors such as Tirone David, Wilbert Keon, and others.

More recently, Canada's creative medical tradition was sustained in remarkable fashion by James Till and Ernest McCulloch, who conducted highly original research on stem cells and regenerative medicine at the Princess Margaret Hospital in Toronto and other medical facilities in Ontario. They demonstrated the existence of stem cells more than 40 years ago, and though they received little recognition at the time, are now deemed "the fathers of stem cell research" in Canada. They were inducted into the Canadian Medical Hall of Fame in 2006.

Working at the Ontario Cancer Institute in the early 1960s, McCulloch and Till published a seminal paper in 1961 on what were called "colony-forming cells." This paper is generally recognized as the foundation on which present-day stem cell research is based, as it laid out many of the principles and concepts still central to this field. One specific example involves bone-marrow transplantation for cancer patients; Till and McCulloch established the theoretical underpinnings for therapies in this area some four decades ago, thereby saving myriad lives.

While their work has been controversial, largely because of the aversion to stem cell research in certain religious, political, and medical circles, their research has had a profound effect on medical practice in all parts of the world. Their creative work put Canada in the forefront of stem cell research, with major contributions being made by the Stem Cell Network in Ottawa, Mickie Bhatia at McMaster University, the McEwan Centre for Regenerative Medicine in Toronto, and by Derrick Rossi, a Toronto-born researcher working at Harvard University. This promises to be an even more topical area in the future, especially with evidence accumulating that Gordie Howe, one of Canada's greatest hockey players, seemed to recover from a severe stroke in his mid-eighties as a result of various stem cell treatments in the United States and Mexico.

Nor is this all. Toronto scientists achieved another medical milestone in stem cell research when Andras Nagy and his team at Mount Sinai Hospital, in conjunction with Keisuke Kaji of the Medical Research Council Centre for Regenerative Medicine at the University of Edinburgh, became the first researchers to reprogram adult human cells into embryonic-like cells without using potentially dangerous viruses that can cause various forms of cancer. This is expected to have a profound effect on overcoming one of the greatest hurdles to using the reprogramming technique in the development of new drugs, finding innovative cures for many diseases, and creating personalized organs and tissues for patients.

Another major contributor in this area is Tak Wah Mak. Son of a successful businessman from southern China, he went to the University of Wisconsin in the late 1960s and completed his Ph.D. at the University of Alberta in the early 1970s. Following this, Mak worked at the Ontario Cancer Institute in Toronto, where most of his research focused on acquiring fundamental knowledge of the biology of cells in normal and disease settings. In 1984, Mak discovered the T-cell receptor and the gene that produces it, generally seen as key to the human immune system. He was made director of the Institute for Breast Cancer Research at Princess Margaret Hospital in Toronto in 2004.

Tak Mak is not the only medical researcher to be born in China but conduct a great deal of pioneering research in Canada. Thomas Ming Swi Chang and Lap-Chee Tsui are two others.

Thomas Ming Swi Chang was born in Swaton, China. While still an undergraduate at McGill University, Chang created the world's first artificial cell in 1957. His idea was to make tiny, ultra-thin plastic microcapsules that could hold biological agents, such as enzymes. If he could control the permeability of the plastic membrane, he could control what passed through the wall of the artificial cell, and thus mimic many of the functions of real cells. After earning his Ph.D. in physiology, Chang created artificial blood, and pioneered a new cellular-based approach to artificial organs. Chang's work on a safe blood substitute gained recognition during the tainted blood crisis of the 1980s.

Lap-Chee Tsui was born in Shanghai in 1950, but undertook most of his research and teaching at the Hospital for Sick Children in Toronto between 1981 and 2002. In 1989, he was acclaimed internationally when he and his creative team identified the defective gene that causes cystic fibrosis. This world-famous geneticist has made many outstanding contributions to research on the human genome. He was president of the Human Genome Organization for a number of years, as well as vice-chancellor and president of the University of Hong Kong.

Another example of medical creativity by Canadians is the work of Alex Mihailidis, a biomechanical engineer who is presently doing research on the creation of mechanical procedures and devices for helping older people, particularly ones who are physically or mentally challenged. Mihailidis and his team at the University of Toronto have invented a "personal emergency response device" that talks directly to elderly people when they are experiencing certain types of medical problems, telling them what to do. They have also created an intelligent anti-collision wheelchair, and a robotic device that enables stroke patients to strengthen their weakened upper body muscles. But their most creative invention to date is "the talking bathroom." It uses a series of visual and verbal aids to help people with dementia wash their hands, through graphic depiction of a series of steps. Mihailidis hopes that many of the technologies he and his team are developing will eventually be standard features in homes, enabling seniors and particularly those suffering from diseases such as dementia, Alzheimer's, Parkinson's, and others to remain in their homes for longer periods of time.

This by no means exhausts the list of creative contributions by Canadians to medicine and health care. Far from it. One of the most fascinating is the creation of the Faculty of Health Sciences at McMaster University in Hamilton and especially the Michael G. DeGroote School of Medicine, which builds on the creativity of other Canadians, most notably William Osler. The focus at McMaster has been on patient treatment and care, just as Osler was concerned with the needs of patients first and foremost. Much of the work at McMaster has centered on training physicians, nurses, physiotherapists, occupational therapists, and other health care professionals to work closely together to provide the finest patient care possible. This "McMaster model" is now being emulated in many other medical centres and universities throughout the world. Appropriately enough, all this activity is taking place very near where Osler grew up in Dundas, Ontario.

Two key contributors to the developments at McMaster University were John Evans and Fraser Mustard, who both died recently in their eighties after outstanding careers in many different fields. Both men were tackles on the same University of Toronto Varsity Blues football teams when they went to university, but got back together later in life to collaborate at McMaster. Evans was also president of the University of Toronto, a founder of MaRS in Toronto, and chairman of the Rockefeller Foundation in the United States. Fraser Mustard was founder of the Canadian Institute for Advanced Research, and was world-renowned for his research on blood platelets, vessel injury, and the effects of Aspirin while he was working at McMaster University. He was also internationally recognized for his advocacy for early childhood education.

As these examples confirm, there has been a strong connection in Canada between medical innovation and caring and compassion. Canadians have directed their energies toward helping their fellow citizens, in the process manifesting a great deal of concern for others. While it would be a mistake to push this argument too far, it does help explain why the country has one of the most creative and effective health care systems in the world, despite the problems posed by funding shortfalls and an aging population.

MEDICARE AND THE DEVELOPMENT OF CANADA'S SOCIAL SECURITY SYSTEM

As important as doctors, nurses, researchers, and hospitals have been to the development of Canada's health care system, some of the most important contributions have come from governments and politicians.

The best example of this is Tommy Douglas. He was born in Falkirk, Scotland in 1904, the same year that Sir Wilfrid Laurier made his famous speech to the Canadian Club in Ottawa in which he declared that "Canada will fill the twentieth century." As matters turned out, Douglas spent much of his life striving to ensure Canada held a leading place in the twentieth century, by working diligently to improve the country's health care and social security systems. His political career spanned four decades, and he is often described as a politician who was concerned first and foremost with people and their specific problems and needs. Such needs were legion.

In 1929, Douglas was invited to come to the Calvary Baptist Church in Weyburn, Saskatchewan as a student minister. The church also invited Stanley Knowles, someone else who became a well-known and compassionate politician. Although the congregation chose Douglas over Knowles, the two men established a close friendship that endured for more than half a century.

During his long and distinguished career as an MP and MPP, Douglas made many creative contributions to the development of Canada's health care and social security system. These contributions spanned the gamut of possibilities: Medicare, his most creative achievement as the first government-operated health care program in North America and one of the first in the world; public automobile insurance; electrification of rural areas; development of the Canadian Wheat Board; old age pensions; and numerous other initiatives. He fought valiantly and tenaciously for the rights of citizens, the development of labour unions and collective bargaining, and the realization of workers' rights in Canada.

Douglas was ideally suited to this task. He grew up in a family with strong ethical values and religious convictions. He also experienced extreme poverty and hardship as a youth in Scotland, and later as an adult in Saskatchewan during the Depression. Small wonder this pioneer of democratic socialism in Canada, first federal leader of the NDP, fighter for human rights and freedoms, and leader of Canada's first socialist government in Saskatchewan was described as "a little giant of a man who stirred up Weyburn, the province of Saskatchewan, and the nation." There is no doubt that Canada is a more caring and compassionate country today as a result of Douglas's efforts, with much more commitment to the needs and rights of others as well as to a more equitable distribution of wealth. Without Douglas, Canada would not have the highly developed social system it does today. Universal health care, old age security, unemployment insurance, worker's compensation, and social welfare assistance—all these achievements were spurred on by Douglas's courage, conviction, creativity, and determination. It is not surprising that when Canadians were asked to select the "greatest Canadian" of all in a CBC television program in 2004, they selected Douglas first and foremost.

Douglas transformed the entire approach to health care in Canada by claiming that health care is a basic right of every Canadian and a fundamental responsibility of the country's governments. Eventually, politicians of all stripes and citizens from all walks of life agreed, especially when they were persuaded by Douglas's persistence, humour, and ability to make Medicare a reality. This opened the doors to a profuse array of improvements in the country that were social and humanistic in character and not just economic and industrial.

Douglas also set a marvellous example for other politicians to follow. One of the most effective of these is Roy Romanow, another politician from Saskatchewan. He followed in Douglas's footsteps by heading up a comprehensive assessment of Canada's health care system in 2001–02. He was also premier of the New Democratic government in Saskatchewan from 1991 to 2001. He is well-known as one of three politicians who hammered out the "Kitchen Accord" that led to patriation of the Canadian Constitution and the signing of the Charter of Rights and Freedoms in 1982. (The others were Roy McMurtry and Jean Chrétien.)

Despite creative contributions from people like Douglas, Romanow, medical doctors, health care providers, and others, the origins of the country's health care and social security systems can be traced even further back, to the end of the nineteenth century. It was at this time that Canadians and people elsewhere in the world were starting to become aware of the need for a *public* social security system, largely as a result of the failure of the marketplace to provide a reasonable measure of social security in general and health care in particular.

The idea of a "social minimum" emerged slowly but surely in the Western world in response to this problem. L. C. Marsh, a major pioneer in the development of Canada's social security system, saw this as "the realization that in a civilized society, there is a certain minimum of conditions without which health, decency, happiness, and a 'chance in life' are impossible." It was an idea that had its origins in the undesirable aspects of the Industrial Revolution, including high levels of poverty and child labour, as well as the overall poor health of working-class people in industrial countries.

While pressure was building in the early years of the twentieth century to provide some measure of social security in Canada, the country's governments were reluctant to act. Moreover, there was confusion over which level or levels of government should be responsible. Although the BNA Act assigned responsibility for this area to the provinces, strong pressures were being exerted on federal and municipal governments to get involved as many social problems were national rather than provincial in nature, and poverty was most conspicuous at the municipal level.

Despite these factors, it was a provincial government that introduced the first real social security legislation in Canada. The Ontario government introduced a Workman's Compensation Act in 1914. This enabled workers to receive cash income, medical care, and rehabilitation services when they were injured on the job or experienced certain types of "occupational diseases," despite the fact that they were unable to sue employers in court over this. This legislation acted as a model for similar laws in Nova Scotia, British Columbia, Alberta, and New Brunswick, and was followed, in 1916, by the provision in Manitoba of a Mother's Allowance, which provided assistance for women who faced difficulties raising their families after their husbands had gone to fight in World War I. Though the federal government did not take the lead on social welfare measures, it did assume some responsibility for war pensions and the rehabilitation of veterans.

Many thought the election of William Lyon Mackenzie King in 1921 would usher in a new era in social legislation. After all, King had set out a vision for "a new social order" in Canada when he was an educator, and had campaigned vigorously on a platform of old age pensions, unemployment insurance, and health care. Unfortunately, however, these hopes were not realized, although the federal government did launch the country's first old age pension program in 1927, thanks to the work of J. S. Woodsworth and a small group of independent members of Parliament. It paid the modest sum of $20 a month to qualified recipients, and costs were shared with the provinces. However, recipients had to pass a rigorous and humiliating "means test" in order to receive this assistance, and eligibility was restricted to people over 70. Nevertheless, the program's launch signalled the fact that the federal government was prepared to assume some responsibility for the poor, the elderly, and the needy in

Canada, and was willing to share the costs of certain types of social programs with the provinces.

The Great Depression, which stretched from 1929 to 1939, proved to be a disaster for Canada as far as social security was concerned. Aside from some small payments the federal government made to the provinces between 1930 and 1939, largely for relief of the unemployed, virtually no assistance was forthcoming from any level of government. It was only when Mackenzie King appointed the Rowell-Sirois Commission in 1937 to undertake a detailed assessment of Dominion-provincial relations that recognition was made of the need for governments to act in the social and not just the economic realm. But it took the outbreak of World War II in 1939, and especially preparations for post-war recovery, to bring about significant improvements in Canada's embryonic social security system. As L.C. Marsh noted, concern for social security was in the air during the Second World War as never before, particularly after Winston Churchill and Franklin Roosevelt signed the Atlantic Charter in 1941, signaling a common desire to bring about the collaboration of all nations in realizing improved labour standards, significant economic progress, and a real measure of social security.

Many of Canada's present social programs date from this era. For example, in 1940, the federal government introduced unemployment insurance. In order to be eligible, people had to have been previously employed, willing to work, and prepared to sign a claim indicating that they were out of work. It was at this time that L.C. Marsh wrote his pioneering *Report on Social Security in Canada* as research director of the Advisory Committee on Reconstruction—the James Committee—appointed by the federal government. It called for a "comprehensive and integrated social security system for Canada" to provide a reasonable measure of social security for all Canadians from cradle to grave, largely through measures such as unemployment insurance, sickness benefits, free medical insurance, pensions for widows and the permanently disabled, old age pensions, and funeral benefits. While the report was short on details about how these proposals were to be implemented and paid for, it did set out a "social vision for Canada" that guided developments in the post-war period.

This is when Tommy Douglas arrived on the scene. He and his CCF government in Saskatchewan made a major contribution to the realization of this vision when they introduced the first hospital insurance plan in 1947. This immediately created demands from people in other provinces for similar plans. The federal government responded to these demands by promising that it would share the cost of hospital and diagnostic services with the provinces in 1957, thereby making it possible for other provinces to follow the pioneering example set by Saskatchewan. Nevertheless, Saskatchewan maintained its lead in this area by introducing medicare in 1962, making it the first government in North America to offer a universal, publicly funded medical insurance plan covering visits to doctors and various types of medical specialists. The federal government responded to this by passing the Medical Care Act in 1966. This legislation committed the federal government to contributing funding to all provincial plans that met federal goals, objectives, and priorities. By 1968, all provinces and territories in Canada had finalized cost-sharing agreements with the federal government, and by 1971 had launched medical insurance plans of their own.

The 1960s saw a number of other creative social policy developments. The Canada Pension Plan (and its Quebec counterpart) was created in order to meet two major objectives: first, to improve living standards for the elderly, and second, to enable Canadians to remain in the plan regardless of whether they changed jobs or geographical location. This latter feature of the plan helped to improve labour mobility in Canada. This period also witnessed the extension of youth allowances from 16 to 17 for those who remained in school, improvements in the pensions of older Canadians with little or no other income through the introduction of the Guaranteed Income Supplement, and the introduction of the Canada Assistance Plan to share the cost of provincial social assistance programs.

Not a great deal of effective social security legislation has been passed since that time. Moreover, there has been a great deal of friction between the federal and provincial governments over cost-sharing arrangements, authority over specific programs, downloading of certain services, and reallocations of funds and responsibilities. These problems have been compounded by a series of difficult economic and financial problems, including a couple of major downturns in economic activity, globalization, the deregulation of markets, rapidly changing demographic conditions, shifts in political ideologies and parties, and recent financial breakdowns and recessions. Nor are these the only problems with which federal and provincial governments have had to contend. Throughout much of this period, there have been serious concerns about the size and growth of public debts and deficits and the need to balance expenditures and revenues more effectively. These problems have all taken their toll on Canada's health care and social security system in one way or another.

Despite this, government expenditures on social security in Canada have remained remarkably stable over the last 50 years. At the end of the 1970s, spending on social security programs amounted to roughly 53 percent of all government expenditure. It is roughly the same percentage today, despite the concerns of some over "the dismantling of Canada's social security system." The country's governments remain deeply committed to health care and social security, although the system has undergone countless changes over the last half-century and is today more focused on childhood development and advanced educational training than in the past. Canada's social situation is changing rapidly, and it is imperative for the various levels of government to stay on top of these changes, particularly in view of the country's aging population.

SOCIAL ACTIVISM AND ACTIVISTS

Canadians have also demonstrated a great deal of creativity in the area of social activism over the course of the country's history. As in other areas, both individuals and groups and institutions have played a role.

One of the best examples dates from the late 1960s and early 1970s. About the same time that many Canadians were packing up to go to Expo in Montreal, a film crew from the National Film Board was heading to Fogo Island to work on a highly creative project in social activism in co-operation with the Extension Department at Memorial University. Both events—one large and highly visible, the other small and seemingly insignificant—were destined to make valuable contributions to the country's development. While Expo's objective was to heighten aesthetic awareness of cultures in general and Canadian culture in particular, the objective of the Fogo Island project was to involve local citizens and community groups in public and private decision-making and creative problem-solving, and to utilize lobbying and advocacy techniques to achieve practical and concrete results.

Fogo Island is located off the northeast coast of the island of Newfoundland. In 1967, many communities on Fogo Island were experiencing difficulty making ends meet. Residents could eke out only a slim existence from fishing, largely because of stiff competition from highly mechanized producers, devastating fluctuations in prices, and insufficient marketing. The result was high unemployment and the humiliation of having to live on welfare for a substantial part of the year. What was creative about the

Fogo Island project was the opportunity it provided to citizens and community groups to use the media in highly inventive ways to document their problems, as well as to engage in various types of political and social activism. To do this, the NFB and Memorial University gave people cameras, tape recorders, and other audio-visual equipment and encouraged them to make their own films. When they had completed this process, they organized meetings with politicians to show their films and vent their frustrations and concerns. This eventually led to residents getting what they wanted most: a co-operative to replace the commercial fishery.

This proved to be an excellent example of social activism because it was initiated by institutions but carried out by citizens and community groups. While it was not without its problems and involved a certain amount of conflict and confrontation—something which is not unusual in social activist projects and often very necessary—the results were so successful that the Fogo Island project grew into one of the most important programs the National Film Board ever initiated. The program was called Challenge for Change/*Société Nouvelle* and was duplicated by many communities and community groups across the country. As the commissioner of the National Film Board said at the time, "If the Film Board had done nothing else in its thirty-five years, this project alone would have assured its place in history."

Spurred on by the success of the Fogo Island project and Challenge for Change/*Société Nouvelle*, the federal government launched a number of other highly creative and very successful programs designed to put public funds into the hands of citizens and community groups to carry out projects of their own choosing and design. It was a risky venture, but one that produced such highly valuable and socially inventive initiatives as Opportunities for Youth (OFY), the Local Initiatives Program (LIP), the Local Employment Assistance Program (LEAP), and New Horizons. These initiatives were all designed to tackle pressing economic and social issues, including high rates of unemployment among the country's young people, poverty in selected regions, the need to re-train middle-aged workers, and the desire of seniors to find new avenues for exploration and discovery. Many of these undertakings led to the establishment of permanent organizations and activities in the decades to follow.

Despite the contributions to social activism from initiatives like this, most such contributions have come from individuals rather than groups or institutions. Indeed, Canada boasts a long list of highly creative social activists, including Emily Stowe and Adelaide Hoodless, who were discussed earlier because of their contributions to education, as well as Alphonse Desjardins, Moses Coady, Jean Vanier, Doris Anderson, Terry Fox, Rick Hansen, Clara Hughes, Henry Enns, June Callwood, Craig and Marc Kielburger, Maude Barlow, and others. Each of these activists has been concerned with caring, sharing, and compassion in one form or another. This has led to the realization of many creative ideas, which in turn have led to the founding of new organizations, agencies, activities, and programs that are now permanent fixtures on the Canadian and international scene.

Alphonse Desjardins was a journalist and French-language stenographer in the House of Commons when he created the Caisse populaire with his wife Dorimène Roy in Lévis, Quebec in 1900. The Caisse was a cooperative savings and loan organization patterned along the lines of some of the saving and loan companies popular in Europe at that time. It encouraged people of modest means to save for the future by providing them with the credit they needed for economic necessities, much as small-loan cooperatives in Africa, Asia, and Latin America do today. The Caisse populaire proved so popular with the government of Quebec and the Church that when Desjardins died in 1920, there were more than two hundred offices in Quebec as well as in other parts of Canada and areas in New England with large francophone populations. The Caisse has grown steadily since that time, and was also a forerunner of the credit unions popular in North America today.

Like Alphonse Desjardins, Moses Coady was concerned with the welfare and well-being of the less fortunate. Coady was born in North East Margaree, Nova Scotia in 1882 and died in Antigonish, Nova Scotia in 1959. He was a teacher and priest who developed a program to assist the poor in depressed areas of the Maritimes. As director of extension programs at St. Francis Xavier University, he created the "Antigonish Movement," a program since adopted elsewhere in the world to help poor people improve their social and economic situation. His book *Masters of Their Own Destiny*—the title of which says a great deal about the central objective of Coady's life and work—documents the development of the Antigonish Movement in detail and has been translated into many languages.

Jean Vanier is another well-known Canadian social activist. Born in 1928 the son of Pauline and Georges Vanier—the latter served as Governor-General of Canada from 1959 to 1967—Jean Vanier served in the British and Canadian navies and then studied philosophy and theology at the Monastery of Le Saulchoir and the Institut Catholique in France. After teaching at several universities in Europe, he established a home for mentally challenged people in 1964 in Trosly-Breuil, north of Paris. The home was called *L'Arche*—The Ark—and became so popular that there are now many such institutions located in different parts of the world with no end in sight. Vanier is also a prolific author whose books include *Tears of Silence* and *Community and Growth*. His writings and life have been devoted to creating respect for people less fortunate than himself and sharing everything he has with others, particularly the mentally and physically challenged. He is strongly committed to the belief that every person is precious in his or her own right and should be loved and valued for who they are and what they are able to contribute to their communities and society.

Doris Anderson, another Canadian social activist with strong convictions and beliefs, was born in Calgary. From 1957 to 1977, Anderson was editor of *Chatelaine* magazine. Long before the world had heard of Betty Freidan or *Ms.* magazine, Anderson was a powerful advocate for women's rights and social justice. She transformed *Chatelaine* into a magazine concerned with the problems confronting Canadian women, such as pay equity, divorce, abortion, domestic violence, and so forth. Anderson was later appointed chair of the Canadian Advisory Council on the Status of Women in 1979 and served as president of the National Action Committee on the Status of Women from 1982 to 1984. In these roles, she worked tirelessly for gender equality and its inclusion in the Canadian Constitution and the Charter of Rights and Freedoms. In 1981, Parliament was on the verge of passing a Charter of Rights that Anderson felt drastically undermined the status of women. As president of the National Advisory Council on the Status of Women, she immediately organized a conference so that women could discuss what was at stake and what had to be done. When the federal government pressured her to cancel the conference, she resigned her post in protest. This instantly triggered an uprising among women in Canada that led to the holding of an ad hoc conference on the status of women. The political fallout from this was so intense that the federal government was forced to back down and include a clause in the Charter stating that women and men are equal under the law.

While many social activists have made their presence felt in Canada, none is more remembered—or more revered—than Terry Fox. When Canadians were asked by the CBC to select the greatest Canadian of all time, Terry Fox came a close second to Tommy Douglas.

Fox was studying kinesiology at university in 1977 when he discovered that he had a rare form of bone cancer called osteogenic sarcoma. This led to the amputation of virtually all of one leg. While he was recuperating, he struck on the idea of creating a "Marathon of Hope" to raise money for cancer research. It involved running across Canada from coast to coast. He started his run in St. John's, Newfoundland on April 12, 1980. With unbelievable courage and conviction, he ran through the Atlantic provinces, Quebec, and the greater part of Ontario before he was forced to give up his run in Thunder Bay on September 1, after it was discovered that the cancer had returned and spread to his lungs. He had run some 5,373 kilometers and raised more than $1.7 million for cancer research when this happened.

While this amount fell short of Terry's goal of raising one dollar for every Canadian (or roughly $30 million in total), the Terry Fox Run has now become an annual event in Canada and many other parts of the world and has raised more than $500 million for cancer research—an amount far exceeding Terry's original goal. Canadians have been so utterly taken with the caring, sharing, and compassion Terry demonstrated throughout his life that they have never forgotten him. He epitomized everything that is best in the Canadian character. Douglas Coupland, who has done so much to keep Fox's memory and accomplishments alive through the various images he has created of Terry and the book he has written about him, captured this heroic individual's spirit most effectively in the summer of 2003 in an article he wrote for *Maclean's* magazine: "There is not a soul in the land who could feel anything but pride towards the man's memory. How could they not? Terry loved his family and country, and he knew that as a people we have huge untapped reservoirs of kindness and strength."

Like Terry Fox, Rick Hansen has also endured mental and physical hardship to raise money for a worthwhile social cause. Much like Fox, Hansen displayed great athletic ability when he was young. However, a car accident when he was 15 left him paralyzed from the waist down, forced to use a wheelchair. Inspired by Fox and his ambitious Marathon of Hope, Rick Hansen began his own "Man in Motion Tour" at a mall in Vancouver in 1985. While the tour was initially ignored, it soon took hold and gathered momentum. By the time it was completed in 1987, Hansen had logged more than 40,000 kilometers across 34 countries, returned to B.C. Place Stadium in Vancouver to a triumphant standing ovation, and raised more than $26 million for spinal cord research. Since then, Hansen has created the Rick Hansen Foundation, married and had four children, written several books, been elected to Canada's Sports Hall of Fame and the Canada Walk of Fame, and raised more than $200 million for his worthy social undertaking. And this is not all. He is still an outstanding athlete, has won many national and international competitions and six medals at the Paralympics (including three gold medals), and is a frequent commentator on radio and television.

The tradition begun by Terry Fox and Rick Hansen was carried on in remarkable fashion in 2014 by Clara Hughes, winner of numerous gold, silver, and bronze medals for speed skating and cycling at the Olympic Games, the Commonwealth Games, the World Championships, the Pan American Games, and the World Cup. Starting on March 14 in Toronto and finishing on July 1 in Ottawa, Hughes covered more than 11,000 kilometres from the Atlantic to the Pacific and the Arctic during "Clara's Big Ride." Hughes's remarkable accomplishment was designed to create awareness of mental illness and depression. What made Hughes's efforts especially poignant was the fact that she herself suffered from depression and was consequently the ideal person to raise this issue and discuss it with others.

The highly creative contributions made by physically or mentally challenged Canadians to the country's social development are documented by Henry Enns and Alfred H. Neufeldt in their book *In Pursuit of Equal Participation: Canada and Disability at Home and Abroad*. Canadians have been especially active in this area since 1951, when the first National Conference on Rehabilitation of the Physically Disabled took place. This conference eventually resulted in the Vocational Rehabilitation of Disabled Persons Act, passed into law in 1961. It also acted as a real stimulus to the creation and development of many organizations for the disabled throughout the country, including the Council of Canadians with Disabilities (CCD), the Canadian Association of Community Living (CACL), the Canadian Rehabilitation Council for the Disabled (CRCD), and others.

Through these and other organizations, as well as through the efforts of people like Gustave Gingras, Walter Dinsdale, Allan Roeher, Henry Enns, Jim Derkson, Marie Barile, and others, the country and its citizenry have been real pioneers in developing many creative approaches to assisting people with different types of disabilities, including the community-based approach to care as well as greater collaboration between the public sector and the private sector in this important field. The country also played a leading role internationally, and was the driving force behind the creation of Disabled People's International (DPI), the global non-governmental organization in this area. Like the International Association of Adult Education, this organization has its origins and head office in Canada.

It is fitting at this point to turn to June Callwood, a well-known and highly creative social activist who was concerned with helping people with difficult problems, especially young people, people suffering from various illnesses, and the poor.

Callwood's life was taken up with three callings: fighting for social justice; embracing numerous social causes and concerns; and writing many books and articles. Over the course of her life, which spanned 82 years, she was involved in countless social undertakings, including active involvement in the development of the Civic Liberties Association of Canada, Connecting Seniors of Canada, the Writer's Union of Canada, the Canadian Campaign for Prison System Improvements, the Toronto's Children's Network, and others. But she is best known for founding a number of key social institutions in Toronto that are devoted to helping those with health problems, such as Casey House, a hospice for people suffering from HIV/AIDS, Nellie's Hostel for Women, and Jessie's Centre for Teenagers. Moreover, she authored more than 30 books, including *Canadian Women and the Law*, *Portrait of Canada*, *Emma*, *June Callwood's National Treasures*, *The Man Who Lost Himself: The Terry Evanshen Story*, and others. She also wrote articles for the country's leading newspapers and magazines.

Despite her many accomplishments, Callwood experienced her fair share of disappointments and setbacks along the way. One of the greatest was the battle she and others waged against poverty, especially child poverty. Indeed, if there is one area where Canada's well-deserved reputation for caring, sharing, and compassion comes up short, it is in the area of alleviating poverty, especially among young people, children, and the elderly.

Craig and Marc Kielburger are also well-known Canadian social activists who have garnered a great deal of international attention in recent years. This is especially true of Craig, whose life was transformed at a very early age when he read a newspaper article about Iqbal Masih, a child slave in Islamabad, Pakistan who was murdered. Shortly after this, he founded a non-profit organization called Free the Children. It has since become one of the largest and most successful organizations in the world for "children helping children" through education and social development, having built more than 450 schools in various parts of the world since 1995.

Craig Kielburger is not only an accomplished social activist. He is also an award-winning author and popular speaker who has been nominated for a Nobel Peace Prize on several occasions. Among his most recent books is *Me to We*, which he co-authored with his brother Marc, a passionate plea for more kindness and understanding in Canada and the world. As the title suggests, the book is about making the shift from a world based on egoism, materialism, and concern for the self to a world based on altruism, sharing, and concern for others. It is perhaps not surprising that a book of this sort was written by two Canadians. Nor is it surprising that their We Day rallies attract thousands of young people every year.

The final social activist we will discuss is Maude Barlow. Born in 1947, Barlow learned a great deal about social activism when she was young from her father, Bill McGrath, who was well known in Ottawa for his efforts to fight wartime atrocities and to promote reform of Canada's prison system following his return home after the Second World War.

Early in her career, Barlow was active in the feminist movement in Canada, as director of the Office of Equal Opportunity for the city of Ottawa and advisor on women's issues to Pierre Trudeau's Liberal government. Later, she fought the Mulroney Government over the North American Free Trade Agreement (NAFTA) and then became an active participant in the quest to create a strong, independent, and sovereign Canada through her work as national chairperson of the Council of Canadians, a position she still holds today.

In recent years, Barlow has become active in the grassroots movement to ensure that all citizens in the world have sufficient access to water, as well as to prevent the depletion, pollution, diversion, and commodification of water by large corporations. This has led her to travel to many parts of the world to speak about the present water crisis, as well as to create the Blue Planet Project, intended to protect the world's fresh water from the growing threats of international trade and privatization.

In recognition of her efforts, Barlow was accorded the Right Livelihood Award in 2005—an award that some regard as "the alternative Nobel Prize" because it honours people "offering practical and exemplary answers to the most urgent challenges facing us today." She has received numerous awards since then, such as the EarthCare Award from the Sierra Club in 2011. She is also the author of numerous books, including *Take Back the Nation, Global Showdown: How the New Activists Are Fighting Global Corporate Rule, Too Close for Comfort: Canada's Future within Fortress North America, Blue Covenant: The Global Water Crisis and the*

Coming Battle for the Right of Water, and, more recently, *Blue Future: Protecting Water for People and the Planet Forever*. The very titles of these books say a great deal about the type of creative social activism she has engaged in over the years.

There is one final area where Canadians have exhibited a great deal of creativity in the social and social activist realm—the area known as "indicators of well-being." Development of such measures is imperative because traditional indicators like gross domestic product and per capita income do not provide accurate measures of the overall quality of people's lives.

To address this problem, a project called the Canadian Index of Well-being was created in 2002 by the RBC Foundation and the Atkinson Charitable Foundation. (The latter is one of the most socially active organizations in Canada.) The aim of this highly innovative project was to create a more comprehensive way of measuring societal progress, not only in Canada but throughout the world. In order to do this, the project established eight *societal domains*—living standards, healthy populations, community vitality, ecosystem health, time use, educated populace, civic engagement, and culture, arts, and recreation—and is in the process of developing effective indicators to measure well-being in each domain. Now at its new institutional home at the University of Waterloo, the project is attracting a great deal of international attention as it forges partnerships between various national and international organizations.

It is clear from the many individuals and initiatives discussed in this chapter that Canadians have been—and remain—at the cutting edge of creative developments in health care and social welfare. In the process, they have reinforced their reputation as a caring, sharing, and compassionate people living in one of the most socially advanced countries in the world.

Canadian Creators

Sandford Fleming
Originator of Universal Standard Time and Railway Pioneer
(Chapter Three)

Abraham Gesner
Petrochemical Pioneer
(Chapter Four)

Adam Beck
Hydroelectricity Pioneer
(Chapter Four)

Adelaide Hunter Hoodless
Founder of the Women's Institute Movement
(Chapter Five)

Nellie McClung
Social Activist,
Politician,
Author
(Chapter Five)

Elizabeth McMaster
Philanthropist,
Founder,
Hospital for Sick Children
(Chapter Six)

William Osler
Medical Pioneer
(Chapter Six)

Tommy Douglas
Medicare Pioneer
(Chapter Six)

Reginald Fessenden in his laboratory at Brant Rock, Mass., in 1906
(Chapter Three)

J.-A. Bombardier in 1943 explaining the workings of the Bombardier-built military snowmobile (Chapter Three)

Thomas Ahearn
Inventor of the Electric Oven
(Chapter Four)

Arthur McDonald
2015 Nobel Laureate in Physics
(Chapter Four)

Samuel Cunard
Steamship Pioneer
(Chapter Three)

William Stephenson
Inventor and Espionage Agent
(Chapter Three)

Charles H. Best and Frederick Banting
Discoverers of Insulin
(Chapter Six)

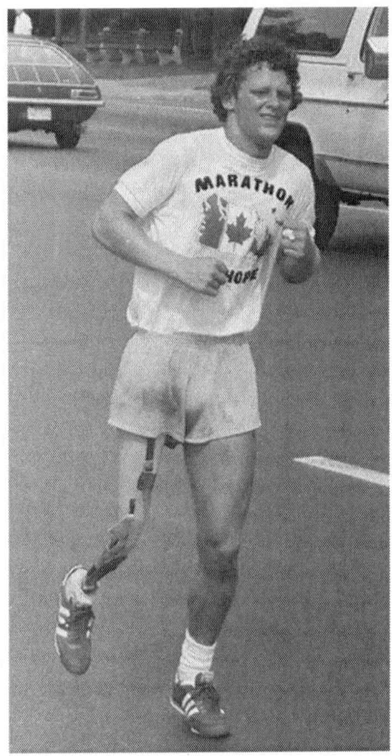

Terry Fox
Medical Advocate (Chapter Six)

Lucy Maud Montgomery
Author
(Chapter Seven)

Canadian Creators

Clara Hughes
Athlete, Social Activist
(Chapters Six, Eight)

Alice Munro
Author,
Nobel laureate
(Chapter Seven)

Margaret Atwood
Author
(Chapter Seven)

Céline Dion
Singer
(Chapter Seven)

Oscar Peterson
Jazz Pianist,
Composer
(Chapter Seven)

James Naismith
Inventor of Basketball
(Chapter Eight)

CHAPTER SEVEN

The Arts and Entertainment

For many Canadians, creativity manifests itself in the arts and entertainment more than anywhere else. This is because artists and entertainers possess the ability to create and perform works that are unique and say a great deal about Canada, Canadians, and Canadian culture. Everything is there in one form or another: people, places, events, traditions, communities, regions, history, geography, landscape, and the nature of the country as a whole.

FROM THE INDIGENOUS PERIOD TO CONFEDERATION

As in other areas we've considered, creativity in this field can be traced back to the Indigenous peoples. Although most of their efforts were channeled into ensuring their survival, they were active and gifted artists, as the rock paintings and petroglyphs of the Ojibwa, the myths, legends, and dances of the Cree, the costumes of the Micmacs, the totem poles of the Haida, the masks of the Kwakiutl, and the stone carvings of the Inuit readily confirm. Canada would not have the profuse legacy of Indigenous aesthetic works it does today without major contributions from painters, carvers, singers, and printmakers such as Pitseolak Ashoona, Kenojuak Ashevak, David Ruben Piqtoukun, Susan Aglukark, Norval Morrisseau, Benjamin Chee Chee, Allen Sapp, Bill Reid, and others. Places like Cape Dorset and Nunavut are known internationally for their artistic creations and aesthetic capabilities.

In a similar fashion, the fact that they had numerous economic and material needs to address didn't deter the first European settlers from addressing their artistic and entertainment needs. When the Order of Good Cheer was created at Annapolis Royal by the first French settlers more than four centuries ago, music, song, and dance played a prominent role along with good food and drink. It was at this time that Lescarbot composed the verses for *Les Muses de la Nouvelle France* and wrote *Neptune's Theatre*, generally regarded as the first theatrical performance by Europeans in North America. It was performed at Port Royal in 1606.

As settlement moved westward from Annapolis Royal to Quebec and Montreal, the Church and the Jesuits played a prominent role. By the middle of the seventeenth century, the *Ecole des Arts et Métiers* had been created in Quebec to teach painting, sculpture, carpentry, and weaving in addition to agriculture. It played a crucial role in the evolution of early French religious painting, statue-making, silverwork, embroidery, and leather work. Only later, after many subsequent achievements in the arts and crafts, was it realized what a solid foundation had been laid by early French settlers and religious leaders in this area.

Between 1600 and 1867, numerous advances were recorded in the artistic life of the country, not only by the French but also by the English, Irish, Scots, Germans, Ukrainians, Scandinavians, United Empire Loyalists, and others who came to Canada. Some of the biggest advances were in music. Both sacred and secular music flourished. Sacred music included a great deal of liturgical singing and organ music, as well as some large oratorios. Secular music progressed apace: the folk songs of the habitants, trappers, and voyageurs of Quebec, as well as the fishermen and farmers of Newfoundland, Nova Scotia, and New Brunswick, developed first, as documented admirably and diligently by Marius Barbeau, Helen Creighton, and others. Later, bands played an important role, not only for military and religious occasions and performances in public squares, but also for theatrical events. When Charles Dickens visited Montreal in 1842, for example, he saw a play performed with music by the band of the Twenty-third Regiment. Music also provided the perfect complement to the many dances that were popular at that time, including cotillions, quadrilles, polkas, mazurkas, square dances, jigs, and hornpipes. There were composers, too, like John Quesnel, who wrote several drawing-room operas such as *Colas and Colinette* and a number of plays, as well as Calixa Lavallée, who composed the music for the country's national anthem.

In literature, Nova Scotia in general—and Halifax in particular—took the lead. It was in Halifax that Canada's first literary periodical, the *Nova Scotia Magazine*, was launched in 1799. Nova Scotia was also home to some of the country's earliest and finest authors, including Oliver Goldsmith (the great-nephew of the famous eighteenth-century Irish writer), Joseph Howe, and especially Thomas Chandler Haliburton. Haliburton was a humourist who produced Canada's first internationally successful book—*The Clockmaker*—recounting the exploits and escapades of the notoriously funny Samuel Slick. It was published in 1836, and while it was one of Canada's first literary forays into the realm of humour, it was certainly not the last. In fact, Canada has made creative contributions to humour and comedy out of all proportion to the size of the country's population.

It was not long after these auspicious beginnings in Nova Scotia that Susanna Moodie, Catharine Parr Traill, and John Richardson appeared on the scene. While Traill and Moodie came from England and Richardson from the United States, they wrote about the trials and tribulations of life and living in Canada as immigrants in such books as *The Backwoods of Canada*, *Roughing It in the Bush*, *Life in the Clearings*, and *Wacousta*. What is most significant about these books is the fact that their authors were concerned first and foremost with showing what was taking place in Canada at the time, as well as demonstrating the intimate connection between people, the natural environment, and community life.

In addition to writing books, the aforementioned authors also wrote for literary magazines such as Montreal's *Literary Garland*. Periodicals like these did much to help struggling writers by publishing their plays, short stories, poems, and articles. Another important early Canadian author is Louis-Honoré Fréchette, born in Lévis in 1839. He served in the House of Commons from 1874 to 1878, but is best known today as one of the principal pioneers of literary developments in Quebec, particularly with the publication of *La Voix d'un exilé* and *La Légende d'un peuple*, which were concerned with the needs and aspirations of French Canadians.

Although theatre progressed more slowly, it was also in an active state of development by the first half of the nineteenth century. Canada's first real theatre opened its doors in Halifax in 1787, and Saint John had a professional theatrical group producing plays of a high calibre by 1816. Although plays such as those of Molière and Racine were produced in Quebec prior to this time, the first real theatre to be built in Quebec was Montreal's Theatre Royal, constructed in 1826. In the decades to follow, many theatres were built in Upper and Lower Canada to house touring groups from England and the United States, as well as to provide opportunities for local resident groups. As a result, a solid foundation was laid for Canada's future theatrical development.

In painting, Quebec City played the dominant role, largely as a result of painters like Légaré, Plamondon, Hamel, Triaud, and others. Following in their footsteps were such highly creative talents as Cornelius Krieghoff and Paul Kane, whose works were destined to have an important impact on Canadian painting in the century to follow. In the crafts, which formed such a pivotal part of the country's culture at the time, every community had its fair share of creative talents, as well as a pressing need for them. While many things could be imported from abroad, many others had to be created here in Canada. As a result, skilled artisans, who made everything from household goods to religious relics and monuments, were in great demand. Churches, schools, farm houses, barns, factories, and other buildings had to be erected, generating a demand for architects, stonemasons, carpenters, carvers, designers, and planners.

CONFEDERATION TO CENTENNIAL

By the time of Confederation, Canada had built up an impressive array of artistic works that included songs, dances, musical works, plays, stories, paintings, craft objects, architectural edifices, and historic sites and monuments. While some of these works had an Indigenous quality about them, the large majority were cast squarely in the European tradition. Most of the country's musical, theatrical, and dance groups, for instance, performed compositions, plays, and ballets by well-known European masters. As a result, there was a German ring to the music, a Scotch and Irish flair to the dances, and a French or British tinge to the theatrical works. Because of the desire to emulate European tastes and traditions, a uniquely Canadian creativity and expression did not manifest themselves until much later.

Nevertheless, the arts expanded rapidly after Confederation. Some of the most important developments took place in literature. Capitalizing on the tradition established by Goldsmith, Haliburton, Moodie, Traill, Fréchette, and others, a new group of creative talents emerged who are deemed in retrospect to be pioneers in the development of a more distinctive Canadian style of literature. These authors included Charles Mair, Charles G. D. Roberts, Bliss Carman, Archibald Lampman, Charles Gordon (under the pen name Ralph Connor), Lucy Maud Montgomery, Stephen Leacock, Robert Service, Louis Hémon, Frederick Philip Grove, and others.

Montgomery wrote Canada's most successful novel, *Anne of Green Gables*, during the first decade of the twentieth century. Leacock, who is generally regarded as Canada's greatest literary humourist, satirized social situations and pretensions as well as literary practices and political fads in books like *Literary Lapses* and especially *Sunshine Sketches of a Little Town*, published in 1912. Service, a bank teller from the Yukon, immortalized three memorable Canadian characters—Sam McGee, Dan McGrew, and "The Lady known as Lou"—in books like *Songs of a Sourdough* which appeared in 1907. Hémon, an immigrant from France, wrote *Maria Chapdelaine*, a book that acquainted English Canadians with French Canada; it was published in France in 1913. And Grove, an immigrant from Germany who settled in Manitoba, wrote books like *Over Prairie Trails* and *Fruits of the Earth* that were published in the 1920s and '30s.

About the same time, Canadians were making some highly creative and very remarkable contributions to the development of theatre and film in the United States. Donald Brian, an actor, dancer, and singer born in St. John's, Newfoundland in 1877—many decades before Newfoundland became part of Canada—went to New York, where in 1907 he was crowned "The King of Broadway" by the *New York Times* when he was still only 18 years old. He had lead roles in more than 20 Broadway productions, worked closely for many years with George M. Cohan, the great American theatrical figure, had major roles in two Jesse L. Lasky films, and is reputed to have helped President Theodore Roosevelt act more relaxed in public in addition to teaching Frank Sinatra how to dance and entertain U.S. troops in England along with Bob Hope.

He was not the only Newfoundlander to make it big in New York in show business. John Murray Anderson was born in St. John's in 1886, educated in Newfoundland, Scotland, and Switzerland, and then moved to New York, where he made his mark working as writer, director, and producer of *The Greenwich Village Follies* in 1919. He was also involved in the *Ziegfeld Follies,* Radio City Music Hall, the Ringling Brothers Circus, and taught Lucille Ball and Bette Davis in his acting school in Manhattan.

As these creative developments were taking place on the East Coast of the United States, comparable, if not even more remarkable, developments were taking place on the West Coast. There, a number of Canadians were making seminal contributions to the early development of Hollywood. One of the most important of these was Sidney Olcott, who was born in Toronto. As an actor and screenwriter, but much more importantly as a film maker, producer, and director, Olcott was active from the very dawn of Hollywood, making several silent films, most notably the first version ever of *Ben Hur* (1907) and *From the Manger to the Cross* (1912). The latter film grossed over a million dollars, and is claimed to have had a strong impact on the development of such world-famous directors as D. W. Griffith and Cecile B. DeMille.

Olcott was viewed by many as the greatest film director of the era. He paved the way for many other Canadians to follow in his footsteps, including Louis B. Mayer, founder of Metro-Goldwyn-Mayer Studios (better known as MGM), Jack Warner, founder of Warner Brothers Studios, and Mack Sennett, who established the Keystone Kops. These individuals, and other Canadians, played important roles in the making of such popular films as *Casablanca*, *Gone With the Wind*, *The Wizard of Oz*, and virtually all of the Charlie Chaplin, Buster Keaton, Gloria Swanson, and Marie Dressler movies. Their contributions, and those of others, are described at length by another person who had a long association with Canada and Hollywood, Charles Basil Foster, who was born in England but spent the bulk of his life in Canada. A publicist, Foster worked closely with such well-known actors as Marilyn Monroe, Richard Burton, Boris Karloff, and Errol Flynn. He was also the publicist for the world's longest running play, Agatha Christie's *The Mousetrap*. Two of his books document the remarkable impact Canadians had on the origins and early development of Hollywood: the first is *Stardust and Shadows*, which is about the silent film era; and the second is *Once Upon a Time in Paradise*, which is about Canadian contributions to Hollywood from the late 1920s to the 1950s. A third book by Foster—*Donald Brian: King of Broadway*—documents Brian's multifarious contributions to Broadway.

This by no means concludes the story of Canada's contributions to the film industry. While the Frenchman Lumière brought the first moving picture to Canada in 1896, two Canadian brothers—Andrew and George Holland from Ottawa—were the first to open a movie house in North America. It was called a "kinetoscope parlour," opening in the United States in 1894 and grossing over $16,000 in the first year. About the same time, James Freer from Manitoba purchased a combined camera, projector, and printer and became Canada's first film-maker, and one of the first in the world. He made a number of short films about trains and farm life in Manitoba, where he and his family lived in the latter part of the nineteenth century. Interestingly, Ernest Ouimet, a Canadian labourer who eventually became an entertainment mogul, opened the Ouimetoscope Theatre in Montreal soon after this. It was followed by a second Ouimetoscope Theatre in 1907. It had over a thousand upholstered seats, a refreshment bar, and an orchestra, and was the first large moving-picture palace—called a "grind house" at that time—in all of North America.

§ § § § §

It was also during the early twentieth century that Canada's governments, and especially the federal government, began to lay the foundations for the country's system of heritage conservation institutions in general, and art galleries, museums, libraries, archives, historic sites, and monuments in particular, something we discussed earlier. At the federal level, the National Gallery of Art, the Dominion Archives, and the Historical Sites and Monuments Board were all established about this time.

These developments were complemented by others at the provincial and municipal level, as well as in the private sector. In music, many important musical organizations were formed in the late nineteenth and early twentieth century, including the Montreal Symphony, the Toronto Symphony, the Toronto Conservatory of Music, the Vancouver Symphony Society, the Mendelssohn Choir, and others. In theatre, Winnipeg had four theatres—the Winnipeg Theatre, the Winnipeg Opera House, the Dominion Theatre, and Walter Theatre—as early as 1900, thereby establishing its reputation as a gateway to the arts in western Canada and a creative pioneer in Canada's artistic development. In the decades to follow, this city became home to many creative talents, including Dr. Ferdinand Eckhardt, director of the Winnipeg Art Gallery for many years and the husband of the internationally known musician and composer Sonia Eckhardt-Gramatté; John Hirsch and Tom Hendry, who were co-founders of the Manitoba Theatre Centre; Izzy Asper, founder of media company Canwest Global Communications; and Victor Feldbrill and Bramwell Tovey, both musical directors of the Winnipeg Symphony Orchestra. Tovey was also the founder of Winnipeg's highly successful and creative New Music Festival.

While theatrical touring in the late nineteenth and early twentieth century was done largely by British and American companies, thus limiting the development of Canadian theatre and the creation of a more indigenous repertoire, many amateur theatre groups were formed and flourished, including the Little Theatre Association, the Shakespeare Society, the Players Club of Hart House, and others. Moreover, and certainly more importantly as far as the development of theatre in Canada is concerned, the Dominion Drama Festival was founded towards the end of this period in 1932. It played a seminal role in the development of theatre across the country until well into the 1960s, primarily by providing a showcase for dramatic works and talents and the only coast-to-coast hook-up for Canada's theatrical community.

The development of other arts service organizations also continued. By the early 1930s, many such organizations had been created, including the Canadian Authors Association, the Société des Écrivains Canadiens, the Sculpture Society of Canada, the Canadian Society of Painters in Water Colour, the Royal Canadian Academy, and others.

Nevertheless, by far the most creative development of this period was the formation of the Group of Seven. Following in the footsteps of Tom Thomson, who is generally regarded as Canada's greatest landscape painter, the Group rejected European styles and traditions and endeavoured to create a style of painting that was "uniquely Canadian," although they were influenced greatly by the Impressionists. They travelled to many parts of Canada and into the Far North to paint the country's magnificent forests, mountains, landscapes, waterways, tundras, and wilderness areas. Comprised of Franklin Carmichael, Lawren Harris, A. Y. Jackson, Frank H. Johnston, Arthur Lismer, J. E. H. MacDonald, and Frederick Horsman Varley, the Group had a vision of Canada—and a vision of the role that the arts and artists should play in the realization of this vision—that they were anxious to share with all Canadians.

The best place to see works by the Group of Seven is in the McMichael Canadian Art Collection in Kleinburg, Ontario. Located in a huge log cabin evocative of earlier periods in Canadian architectural history, the collection and gallery were created by a wealthy industrialist, Robert McMichael, and his wife Signe. Located in a magnificent setting northwest of Toronto, the gallery houses some of the best paintings of the Group of Seven, as well as an outstanding collection of works by other Canadian artists. It also displays a number of paintings by Indigenous artists and by Emily Carr, who is well known for her paintings of Indigenous villages and totem poles on the West Coast, her depictions of the magnificent forests of British Columbia, and her books such as *Klee Wyck*, which was written after her painting career ended and won a Governor-General's Award.

What is most significant about the Group of Seven is the effect it had on the development of the arts in Canada. The Group's belief that the arts must flourish before Canada could become a real home to Canadians struck a responsive chord with many in the arts community, as well as with the general public. Slowly but surely, Canadian artists began to look at Canada in a new way, focusing more on Canadian styles, traditions, and values, and less on those imported from Europe.

If the Group of Seven had a remarkable impact on the development of the arts in Canada, so did the Canadian Broadcasting Corporation. As noted earlier, it provided an incredible impetus to the development of the arts at a time when few opportunities for artists and arts organizations existed in Canada, and the arts occupied a marginal rather than mainstream place in Canadian culture.

While it may come as a surprise, many of Hollywood's best-known film and television actors over the years have been or are Canadian. Many got their start at the CBC, such as Lorne Greene, Pa Cartwright in *Bonanza*, William Shatner, Captain Kirk in *Star Trek*, and Christopher Plummer, co-star with Julie Andrews in *The Sound of Music*.

But they are merely the tip of a much larger iceberg. Though not all of them worked at the CBC, a longer (though still incomplete) list of Canadian actors who have made it big in Hollywood includes Mary Pickford, Marie Dressler, Walter Pidgeon, John Ireland, Raymond Massey, Raymond Burr, Fay Wray, Barry Morse, Chief Dan George, Jay Silverheels, Kate Reid, John Candy, Leslie Nielson, Donald Sutherland, Michael J. Fox, Dan Aykroyd, Geneviève Bujold, Mike Myers, Jim Carrey, Victor Garber, Keiffer Sutherland, and Jill Hennessy. As well, many of Hollywood's outstanding directors, producers, script writers, and composers have been or are Canadian, such as Bernard Slade, Harry Rasky, Ivan Reitman, Lorne Michaels, Ted Kotcheff, James Cameron, Norman Jewison, Graham Yost (son of Elwy Yost, long-time host of TV Ontario's extremely popular *Saturday Night at the Movies*), Howard Shore, and others.

While not all of Canada's film and acting talents have been able to take advantage of opportunities provided by the CBC or make it big in Hollywood, virtually every Canadian involved in the production, distribution, and development of films or television in the early years was able to profit in one form or another from the fact that Canada possessed—and still possesses—one of the oldest and finest public broadcasting systems in the world. People involved in this system have gone to great lengths from the beginning to support the country's creative film, acting, television, and broadcasting talents and give them opportunities to hone their skills in Canada.

The country's artistic community, though extremely small in size when the CBC was created in the 1930s, was vocal and aggressive in promoting the development and funding of the arts in Canada, especially at the federal level. Indeed, despite the geographical challenges it has faced, the arts community has at various times acted with a great deal of vision, clarity, unity, and determination. One such time was when the *Artists' Brief* was presented to the Special Committee of the House of Commons on Reconstruction and Re-establishment—the Turgeon Committee—in 1944. The Brief was prepared by an assembly of Canada's leading artists, administrators, and volunteers, including Sir Ernest Macmillan, Herman Voaden, and John Coulter, and spearheaded by the Canadian Arts Council, which later became the Canadian Conference of the Arts (CCA). According to one observer, the Brief was "one of the most businesslike statements ever submitted to a parliamentary committee. No redundancy. No exaggeration. No class-consciousness, axe-grinding, self-seeking argument. Nothing but honest common sense, clearly stated and sincerely argued."

The Brief called for numerous changes in the country's artistic life, such as the creation of a government agency to fund the arts, effective copyright legislation, improvements in town planning and industrial design, promotion of the arts abroad, and construction of community arts centres across the country. This latter proposal was especially attractive to members of the Turgeon Committee because it would have provided an effective link between amateurs and professionals, made all levels of government responsible for the arts and not just the federal government, and addressed such difficult problems as the vast size of the country, the dominance by central Canada, over-reliance on foreign producers, organizers, and philanthropists, and the importance of towns and cities in Canada's arts development.

By the time the *Artists' Brief* was presented to the Turgeon Committee, a whole new wave of authors had appeared on the scene, including Morley Callaghan, E. J. Pratt, W. O. Mitchell, Hugh MacLennan, Anne Hébert, Gabrielle Roy, and others. Callaghan, whose concern with "the little guy" was legendary and who was reputed to have defeated Ernest Hemingway in a boxing match, wrote about crime, deprivation, and a variety of secular and sacred issues in the country's rapidly evolving urban centres in books such as *They Shall Inherit the Earth*, *Strange Fugitive*, and *The Loved and the Lost*. Pratt, a professor at the University of Toronto originally from Newfoundland, wrote numerous poems and books such as *The Titanic* and *Brébeuf and His Brethren*, which were published between 1935 and 1940. Mitchell, a much loved literary figure from western Canada who was also a great raconteur and humourist in the tradition of Stephen Leacock and Thomas Chandler Haliburton, wrote about farm life on the prairies in books like *Who Has Seen the Wind* and long-running CBC radio and television programs like *Rawhide* and *Jake and the Kid*. MacLennan, preoccupied with the rift between French and English Canadians, published *Two Solitudes* in 1945; it rapidly became a best seller. Hébert, an outstanding Quebec poet, playwright, and novelist, wrote *Kamouraska*, which won the *Prix des Libraries* in France and was eventually made into a movie by the well-known Quebec filmmaker, Claude Jutra. And Gabrielle Roy, another well-known French-Canadian author, but this time from Manitoba, wrote *Bonheur d'occasion* (*The Tin Flute*) (1945) and *La Petite Poule d'eau* (*The Little Water Hen*) (1950); both won a number of coveted French literary awards.

These artists, and others, were hoping for much more government support for the arts when World War II ended in 1945. Many factors contributed to this hope. One was the rapid growth of the arts themselves, spurred on by the euphoria over the end of the war, the return of the troops from abroad, the excitement of post-war recovery, and the prospects for peace. Another was the movement among Canadian artists and arts administrators to break the centuries-old shackles of amateurism, and, in Quebec, the publication of *Refus global*, which called for the liberalization of Quebec through the freeing of the arts from the traditionalism of the Church and the conventionalism of education. Yet another factor was pressure for a much greater commitment to the arts, better utilization of the country's artistic talents, the desire for increased professionalism, and more effective use of artistic and financial resources. All these factors, and others, set the stage for the Royal Commission on National Development in the Arts, Letters, and Sciences—the Massey-Lévesque Commission—from 1949 to 1951, as well as the creation of the Canada Council in 1957.

From the outset, the Canada Council (now the Canada Council for the Arts) was concerned with two issues of fundamental importance to the development of the arts in Canada. The first was the creation of the highest standards of excellence, and the second the establishment of a corps of professional artists and arts organizations across the country capable of meeting these standards. While such an approach downplayed the artistic needs of citizens, the need for more Canadian content, the development of the arts at the municipal, provincial, and regional level, the necessity of arts education in the schools, and the creation of artistic facilities across the country, even the staunchest critics of the Council were forced to admit that the Council had few viable alternatives at that time. A corps of professional artists and arts organizations as well as high standards of professionalism and excellence were imperative if the Council was to fulfill its mandate.

The Council was created just in time. For another wave of artists and arts organizations had appeared on the scene that desperately required financial support. Included among the organizations were the Stratford Festival, the Théâtre du Nouveau Monde, the Théâtre du Rideau Vert, the Manitoba Theatre Centre, the Royal Winnipeg Ballet, the National Ballet of Canada, the Canadian Opera Company, the Playhouse Theatre in Vancouver, the Neptune Theatre in Halifax, the Citadel Theatre in Edmonton, the Crest Theatre and the Canadian Players in Toronto, and others. While some of these organizations were created from scratch, others existed in a semi-professional state by the time the Canada Council arrived on the scene. Nevertheless, the financial assistance provided by the Council made it possible for these organizations, and many others, to become more professional in their operations in both artistic and administrative terms. Not only were they able to pay artists higher salaries and extend their seasons, but they were also able to engage in more planning, marketing, administration, and promotion of their artistic works.

While the founding and development of each of these organizations was creative in many ways, the ingenuity required to bring them into existence and nurture them through the formative stages of their development is best epitomized by the Stratford Festival. It was created primarily by Tom Patterson, who, like many of Canada's creative talents, had a dream and wanted to turn that dream into a reality. Returning home from the Second World War, he envisaged a major festival for the arts—a Shakespeare Festival—in his home town of Stratford, Ontario.

Virtually no one in Stratford thought this was possible. However, with the town's livelihood at risk because of cuts to the railroad yards that had sustained the town for so long, people were willing to listen to Patterson and give him a chance. This was the opportunity that Patterson, a journalist, needed and instantly seized. After a seemingly endless battle, he convinced Stratford City Council and a number of key authorities in the town that his dream for a major arts festival in Stratford was not far-fetched. Networking with Dora Mavor Moore, the granddame of Canadian theatre at the time, and many other theatrical professionals and practitioners throughout the country, Patterson eventually came into contact with Tyrone Guthrie, one of the world's greatest actors and theatre directors.

Patterson and his entourage managed to convince Tyrone Guthrie to come to Stratford to assess the situation for himself. He liked what he saw, but there was a major problem. Stratford lacked a suitable facility to put on plays. After a great deal of discussion and debate, the group decided to open the first season in a tent! They ordered a huge canvas tent from a company in Chicago, and the first season opened on July 13, 1953. When Alec Guinness, the world-renowned British actor, uttered those immortal words from Shakespeare's *Richard III*—"Now is the winter of our discontent / Made glorious summer by this sun of York"—the Stratford Festival was born.

Things moved quickly after that incredible first summer. A world-famous designer, Tanya Moiseiwitsch, was brought to Stratford to design an amphitheatre with the kind of "thrust stage" Guthrie envisaged. It was built in the parklands on the Avon River. Many internationally known actors and actresses, such as the aforementioned Guinness and Irene Worth, were recruited at the beginning to ensure that the Festival achieved a high level of artistic excellence, as well as visibility and credibility. In later summers, actors of the international stature of Alan Bates, Jessica Tandy, Hume Cronyn, Maggie Smith, William Hutt, James Mason, Christopher Plummer, Colm Feore, Douglas Rain, Peter Ustinov, Donald Sutherland, and many others came to Stratford to perform works by a variety of playwrights, most importantly Shakespeare, but also including Molière, Beckett, Chekhov, Ibsen, and O'Neill. The Festival never looked back after the early years, and has gone on to achieve a great deal of international acclaim as one of the most outstanding theatrical organizations in the world.

While developments like these were occurring on the institutional side of the arts, comparable developments were taking place on the individual side. Many well-known Canadian artists got their start at this time. In music, John Weinzweig, Jean Papineau-Couture, André Prévost, Harry Somers, Harry Freedman, R. Murray Schafer, and Violet Archer arrived on the scene. Their compositions were much more indigenous in character than those of their predecessors, as is apparent from works like John Weinzweig's *Red Ear of Corn*, Jean Papineau-Couture's *Nuit polaire* (*Polar Night*) and *Paysage* (*Landscape*), Harry Somers's *North Country Suite*, Harry Freedman's *Tableau* and *Image,* Godfrey Ridout's *Fall Fair*, Violet Archer's *Northern Landscape*, and somewhat later, Victor Davies' *Mennonite Piano Concerto* and R. Murray Schafer's *North/White*, *Princess of the Stars* and *Music for Wilderness Lake*. Clearly the search was on for more indigenous and creative forms of musical expression that were evocative of the country's geography, climate, landscape, and peoples.

The same trend was evident in opera. While interest in European operas had predominated for more than a century, attempts were made in the 1950s to create "Canadian operas," including Healey Willan's *Deirdre* in 1951 followed, in 1967, by the production of *Louis Riel*. The latter was created by Harry Somers, Mavor Moore, and Jacques Languirand, and concerned the famous Métis leader Louis Riel who was hanged in what is now Saskatchewan in the late nineteenth century under controversial circumstances for leading what was deemed to be an uprising against the Government of Canada.

Theatrical developments followed a similar pattern. Whereas the early years were dominated by preoccupation with European plays and playwrights, attempts were made to create a more indigenous repertoire consistent with the character of Canada and its citizens. Here, the lead was taken by George Ryga, a playwright of Ukrainian descent who was best known for his play *The Ecstasy of Rita Joe* about the plight of the Indigenous peoples in Canada.

Painting also experienced some significant changes. A new generation of painters was making its presence felt. This new generation was less concerned with landscapes than the Group of Seven, but still very much interested in creating paintings that were characteristic of Canada, though in a more contemporary sense. Included among these artists were Greg Curnoe, Dennis Burton, Graham Coughtry, Joyce Wieland, Michael Snow, Roy Kiyooka, Kazuo Nakamura, Jack Shadbolt, Harold Town, and others. While Quebec had also had its fair share of painters in the landscape tradition—most notably James W. Morrice, Ozias Leduc, Maurice Cullen, and Clarence Gagnon—painting in Quebec began to move in some different but highly creative directions after World War II. The impetus here was provided by Alfred Pellan and a group of artists known as the *Automatistes*, several of whom were engaged in writing *Refus global*, as noted earlier. The group included Jean-Paul Riopelle, Marcel Barbeau, Fernand Leduc, and Paul-Émile Borduas. Many of these artists had lived in Paris for significant periods of time, became well-known for abstract expressionism and geometric designs, and paved the way for the next generation of Quebec painters, including Guido Molinari, Claude Tousignant, Yves Gaucher, and others.

This period also saw the emergence of many talented writers, among them Margaret Laurence, Marian Engel, Adele Wiseman, Timothy Findley, Rudy Wiebe, Alice Munro, Margaret Atwood, Leonard Cohen, James Reaney, and Marie-Claire Blais. The period also saw growing success on the part of writers already established, such as Morley Callaghan, Hugh MacLennan, Robertson Davies, Pierre Berton, Farley Mowat, Mordecai Richler, W. O. Mitchell, Northrop Frye, Dorothy Livesay, and others. While not all of these authors were able to take advantage of support provided by the Canada Council, there is no doubt that the Council did assist many authors at this time through its program of grants.

Indeed, Canada was one of the first countries in the world—if not *the* first—to provide public support to individual artists on a substantial basis. This sent a clear signal that the Canada Council was serious about its intention to be creative in its funding and administration of the arts. The same was true of the Ontario Arts Council, founded in 1963. This message was further amplified when York University created what is viewed by many as the world's first academic program for training arts managers, administrators, and policy-makers. The Program in Arts Administration (now Arts and Media Administration) was established at the graduate level in 1969. It resulted from a major recommendation in the *Ontario Theatre Study Report*, and combined practical training with academic experience. The program produced many excellent arts managers, administrators, and policy-makers, as well as a number of seminal reports on the administration, funding, and development of the arts in Canada.

CENTENNIAL CELEBRATIONS TO CANADA'S ARTISTIC RENAISSANCE

If the Canada Council did a great deal to stimulate artistic activity in the middle years of the twentieth century, so did the centennial celebrations of 1967.

Expo was without doubt the jewel in the crown of the centennial celebrations. It took place in Montreal, and proved the ideal vehicle for opening the doors to a vast panorama of domestic and international possibilities. Of those with the good fortune to attend Expo, who will ever forget the creative ingenuity of the Canadians in pavilions like Labyrinth and Man and His World, or the artistic achievements of the Czechs and the Asians?

Many developments were required to make the centennial celebrations a success. Some of the most important ones took place prior to 1967. Included were the reorganization of the Department of the Secretary of State in 1963, the establishment of a Cultural Affairs Division in the

Department of External Affairs in 1966, and the creation of the Centennial Commission in 1966. If Canada was to celebrate one hundred years of Confederation and make its mark on the world, infrastructure equal to the challenge was needed. With these changes, the federal government served notice that it intended to play an active role in the domestic and international development of the arts in Canada.

If Expo was the jewel, the centennial celebrations were the crown. These were truly national celebrations. There was hardly a town, city, or village of any size or in any part of the country that did not seize the opportunity to create something of lasting value to commemorate the country's one-hundredth birthday. Thanks to support provided by the federal government, the Centennial Commission, and provincial and municipal governments, countless towns and cities built art galleries, museums, concert halls, theatres, auditoria, sports complexes, libraries, and recreational centres, laying the foundations for a solid network of artistic, athletic, and recreational facilities across the country. Moreover, hundreds of amateur, semi-professional, and professional artists and arts organizations were provided with opportunities to perform and tour.

The centennial celebrations signalled the beginning of a new phase in the artistic life of the country. Though artists and arts organizations had been steadily sharpening their skills and expanding their repertoires prior to 1967, no one was quite sure how they would stand up to international scrutiny. Expo proved beyond a shadow of a doubt that Canadian artists could take their rightful place alongside the best in the world. This gave Canada's arts community a confidence it lacked before Expo but has retained ever since.

For the public, the centennial celebrations were a watershed with respect to public involvement in the arts. Prior to 1967, there had been an elitist quality about the arts and arts audiences in Canada. Since the centennial year, the arts and arts audiences have been much more diversified and populist in nature. The reason is not difficult to determine. People from many different socio-economic classes, educational backgrounds, and regions of the country had the opportunity to enjoy artistic activities as a result of Expo and the centennial celebrations. This had the effect of dramatically increasing audiences for the arts, as well as extending those audiences well beyond the rich, the privileged, and the well-educated.

For politicians and governments, the centennial celebrations demonstrated that the arts had a crucial role to play in Canada's development. This realization opened the doors to a new awareness in political circles of the essential role the arts play. It was no longer a matter of determining whether governments should be involved in Canada's arts development, but, rather, what form and direction this involvement should take.

The federal government was quick to capitalize on the success of Expo and the centennial celebrations. Between 1967 and 1973, it initiated a series of highly creative improvements in the country's artistic and cultural life. In the space of a few short years, it passed the Broadcasting Act of 1968, created the Canadian Radio-Television Commission (now the Canadian Radio-Television and Telecommunications Commission), set up the Canadian Film Development Corporation (now Telefilm Canada), and completed the building of the National Arts Centre. It also set out the principles underlying national cultural policy, which included pluralism, democratization, decentralization, federal-provincial cooperation, and international outreach. The objective behind these guidelines was unequivocal. It was to make the country's rapidly expanding constellation of artistic assets accessible to all Canadians, regardless of age, gender, economic situation, religious affiliation, educational level, ethnic background, or geographical location. As a result of these initiatives, and others, this era is generally regarded as one of the most fertile and prolific periods in Canada's arts development.

Specific policies were also designed for publishing, film, and museums. In publishing, the emphasis was on increasing the production and distribution of Canadian books through such measures as grants to publishers, increased government purchases of books by Canadian authors, funding assistance for translations, especially from French to English and English to French, and enhanced representation at international book fairs. Film production and distribution were given a boost through greater use of Canadian films by government departments and agencies in general and the CBC in particular. Some regional offices were added by the National Film Board, and more financial assistance was allocated to the Canadian Film Development Corporation. For museums, a number of programs were established, including the system of associate museums linked to the national museums in Ottawa that was mentioned earlier, development of a series of exhibition centres in the more remote parts of the country, the use of museum-mobiles to travel from community to community, and the establishment of a major conservation institute and heritage information and retrieval network.

Two other federal programs were also created at this time that were mentioned earlier but deserve to be expanded upon here because they played such a crucial role in Canada's coming of age artistically. These were Opportunities for Youth (OFY) and the Local Initiatives Program (LIP).

When OFY and the LIP were begun, no one thought they would have a major impact on the artistic and cultural life of the country. After all, they were designed to achieve very different goals and objectives, namely combating lagging rates of economic growth as well as high levels of unemployment among the country's young people and seasonal workers. Contrary to expectations, however, these two programs opened the doors to a cornucopia of possibilities, largely because they provided citizens with opportunities to create activities of their own choosing and undertake projects very different from those already in existence. Although estimates vary depending on how "art" and "culture" are defined, there is general agreement that the proportion of artistic and cultural projects in the two programs was extremely high—anywhere from 20 to 60 percent, depending on the definition used. In retrospect, the reason for this is clear. The demand for artistic activities and opportunities in Canada was running far ahead of the supply in virtually all parts of the country.

As a result of opportunities provided by OFY and LIP and many other developments, a new wave of artists and arts organizations made their appearance on the scene in the mid- to late 1970s and early '80s. Many of the organizations were theatrical and highly creative in character, such as Vancouver's East Cultural Centre, Toronto's Factory Lab Theatre, Free Theatre, Theatre Passe Muraille, and Tarragon Theatre, and Newfoundland's Mummers Theatre. Not only did these (and other) organizations become permanent fixtures on the Canadian cultural scene in the decades to follow, but they also committed heavily to producing Canadian plays and reaching new audiences.

It was at this time, for example, that Vancouver's East Cultural Centre produced *Billy Bishop Goes to War* by John Gray and Eric Peterson. In Toronto, the Factory Lab Theatre produced four plays by George F. Walker: *Prince of Naples, Nothing Sacred, Escape from Happiness*, and *Love and Anger*, while Theatre Passe Muraille mounted *The Farm Show* and Tarragon Theatre produced *Creeps* by David Freeman, *The Mercer Plays* by David French, *The Donnellys Trilogy* by James Reaney, *One Night Stand* by Carol Bolt, *White Biting Dog* by Judith Thompson, and *Hosana, Forever Yours, Marie-Lou,* and *Bonjour* by Michel Tremblay. Such developments came at an important time. Plays by Canada's own creative talents reached the stage at a time when concern was running high about the appalling lack of Canadian content in the arts and academic affairs, the adverse socio-economic conditions confronting artists and arts organizations, and especially the influx of countless artistic products, productions, and influences from the United States.

While developments like this were taking place at the national and local levels, some interesting initiatives occurred at the provincial level, too. Between 1970 and 1980, many provincial governments set up ministries of culture or their equivalents to complement the arts councils, cultural branches of other government departments, and support mechanisms created earlier. The objective was to expand provincial government involvement in the arts in Canada, as well as to consolidate many diverse activities under one roof, such as the arts, crafts, sports, recreation, communications, heritage, and citizenship.

Quebec was in the forefront of these developments. Not only was the Ministère des Affairs culturelles reorganized and expanded, but it released the first comprehensive governmental report on cultural policy ever produced in Canada. Entitled *Pour l'évolution de la politique culturelle* (*Towards the Evolution of a Cultural Policy*) and released in 1976, the report called for a greatly expanded role for the arts and culture in Quebec. Then, in 1977, the Quebec government passed Bill 101, setting out regulations governing language in Quebec, further strengthening the bonds between language, culture, and the arts in that province. Quebec also created a super-ministry for cultural affairs about this time and appointed Camille Laurin as Minister of State for Cultural Development. He promptly sanctioned the creation of regional cultural councils in Quebec—councils that were similar in some ways to the Maison de la culture created by André Malraux in France, and which were designed to provide artistic programs and advise the government on cultural matters.

Laurin also sanctioned the preparation of another comprehensive report on cultural policy in Quebec. Entitled *La politique québécoise du développement culturel* (*A Cultural Development Policy for Quebec*), it took a broader and deeper view of culture in general and Quebec culture in particular. This view encompassed education, the environment, science, architecture, food, and dress in addition to the arts, heritage, and language, thereby defining culture in far more expansive terms as a "dynamic and organic whole" and an "overall way of life." The justification for this was provided by the policy's principal author, Fernand Dumont, who said, "I have always considered a collective project as something mainly cultural. The economy is not an end in itself: culture is." Not surprisingly, the report began with these words:

> More and more countries are today beginning to rethink their cultural programs, and to draw up policies encompassing the whole of their culture. Quebec too is involved in this process.

While the Quebec government was moving farther and faster in recognizing the pivotal role played by the arts and culture in the lives of people and affairs of society, it was not the only provincial government on the move at this time. Alberta, Ontario, Saskatchewan, and Nova Scotia all set up ministries or departments of culture between 1970 and 1980. As a result, by 1980, virtually every province in the country had at least one, and in some cases two, public administrative institutions to advance the artistic cause and promote cultural development. While this same claim could not be made for the large majority of municipalities—except for Vancouver, Calgary, Toronto, and Montreal, all of which had an arts council, a municipal department, or both—there was nevertheless a significant increase in municipal funding for the arts in Canada. This served to demonstrate the growing importance that Canadian municipalities attached to the arts and culture—an importance that has grown steadily to the present day.

Interestingly, Canada and Canadians proved ground-breakers in this area as well. While most countries in the 1980s had either an arts council *or* a government department to promote and administer the arts and culture, at the federal level Canada had both, namely the Canada Council and the Department of the Secretary of State. Since that time, this pattern has been adopted or retained not only at the national level, where Canada now has the Canada Council for the Arts and the Department of Canadian Heritage, but also at the provincial and municipal levels. As a result, most provinces and municipalities in the country now have both an arts council *and* a government department to promote and administer the arts and culture. This is another area where Canada has been a real creative pioneer and demonstrated international leadership, since this arrangement allows both for direct involvement in the arts and culture by government through a department or ministry, as well as arm's-length independence and autonomy through an arts council. Increasing numbers of countries are finding this model attractive and emulating it.

CANADA'S ARTISTIC RENAISSANCE

Aided by the developments and initiatives we've discussed, and many others, the arts truly soared in Canada in the late twentieth and early twenty-first century. Many claimed that Canada was in the throes of an artistic renaissance that was being fuelled by the rapid expansion of the arts in all parts of the country as well as a great deal of international attention and acclaim.

This renaissance was most conspicuous in literature. Authors writing about important aspects of Canadian history and culture had already captured the public's attention—for instance, Pierre Berton and his evocative books *Klondike*, *The National Dream*, and *The Last Spike*; Farley Mowat, a strong environmental advocate in books like *People of the Deer*, *Sea of Slaughter*, and *Never Cry Wolf*; Antonine Maillet, whose concern with Acadian life in Canada was expressed in books like *La Sagouine*; and Margaret Laurence, who explored the nature of life in smaller communities and on the Prairies in such novels as *The Diviners* and *The Stone Angel*.

These authors were joined by many others who works also became very popular. Joy Kogawa wrote *Obasan* to cast light on the trials and tribulations of Japanese Canadians who were interned during the Second World War; Mordecai Richler explored growing up in Montreal in *The Apprenticeship of Duddy Kravitz* and *St. Urbain's Horseman*; and Roch Carrier's books *La Guerre, Yes Sir!* and *The Hockey Sweater and Other Stories* hit a chord with many Canadians. To this list should be added many other authors, including Margaret Atwood, Rohinton Mistry, Brian Moore, Alice Munro, Jane Urquhart, Irving Layton, Neil Bissoondath, Rude Wiebe, and Nino Ricci. What is most interesting is the number of authors from ethnic backgrounds and origins other than English or French, a reflection of Canada's increasingly multicultural character. The African-Canadian community has been especially active on the literary scene, with authors like Austin Clarke, George Elliott Clarke, M. Nourbese Philip, Lawrence Hill, Afua Cooper, and others winning many awards, including the Governor-General's Award.

All of these authors, and others, profited from the many new publishing houses springing up across the country. Many of these companies, such as House of Anansi, Coach House Press, Oberon, Porcupine's Quill, ECW, Douglas and McIntyre (now D & M Publishers), Raincoast, Dundurn Press, and others were deeply committed to publishing works by Canadian authors, and, like several of the country's theatrical, musical, and dance organizations, a number of these houses got their start through OFY and LIP grants. Their efforts have been reinforced in recent years by the country's elementary, secondary, and post-secondary schools and public libraries, which are playing a more active role in promoting Canadian books, authors, and literature than they did in the past. The same is true of the publication and promotion of children's books, where Canadian authors and publishers have been in the vanguard of international developments in this area through publishers and related organizations such as Kids Can Press, Citizen Kid, the Canadian Children's Book Centre, Second Story Press, and Tundra Books.

In recent years Canadian authors have captured many prestigious international awards and become global literary figures. An obvious example is Margaret Atwood. As a poet, novelist, scholar, and critic, Atwood is well known throughout Canada and the world for her books on a variety of feminist themes, mythological matters, and human and social endeavours, including *Survival*, *Surfacing*, *The Edible Woman*, *The Handmaid's Tale*, *Cat's Eyes*, and *The Blind Assassin*. A number of these titles have won coveted literary awards, including the Governor-General's Award for *The Handmaid's Tale* and the Man Booker Prize—Britain's top literary award for fiction—for *The Blind Assassin*.

Another internationally known figure, Michael Ondaatje, a Sri Lankan of Dutch-Indian descent who emigrated to Canada in the early 1980s, is the author of numerous books, including *In the Skin of a Lion* and *The English Patient*, which won the Man Booker Prize in 1992. Yann Martel won the Man Booker Prize in 2002 for *The Life of Pi*, Alistair MacLeod won the IMPAC Dublin Literary Award for *No Great Mischief* in 2001, and Carol Shields has won numerous awards for such books as *The Stone Dairies*, *The Orange Fish*, and *Dressing Up for the Carnival*. Authors and books like these have made it possible for both Canadians and people elsewhere to become more familiar with Canada's history, geography, and cultural traditions.

The crowning achievement was undoubtedly the awarding of the Nobel Prize in Literature to Alice Munro in 2013. In many ways, this event epitomizes the rich creativity manifested in Canada's literary community during the last 40 years. Fellow writers have been quick to point out that Munro's literary accomplishments, including the 2009 Man Booker International Prize and three Governor General's awards, are "monumental" and in a "class by themselves." Munro is recognized internationally as someone who revolutionized the short story—"Canada's Chekhov" is how one author put it—through her penetrating examinations of life in small-town southwestern Ontario in such books as *Too Much Happiness*, *The Love of a Good Woman*, *Dance of the Happy Shades*, and others.

It would be a mistake to conclude that Canadian literary creativity is limited to the authors mentioned, or even to the more traditional literary domains. It is also apparent in popular literature and especially comic books (or to use the more current term, "graphic novels"), a genre with much to say about Canada's need for cultural heroes.

It all started in 1933, when Joe Shuster, collaborating with American Jerry Siegel, created the archetypal comic-book superhero, Superman. While Shuster himself moved to the United States at an early age to work closely with Siegel, the comic book and cartoon tradition in Canada was sustained and enhanced considerably in the decades to follow through the creation of such Canadian superheroes as Johnny Canuck, Canada Jack and Canada Jacques, Captain Canuck, Nelvana of the Northern Lights, Cerebus the Aardvark, and others, with contributions by a wide range of artists and authors, including Leo Bachle, Hal Foster, Adrian Dingle, Dave Sim, Todd McFarlane, Chester Brown, Julie Doucet, Joe Matt, Seth, David Collier, and others. This remarkable and highly creative tradition has been documented in detail by John Bell in his book *Invaders from the North: How Canada Conquered the Comic Book Universe*, and Canadian contributions to the genre are recognized with the annual Joe Shuster Canadian Comics Awards.

Music is another field where an artistic renaissance has occurred. Over the last few decades, Canadian musicians have been setting the world on fire, not only in classical but also in popular music. A number of classical composers—such as Gary Kulesha, Marjan Mozetich, Kelly-Marie Murphy, Alexina Louie, Christos Hatzis, and others—have made important contributions to Canada's classical musical tradition, and they have been complemented on the institutional side by such organizations as the Esprit Orchestra, Soundsteams Canada, and the Music Gallery, all of which have made strong commitments to performing works by Canadian composers. However, the country is probably best known internationally for Glenn Gould, the eccentric pianist who hummed while he performed in concert, played Bach and especially the *Goldberg Variations* brilliantly, and told Leonard Bernstein and the New York Philharmonic how the Brahms piano concertos should really be played! His creative achievements on the piano—both in public and later in the recording studio, since he shunned live performances in the later years of his all-too-brief life—did a great deal to pave the way for a new generation of Canadian pianists who have won international acclaim, including Angela Hewitt, Marc-André Hamelin, Louis Lortie, Jane Coop, Janina Fialkowska, Anton Kuerti, Jon Kimura Parker, and others.

These accomplishments were matched in jazz by the incomparable Oscar Peterson, one of the world's most creative jazz musicians, who Louis Armstrong called "the man with four hands" and Duke Ellington dubbed "the maharajah of the keyboard." Peterson was accorded one of Canada's highest honours following his recent death when a bronze statue of him by sculptor Ruth Abernethy was ensconced on Parliament Hill. Mention should also be made here of Phil Nimmons and especially Diana Krall, who is recognized as one of the world's most outstanding contemporary jazz musicians and singers. And while they are active in the world of classical music rather than jazz, Tafelmusik and its talented conductor Jeanne Lamon, who retired recently, should be added to this list of international successes. This remarkable organization has become world famous for its performances of baroque music, often on original instruments.

For many, of course, Canada is better known for its popular than its classical or jazz musicians. Spurred on by the early success of a whole host of creative talents such as Wilf Carter, Hank Snow, Félix Leclerc, Paul Anka, Giles Vigneault, Joni Mitchell, Leonard Cohen, Stan Rodgers, Gordon Lightfoot, Stompin' Tom Connors, Bruce Cockburn, Anne Murray, Neil Young, Rush, The Guess Who, and Blue Rodeo, a new generation of popular singers and musicians emerged in the late twentieth and early twenty-first centuries. Included are such internationally known talents as Céline Dion, Shania Twain, Bryan Adams, Alanis Morissette, k.d. lang, Nelly Furtado, Sarah McLachlan, Michael Bublé, Avril Lavigne, Justin Bieber, K'naan, Drake, Barenaked Ladies, The Tragically Hip, and others. Small wonder recordings by Canadian singers filled four of the top five spots on the American Billboard 200 chart in 2011, including Michael Bublé's *Christmas*, Justin Bieber's *Under the Mistletoe*, Drake's *Take Care*, and Nickelback's *Here and Now*.

Mention should also be made here of David Foster. Winner of numerous Grammy Awards and several times named Producer of the Year, he is known internationally for helping many young singers when they needed it the most, as well as for writing such popular songs as *Somewhere* (Barbara Streisand), *We've Got Tonight* (Kenny Rogers and Sheena Easton), *Because You Loved Me* and *To Love You More* (Céline Dion), *I Will Always Love You* (Whitney Houston), and many others. It is difficult to say why so many Canadian popular singers are famous throughout the world, but there is no doubt that Canada has achieved international acclaim in the area of popular music out of all proportion to the size of the country's population.

To a significant extent, this also holds true for opera. Many of Canada's top opera singers and choreographers have been recognized internationally in recent years. Included here are Ben Heppner, Russell Braun, Michael Schade, Richard Margison, Karina Gauvin, Isabel Bayrakdarian, Measha Brueggergosman, and Robert Lepage, one of the world's most innovative operatic and theatrical designers. These talents are building on the solid operatic tradition established decades earlier by Jon Vickers, Lois Marshall, Léopold Simoneau, Louis Quetico, Maureen Forrester, Mary Morrison, Elizabeth Benson Guy, and Teresa Stratas, virtually all of whom performed in the greatest opera houses in the world and profited immensely from opportunities provided by Canadian opera companies. In recent years, these developments have been enhanced by the development of what is called "music theatre," which is probably best epitomized by the creative achievements of Tapestry New Opera. This highly inventive organization has produced many new music theatre works, including *Nigredo Hotel* by Nic Gotham and Ann-Marie MacDonald and *Iron Road* by Chan Ka Nin and Mark Brownell. This latter work documents the experiences of Chinese immigrants who came to Canada in the nineteenth century to work on the construction of the Canadian Pacific Railway.

Then there is choral music, choirs, and choral conductors. Here, as well, Canada has made its mark. Although Canada has always had a strong tradition in choral music— thanks largely to a keen interest in England's well-known choral tradition and such musical masters as Sir Ernest Macmillan and Healey Willan—choral music did not get a major boost in Canada until Elmer Iseler arrived on the scene in the latter decades of the twentieth century.

According to Walter Pitman, author of *Elmer Iseler: Choral Visionary*, this choral genius not only created the Festival Singers and the Elmer Iseler Singers, but also rejuvenated the Toronto Mendelssohn Choir, one of the oldest choral institutions in the world today. During his tenure, Iseler conducted countless choral concerts in all parts of Canada, as well as in the United States and Europe. His work has been sustained and enriched by the many outstanding choral conductors who have followed in his footsteps, most notably Jean Ashworth Bartle, Robert Cooper, Linda Beaupré, and Lydia Adams in Toronto, Howard Dyck in Hamilton, Noel

Edison in Elora, Gerry Fagan in London, and Jon Washburn in Vancouver. Due largely to Iseler's commitment, creativity, vision, and willingness to feature choral works by Canadian composers in his concerts, Canada now has a large and impressive repertoire of choral music, as well as many first-class choral and creative ensembles in different parts of the country.

Dance is another area where Canada has recorded many creative successes. The impetus for this came from three of Canada's most celebrated classical ballet companies: the National Ballet of Canada, the Royal Winnipeg Ballet, and Les Grands Ballets Canadiens. Interestingly, these three companies were all started by women who came from other parts of the world to pursue their artistic visions and aesthetic dreams in Canada. Celia Franca, originally from England, started the National Ballet of Canada; Gweneth Lloyd and Betty Hey Farrally, also from England, started the Royal Winnipeg Ballet; and Ludmilla Chiriaeff, from Latvia (although her parents were Russian and Polish) started the Les Grands Ballets Canadiens. Their expertise, experience, and international reputations helped considerably to put Canada on the world ballet map. Not only were they able to draw people from some of the greatest ballet companies in the world, but they were also able to persuade world-famous dancers like Rudolf Nureyev, Erik Bruhn, and Mikhail Baryshnikov to come to Canada to perform with Canadian companies.

It wasn't long before Canada was producing international ballet stars of its own. Over the last few decades, dancers such as Karen Kain, Frank Augustine, Rex Harrington, Evelyn Hart, and Veronica Tennant have won many prestigious international awards and danced in major ballet companies all over the world. Such achievements were often made possible, and strengthened, by the creation of the National Ballet School in Toronto. Betty Oliphant, co-founder of the School with Franca, was yet another immigrant from England who came to Canada to realize her artistic dreams. Recognized as one of the finest ballet schools in the world, the National Ballet School has graduated outstanding dancers, directors, choreographers, designers, and teachers. This has produced a solid base for the further development of dance in Canada—development that now includes not only many outstanding classical ballet companies, but also modern, contemporary, and multicultural companies.

In the visual arts, interest has grown steadily in the works of Canadian painters such as David Milne, William Kurelek (who was born of Ukrainian parents but grew up on the Prairies, painted folk scenes evocative of Ukrainian life in Canada, and provided an excellent example for Canadian artists anxious to capitalize on their ethnic roots and multicultural traditions), Christopher Pratt, Mary Pratt, Tom Forrestall, Alex Colville (who produced many paintings in a style known as "hyperrealism" and "magic realism"), Doris McCarthy, and many others. Canada has also been the home of a number of highly creative wildlife artists, such as Glen Loates, Freeman Patterson, and Robert Bateman, who have preferred to focus on the country's wildlife and have earned international reputations for their paintings.

Important developments have taken place in film as well.

Mention was made earlier of Canada's long and distinguished tradition in film. That tradition dates back to the end of the nineteenth century and includes many "firsts," such as the invention of the first panoramic camera, patented by John Connon of Elora in 1887, creation of the first portable film developing system, invented by Arthur Williams McCurdy in 1890, and production of the first commercial motion picture by Clifford Sifton in 1903.

With precedents like these, it is not surprising that Canadians went on to make many creative contributions to film and film-making in the twentieth century, whether here at home or in Hollywood. Among the most important were those in documentary film-making, what John Grierson, the first director of the NFB, called "truth with a hammer," including production of the first documentary film, *Nanook of the North;* cinema verité; multi-screen viewing; and especially animation. Particularly noteworthy in the last category were the contributions made by Norman McLaren, who was born in Scotland in 1914 but came to Canada in 1941 to work at the National Film Board. He was without doubt one of the greatest and most creative pioneers in the development of film animation in the world and won numerous awards for his efforts, including an Academy Award in the United States, the Palme d'Or at Cannes, a number of first prizes at film festivals in Venice, and the Silver Bear in Berlin. He is seen by many as the person who paved the way for the development of animation in general and many of the animated films made by Walt Disney and his company in particular.

McLaren also paved the way for Frédéric Back, who won an Academy Award for his films *Crac* in 1981 and *The Man Who Planted Trees* in 1988, as well as for many highly creative achievements by Sheridan College in recent years. Students and graduates of Sheridan have recorded numerous international successes in animation and computer graphics over the last few decades. Mention should also be made here of IMAX. It is a motion picture film technology that allows the recording and display of images of far greater size and resolution and on substantially larger screens than conventional film systems. This innovative technology was developed by Canada's IMAX Corporation, and especially Graeme Ferguson, Roman Kroitor, Robert Kerr, and William Shaw. It was first used at Expo '70 in Osaka, Japan, and had its first permanent installation at Ontario Place in Toronto in 1971.

Film and photographic achievements like these, as well as Canadians' many contributions to Hollywood films, help to account for the fact that Canada is now well known throughout the world as "Hollywood North." Large numbers of films have been made in British Columbia, Ontario, and Nova Scotia in recent decades. But the most interesting and exciting developments in film have taken place in Quebec. Capitalizing on earlier opportunities provided by the NFB, many outstanding filmmakers and directors have come to the fore in Quebec over the last half century, including Claude Jutra, Michel Brault, Denis Héroux, and Denys Arcand, all of whom have achieved international prominence. Arcand has been especially successful, winning a number of Quebec and international awards in recent years for such films as *Jésus de Montréal* (*Jesus of Montreal*), *Le Déclin de l'empire américain* (*The Decline of the American Empire*), and *Les Invasions barbares* (*The Barbarian Invasions*), which won an Academy Award for Best Foreign Language Picture in 2003.

Unlike Quebec filmmakers, who have produced films in French for a largely French-speaking population, filmmakers in other parts of Canada have found it much more difficult to make, finance, promote, and find audiences for their films. This is because their films, produced in English, must compete with American films, as well as because of the fact that most movie houses in Canada are owned and operated by huge American conglomerates. Nevertheless, some well-known and highly creative filmmakers and directors have emerged in other parts of Canada over the last three or four decades, including David Cronenberg, producer of such films as *The Fly*, *Naked Lunch*, and the controversial *Crash*; Atom Egoyan, a talented film director of Armenian descent who produced *Erotica*, *Remember*, and the equally controversial *Ararat*; Don McKellar, whose film *Childstar* was premiered at the Toronto International Film Festival in 2004; Deepa Mehta, a film-maker of East Indian descent who has produced many popular films, including *Water*, which won several awards; Zacharias Kunuk, an Inuit whose *Atanarjuat: The Fast Runner* received a great deal of critical acclaim and a Caméra d'Or award at the

Cannes Film Festival in 2001; Robert Lantos, founder and director of Alliance Communications and Alliance Atlantis; and Sarah Polley, whose popular *Away from Her* received a 2008 Oscar nomination for Best Adapted Screenplay.

Two final areas deserve mention. The first is comedy, the second the circus. While perhaps not all Canadians consider comedy and the circus (like comic books and cartoons) to be art forms, they most certainly are when produced with flair, imagination, and ingenuity. This is especially true of comedy, which requires subtleties, sensitivities, gestures, and aptitudes that are as demanding as they are rare.

Canada's extraordinary accomplishments in this area did not come out of the blue. As noted earlier, Canada has a long tradition in comedy and humour, one that dates back to Thomas Chandler Haliburton and includes such well-known humourists as Stephen Leacock, W. O. Mitchell, the Happy Gang, Johnny Wayne and Frank Shuster, Al Waxman and his pioneering Canadian sitcom *King of Kensington*, and of course Mordecai Richler and his popular books *The Apprenticeship of Duddy Kravitz, Barney's Version,* and *Jacob Two-Two Meets the Hooded Fang*.

With historical precedents like these, it is not surprising that Canadian comedy continues to thrive. Numerous Canadian comedians have achieved fame for their creative achievements, including Rich Little, Don Harron (and his character Charlie Farquharson), Mike Myers, John Candy, Dan Aykroyd, Jim Carrey, Martin Short, Tom Green, Rick Green, Yvon Deschamps, André-Philippe Gagnon, Mary Walsh, Andrea Martin, Ian and Will Ferguson, Russell Peters, Mark Critch, Rick Mercer, and Dashan, or "Big Mountain," who is incredibly well known in China but is virtually unknown in Canada. Not to be outdone, groups and ensembles have also played a key role, especially CODCO, *Second City TV* (SCTV), *Royal Canadian Air Farce, This Hour Has 22 Minutes, Trailer Park Boys, Red Green Show, Corner Gas, The Rick Mercer Report,* and *Little Mosque on the Prairie*. This latter production was particularly popular with Canadians because of the multicultural character of the country and the show's capacity to poke fun at religious and racial minorities and ethnic customs and traditions in a highly humorous and largely non-confrontational way.

If Canadians are well-known for their creative contributions to comedy, they are also well known for creative contributions to the circus. In fact, Canadians have virtually re-invented the circus in recent years, through the efforts of the world-famous Cirque du Soleil.

This highly creative organization was created in Montreal in 1984 by Guy Laliberté, Daniel Gauttier, Gilles Ste-Croix, and others. It has taken the world by storm, largely through its highly inventive choreography and aesthetic wizardry. Made famous by incredible acrobatic feats, it has transformed the entire approach to circuses in many parts of the world with no end in sight. Its 1300 artists from 50 countries have entertained more than 100 million spectators. In 2015, a majority stake in this remarkable organization was sold to the U.S. private equity firm TPG and other investors, although a commitment was made to keep the organization's headquarters in Quebec.

The arts and entertainment open the doors to a broader and deeper way of looking at and understanding Canada and Canadians. They also form the core of the country's culture and epitomize what life and living in Canada are all about. As such, they shed a great deal of light on how the country and its citizenry have evolved historically, where they stand at present, and where they may be headed in the future.

CHAPTER EIGHT

Sports, Recreation, and the Environment

If the arts and entertainment figure prominently in our understanding of Canadian culture and creativity, so do sports, recreation, and the environment. As Susan Hughes points out in her book *Canada Invents*, "Canada is a country full of people who like to have fun. Canadians have adapted or changed games from other countries to suit their own special needs, and they have come up with their own completely original ideas about how to enjoy themselves."

Although we tend to think of creativity in connection with the arts more frequently than in connection with athletics, creativity is nonetheless central to sports. Individually, creativity manifests itself in the way that athletes train, their strategies for winning, and their preparations for competition. Matches themselves may be more a matter of physical conditioning and technical skills; however, creativity also can be seen in the very way that athletes compete. Consider, for instance, Wayne Gretzky's ability to handle the puck and awareness of what was taking place around him, best embodied, perhaps, in his famous remark that he skated where the puck *would be* rather than where it *was*.

In team sports, creativity often manifests itself in the way a team is put together, including the choice of particular athletes and the chemistry that exists among them. An excellent example is the 2015 Toronto Blue Jays. The team began to gel when Alex Anthopoulos, the general manager, demonstrated a great deal of creativity in selecting and acquiring Troy Tulowitzki, Josh Donaldson, and David Price near the end of the season. Suddenly the team was a playoff contender. Individual skills and personalities meshed well, and produced a team that almost made it to the World Series, for the first time in more than 20 years.

Generally speaking, sports and recreation in Canada fall into two categories. On the one hand, there are activities incorporating some form of competition. These may be individual or collective, amateur or professional, but they usually involve recognition of the winners. On the other hand, there are a variety of leisure-time activities—everything from camping to reading to watching TV—that don't involve such competition.

While Canadians participate in both types of activities, many enjoy ones that involve some form of competition. Canadians have made many creative contributions to the development of sports and athletics over the years, especially for a country that has a relatively small population. This is especially true for sports that are intimately connected to the country's climate and geography, thereby emphasizing once again the importance of *place* in determining the specific character of Canadian creativity. As S. F. Wise put it:

> Canada's sharply defined seasons, its bountiful water resources, both salt and fresh, and the demands its environment placed on such pioneering and survival virtues as strength, endurance and mental and physical toughness, all influenced the manner in which our sports developed. Moreover, organized sport was enormously important to Canadians for the relief it provided from the task of earning a living in a hard country. *To an extraordinary degree, therefore, Canadians have been among the world's most creative innovators in sports.* Both basketball and modern ice hockey are Canadian in origin; both species of North American football owe a good deal to Canadian creativity. Lacrosse is a Canadian adaptation of an Indian game. Modern curling was revolutionized by Canadian-developed techniques; even such activities as ornamental swimming and competitive water-skiing are largely Canadian in origin.

THE DOMINANCE OF HOCKEY

One can't go far in Canada without realizing the enormous importance of hockey. Sometimes the game is called ice hockey in order to differentiate it from field hockey, roller hockey, or ball hockey, but Canadians know it simply as hockey and that's how we'll refer to it here. It is a sport that grips the Canadian imagination like no other activity. Canadians are obsessed with both playing and watching it.

While historians still debate whether hockey was first played in Canada or England—certain types of ball and stick games were played on ice in northern England in the early nineteenth century—there is no doubt that Canada's claim to have invented hockey has a great deal of merit. Not only have Canadians played an indispensable role in the development of hockey over the last century and a half, but the game as it is known and played today derives largely from creative contributions made by Canadians. It makes for a fascinating story.

The principal milestones in the development of hockey are well documented. As far as back as the 1850s, simple versions of hockey were played in Halifax and Kingston, making it difficult to decide where in Canada hockey actually originated, although many claim that it was played for the first time in Windsor, Nova Scotia. Nevertheless, in 1875, the competitive game as we have come to know it was first played in Montreal, with rules set out by W. F. Robertson, Dick Smith, Chick Murray, and especially J. G. Creighton, a student at McGill who wrote the sport's first rule book. The first organized hockey team in Canada was the McGill University Hockey Club. It was created in 1879, and won the first "world championship" game in hockey played at the Montreal Ice Carnival in 1883. It was about this time that the first national hockey association was created. This was the Amateur Hockey Association of Canada, which was followed by the creation of the Ontario Hockey Association in 1890.

Lord Stanley, Governor-General of Canada from 1888 to 1893, was an avid hockey fan, and donated a trophy to be awarded to the country's national champion. It was initially called the Dominion Challenge Cup, later the Stanley Cup. It was won for the first time by the Montreal Amateur Athletic Association in 1893, which won it again in 1894. These early wins were fitting in view of the seminal role Montreal has played in the development of hockey, from the four successive Stanley Cups won by the Montreal Victorias from 1895 to 1898 (when they were led by their superstar speedskater and defenceman Mike Grant) to the many Stanley Cups won by the Montreal Canadiens in the twentieth century. Mention should be made here of Ottawa as well. That city's team, the Silver Seven, won three consecutive Stanley Cups in the early years of the twentieth century. The team was spearheaded by one of the greatest scorers of all time, Frank McGee, who once scored 14 goals in a game against Dawson City.

While hockey remained solely an amateur sport for a long time, pressure built rapidly to professionalize it. In 1908 the Ontario Professional League was created, and a year later, the National Hockey Association was established, becoming the National Hockey League, or NHL, in 1917. Then, in February or March 1923 (the exact date is uncertain), Foster Hewitt broadcast the first hockey game on the radio. He continued as the sport's premier broadcaster for the next 50 years, becoming a legend in

Canada with oft-repeated phrases like "Hello hockey fans in Canada, the United States, and Newfoundland" and, especially, "He shoots, he scores."

As hockey became more established, new scoring sensations emerged, such as Fred "Cyclone" Taylor, Joe "Phantom" Malone, Edouard "Newsy" Lalonde, Aurèle "Little Giant" Joliat, and Howie the "Mitchell Meteor" or "Stratford Streak" Morenz. They were followed by the creation of professional leagues in both the east and the west, and then the "Original Six" teams of the NHL—Montreal, Toronto, Detroit, Chicago, Boston, and New York. Teams in these cities dominated the game for the next 50 years, with a number of them, such as the Montreal Canadiens and Toronto Maple Leafs, winning numerous Stanley Cups, due largely to the emergence of such superstars as Maurice "The Rocket" Richard, Toe Blake, Elmer Lach, Jean Béliveau, and Jacques Plante of the Canadiens, and Lionel Conacher, Syl Apps, "Teeder" Kennedy, Turk Broda, and Johnny Bower of the Toronto Maple Leafs. But others teams in the Original Six also had their superstars, such as Gordie Howe, Alex Delvecchio, Red Kelly, Ted Lindsay, and Terry Sawchuk of the Detroit Red Wings, Eddie Shore of the New York Rangers, Dit Clapper and Milt Schmidt of the Boston Bruins, and Bobby Hull, Ted Lindsay, and Stan Mikita of the Chicago Black Hawks.

The NHL added six new teams in 1967, doubling the league's size. This was followed by the creation of the World Hockey Association in 1972. The WHA was created to capitalize on the growing popularity of hockey in North America and especially the United States, as well as to challenge the supremacy of the National Hockey League. Canada was well represented in the WHA, with teams in Ottawa (later moving to Toronto), Quebec City, Edmonton, and Winnipeg. The new league was able to attract many outstanding players from the NHL, including Bobby Hull, who played for the Winnipeg Jets, Gordie Howe, who played for the Houston Aeros with his two sons Mark and Marty, and Wayne Gretzky, who eventually played for the Los Angeles Kings. But the WHA began to experience financial difficulties soon after it was founded and was forced to pursue a merger with the NHL. Teams in Winnipeg, Quebec, Hartford, and Edmonton were incorporated into the National Hockey League, setting the stage for a dramatic expansion of the NHL in the years to follow, largely south of the border. Today the NHL includes 30 teams. While most are located in the United States, half the league's players come from Canada, 25 percent from the U.S., and the rest from Europe, where a similar expansion in hockey took place in countries like Sweden, Finland, Czechoslovakia, and especially the USSR, now Russia.

A strong amateur system has always been an integral part of the game. This system is made up of teams and leagues categorized according to age categories and other criteria. These teams act as farm teams for the professional teams and provide them with up-and-coming stars. In the early years, and particularly from 1920 to 1961, amateur teams from Canada dominated international hockey. The Winnipeg Falcons won the first world amateur championship held at the Olympics in Belgium in 1920. This was followed by international championships for the Winnipeg Monarchs in 1935, the Trail Smoke Eaters in 1939, the Edmonton Mercurys in 1950 and again in 1952, the Penticton Vees in 1955, the Whitby Dunlops in 1958, and the Trail Smoke Eaters once more in 1961. After this, the Soviet Union dominated international hockey for many years. It won nine out of 10 world amateur hockey championships, although many Canadians claimed its players were professionals because they spent the bulk of their time playing hockey when they were in the Red Army.

This rivalry eventually set the stage for one of the greatest showdowns in sport of all time, the much-hyped eight-game Summit Series in 1972 featuring the best players from Canada and the Soviet Union. The first four games were played in Canada, the last four in the Soviet Union. Canadians were shocked when the Soviet Union won two of the first four games in Canada and tied another. When the series moved to the Soviet Union and the Soviets won the fifth game, Team Canada had its back to the wall. It had to win all three remaining games to win the series. And this is exactly what it did, winning games six and seven and then coming from behind in the last game. Canadians from coast to coast heard the call by Foster Hewitt at 19:26 of the third period in the eighth and final game: "Here's another shot, right in front. . . . *They score! Henderson has scored for Canada."*

The whole country rejoiced. It was one of those rare moments in Canadian sports—indeed in the country's history—that will never be forgotten. While there have been many memorable moments in international men's hockey since 1972—the game-winning goal by Mario Lemieux during a later Canada-Russia series, a game-tying goal by Jordan Eberle at the World Junior Championships between Canada and Russia in 2009 and again between Canada and the United States in 2010, and the "golden goal" by Sidney Crosby at the Olympics in Vancouver in 2010—what made the 1972 series so special was the fact that Canada had regained its reputation in world hockey. It is a reputation that has been maintained since that time, with Team Canada winning both the World Cup and the gold medal at the Olympic Games in Salt Lake City in 2004, the Canadian Junior Team winning five consecutive gold medals at the junior world championships between 2005 to 2009 and again in 2014, and Team Canada winning the gold medal at the Olympic Games in 2010 and 2014.

Canada's reputation in international hockey has been enhanced considerably by the remarkable achievements of the national women's team. Canadian women began their ascent to international prominence in this sport in the 1990s, and what an ascent it has been! While women have been playing hockey in Canada for more than a century, and have achieved numerous "firsts" along the way, it is the rise of the women's hockey team to the pinnacle of international hockey that is most spectacular. Though it has experienced stiff competition from the Americans, it won world championships in women's hockey in 1990, 1992, 1994, 1997, 2000, 2001, 2004, 2007, and 2012, as well as gold medals at the Olympic Games in 2002, 2006, 2010, and 2014. This has made players like Hayley Wickenheiser, Cassie Campbell, Danielle Goyette, Vicky Sunohara, Jayna Hefford, Jennifer Botterill, Cherie Piper, Shannon Szabados, Marie-Philip Poulin, and others household names in Canada.

The Canadian women's team has had its share of "memorable moments" and "golden goals." The most memorable was at the Winter Olympics in Sochi, Russia in 2014, when Marie-Philip Poulin scored the winning goal in overtime to beat the Americans 3–2. What made this feat so astonishing was the fact that the Canadian team was trailing 2–0 with less than four minutes to play, only to come back to tie the game in the final minutes of regulation time with two quick goals—the second of these also by Poulin—before winning in overtime. According to many observers, this game, including Poulin's heroic achievements and particularly the overtime winner, will go down in hockey history as equal to Team Canada's come-from-behind victory in the final game of the 1972 series. Two days later in Sochi, the men's team beat Sweden to also win the gold medal, further confirming Canada's supremacy in world hockey.

As important as these defining moments have been in making hockey "Canada's game," it is really the contributions that Canadians have made to how the game is played and organized, as well as the equipment that is used, that mark the country's most creative contributions to this sport.

Originally the game was played outdoors with snow banks for boards and wooden posts for goals. The first hockey sticks in Canada were made by Indigenous carvers. When the Starr Manufacturing Company of Dartmouth, Nova Scotia started making sticks commercially from birch trees, they called them "MicMac sticks" to honour the original Indigenous carvers. Although the first skates were likely invented in Scandinavia several centuries earlier, in 1857 James Whelpley of New Brunswick invented the first "Long Reach" skate, which was granted a U.S. patent in 1884. Whelpley started manufacturing these skates shortly after he invented them. The blade was 43 centimetres long, and extended beyond the back and front of the boot.

For many years, skates were attached to skaters' boots with straps and buckles. However, in 1865, John Forbes of the Starr Manufacturing Company invented the world's first self-fastening skate by clamping the blade into place under the boot. Most skates were tube skates in those days, since they were lighter and tougher than single-blade skates and not as prone to cracking. It was many years before single-blade skates became popular. Mention should also be made here of the fact that it was Canadian goalies who invented masks for added protection. The first to do so was Clint Benedict of the Montreal Maroons in the late 1920s. However, he abandoned the practice after one game because he found it difficult to wear a leather and wire mask while playing. So it was left to Jacques Plante of the Montreal Canadiens to pioneer the practice of wearing a mask. This occurred in the late 1950s and early 1960s after Plante had been hit in the face so many times with slapshots and sticks that he suffered numerous injuries, including a broken nose, cheekbone, and jaw. Not only do all contemporary goalies wear masks—it would be suicidal in today's game not to do so—but they decorate them with elaborate signs, symbols, and motifs.

Hockey was originally played with nine players on each team and no forward passes. This latter regulation was derived from rugby, as were the on-side and face-off rules. In 1910, the game was divided into three 20-minute periods. Then, in 1912, two of the game's most creative and dynamic players, Frank and Lester Patrick, revolutionized matters by creating the Pacific Coast Hockey Association and bringing Western Canada and especially Vancouver into the equation. The Association lasted for thirteen seasons, and during this time introduced many innovations to the game, such as the forward pass, the penalty shot, the identification of players by the numbers on their jerseys, and the blue line. In addition, in 1916, the number of players per team was reduced from nine to six, the number of players allowed today.

Since that time, many changes have taken place in the game, such as the introduction of the red line and then its elimination, changes in the size of the rink, requirements for goalies' equipment, what is to be done in the event of a tie, and so on. Also noteworthy are the contributions of such hockey commentators as Don Cherry and Ron MacLean. But of all the creative contributions Canadians have made to hockey, none has likely had a greater impact than the introduction of "instant replay." This technology enables rebroadcast of previous events through recorded video, making it possible for a viewer to revisit exciting plays moments after they occur. It also makes it possible for commentators to analyze plays by slowing down the frame count, as well as for officials to assess and reverse calls made in error due to the rapidity of events. This technology can be traced back to 1955, when director George Retzlaff of CBC's *Hockey Night in Canada* used a "wet-film" and "hot-processor" technique to develop footage of goals within 30 seconds in order to replay them. (It is claimed in United States that the first "real" instant replay, using videotape, was aired a decade later on CBS during an Army and Navy football game.) Instant replay is now used in virtually all sports except soccer, as well as in connection with broadcasts of many other events and activities.

LACROSSE, BASKETBALL, AND FIVE-PIN BOWLING

Despite hockey's importance, Canadians have made creative contributions to other sports as well. One such sport is lacrosse.

Like hockey, lacrosse has deep roots in Canada, as well as a tradition that dates back many centuries. While it may have been based on a much older Indigenous game, the version we know today was invented by the Algonquin and Iroquois tribes along the St. Lawrence River and around the Great Lakes. They called it *baggataway*, an Ojibwa word meaning "ball." When played outdoors it is called "field lacrosse," when played indoors "box lacrosse" or "boxla."

The rules governing this sport were originally created in 1860 by George Beers— Canada's "Mr. Lacrosse"—who organized a convention in 1867 that led to the creation of the National Lacrosse Association. He also wrote an 1869 book that generated a great deal of interest in the sport. By the end of the nineteenth century, lacrosse had become Canada's unofficial "national game" and was played in many different parts of the country. This led to the creation in 1901 of the Minto Cup, which (like the Stanley Cup) was named after a Governor General, this time Lord Minto. The Minto Cup was initially awarded to the senior men's amateur lacrosse champions, and then, after the creation of the Mann Cup in 1910, to the championship professional team. With the end of professional lacrosse, the trophy fell into disuse, but since 1937 has been awarded to the amateur men's junior championship team.

Despite the flurry of activity in the late nineteenth and early twentieth century, lacrosse has never gained the following in Canada that hockey has. Nevertheless, it did gain a strong foothold in Ontario and British Columbia, where keen rivalries were created between various teams and leagues. As a result, teams like the Peterborough Lakers, Oshawa Green Gaels, Burnaby Lakers, Victoria Shamrocks, Brampton Excelsiors, Six Nations Chiefs, and the New Westminster Salmonbellies dominated the Minto and Mann cups for many years. Then, in the 1960s and '70s, attempts were made to revive professional lacrosse in Canada. Although these efforts failed, the North American Lacrosse League finally came into existence in the 1990s and was dominated for many years by the Toronto Rock.

In 1994, Parliament declared lacrosse Canada's national *summer* sport. This has caused a great deal of confusion, with no one sure whether lacrosse or hockey is really the country's "national game." Speaking officially, it is lacrosse in the summer and hockey in the winter. However, as every Canadian knows full well, it is hockey that is the popular choice as the country's national sport.

If Canadians played a pivotal role in the development of lacrosse, they actually *invented* basketball. Dr. James Naismith, a Canadian who eventually moved to the United States, invented the sport in 1891 when he was teaching at the International Training School in Springfield, Massachusetts.

Naismith was born in Bennie's Corners near Almonte, Ontario in 1861. Like many young men at the time, he worked on farms during the summer and in logging camps during the winter. He was a keenly motivated and very determined individual, who ultimately became a teacher, athlete, inventor, medical doctor, preacher, professor, administrator, and major contributor to the development of the YMCA in Canada, the United States, and other parts of the world. While he was teaching in Springfield, there was great demand for a game that students could play in the winter to get some badly needed exercise. So Naismith invented basketball and set out 13 rules for the game. The original copy of those rules was recently sold at auction for $ 4.3 million dollars by the Naismith International Basketball Foundation to raise money for charity.

The game was originally played with peach baskets for hoops. It quickly became a success. It was officially recognized as an Olympic sport at the

1936 Games in Berlin. Naismith was at these games, but, by this time, was working at the University of Kansas, where he did a great deal of pioneering work in physical education. In recognition for his outstanding contributions to the creation and development of basketball, Naismith was eventually inducted into the Basketball Hall of Fame in Springfield, Massachusetts. He also played a key role in the creation of the football helmet, as well as many other devices designed to protect athletes and improve their performance.

While basketball was invented by a Canadian, it is Americans who have made it "their game" and put their stamp on it. In fact, Americans have done for basketball what Canadians did for hockey, popularizing it throughout the world and being deeply involved in deciding how the game is played and organized. Despite this fact, Canadians have recorded a number of basketball firsts over the years. Between 1915 and 1940, for example, the Edmonton Grads, a women's team, won four international basketball championships and a total of 502 out of 522 games. Interestingly, Canadian women were back in the news nearly a century later when the country's women's wheelchair basketball team won the gold medal at the world championships in 2014. In addition, Steve Nash, a Canadian from British Columbia, was twice voted the most outstanding player in the National Basketball Association (NBA), and Canada hosted the highly successful NBA All-Star Game and weekend in Toronto in 2016.

And this is not all. More and more Canadian basketball players are playing in the National Collegiate Athletic Association (NCAA) and NBA in the United States. One of these players, Anthony Bennett, made history when he was the first Canadian to go "number one" in the NBA draft in 2013. Other outstanding Canadian players who played on American college teams include Andrew Wiggins at Kansas, who was rookie of the year in the NBA in 2015, Nik Stauskas at Michigan, Tyler Ennis at Syracuse, Trey Lyles at Kentucky, Nick Wiggins (Andrew's brother) at Wichita State, Kevin Pangos at Gonzaga, and many others. To this list should be added Tammy Sutton-Brown, who excelled in professional basketball in the WNBA for many years after having had an outstanding college career at Rutgers and incredible high school career at Markham District High School in Ontario.

Five-pin bowling is another sport invented by Canadians that provides an example of Canadian adaptability, ingenuity, and creativity. Bowling first came to Canada in 1904 when ten-pin bowling was introduced from the United States. It immediately became popular with businessmen in

Toronto who were anxious to play it during their lunch hour. However, there was a problem. The game took too long to play. In order to shorten it so that it could be played during lunch, Tommy Ryan, who owned a bowling alley in downtown Toronto, told his pin boys to set up five pins rather than ten. Along with reducing the number of pins, Ryan eventually reduced the size of both the balls and the pins and encouraged the playing of the game during any time of the day. The popularity of five-pin grew rapidly, and by 1927 the first Canadian five-pin bowling association had been formed. For his efforts, Ryan was elected to Canada's Sports Hall of Fame in 1971, unfortunately ten years after his death.

FOOTBALL, BASEBALL, CURLING, AND ROWING

While Canadians did not invent football, baseball, curling, or rowing, they have made many creative contributions to the development of these sports. Take football, for example. It was originally brought to North America from England in the form of rugby. However, the first football game ever played in North America was between McGill University and Harvard University in Cambridge, Massachusetts in 1874. The game had to be divided into two separate parts because the teams played by different rules! These differences have persisted to this day. The Canadian game is played on a longer and wider field, has 12 players rather than 11, three downs rather than four, and a single point is awarded when a player is tackled in the end zone after a kick or missed field goal. Some feel these rules make the Canadian game more interesting, exciting, and spontaneous, whereas the American game is more staid, controlled, and systematic.

Interestingly, Canada's football tradition is almost as old as its hockey tradition and indeed the country itself. Not only was the Canadian Rugby Football league formed as far back as 1882, but the first Grey Cup game, named after yet another Governor General, Lord Grey, and now emblematic of professional football supremacy in Canada, was played between the University of Toronto and the Parkdale Canoe Club in 1909. Most of the best teams in the country in the first quarter of the twentieth century were university teams. However, beginning in the 1930s, Canadian teams were allowed to import several players from the United States, a practice that still exists today. In 1958, the Canadian Football League (CFL) was formed, and in 1965 the Vanier Cup, symbolic of intercollegiate football supremacy, was created. The Canadian Football Hall of Fame was established in Hamilton in 1972.

Baseball has an even longer history in Canada than football. In fact, the first baseball game in North America—and quite possibly the world—was played in Beachville, near Woodstock, Ontario, on June 4, 1838. After this, many competitions were held between Canadian and American teams, most often in Ontario towns like Guelph and Ingersoll. When the International League was formed in North America, both Montreal and Toronto fielded teams, and Jackie Robinson—the first black player to play in the major leagues—played for the Montreal Royals in 1946. Decades later, major league teams were established in Montreal and Toronto, and in the 1990s the Toronto Blue Jays won two consecutive World Series. Justin Morneau of British Columbia was voted the most valuable player in the American League in 2007 and Joey Votto of Ontario the National League MVP in 2010. They are just two of a number of Canadians who have had outstanding professional baseball careers in the United States.

As impressive as these achievements are, it is really in softball, not hardball, that Canadians have made their greatest mark in baseball. The first amateur softball league, the Ontario Amateur Softball Association, was created in Canada in 1923. Then, in 1949, Tip Top Tailors of Toronto won the world softball championship in Little Rock Arkansas. Canadians have also done very well in Olympic and world championship softball games, winning a gold medal most recently at the Pan American Games in Mexico in 2011 by upsetting the powerful American team by a score of 2–1 in the final.

One other example of Canadian creativity that relates to baseball should be mentioned here since it is so fundamentally connected to the Canadian climate. It is the Sky Dome, or, as it is known today, the Rogers Centre. It is not coincidental that it was a Canadian, architect Rod Robbie, who designed this remarkable facility. The first large sports stadium in the world with a fully retractable roof opened on June 3, 1989. Two days later, the first game in it was played between the Toronto Blue Jays and Milwaukee Brewers. The roof rises to a height of 86 meters at the centre, and opens or closes in about twenty minutes. Since that time, many other cities in the world have created similar facilities with retractable roofs, especially where climatic conditions warrant.

Curling is another sport where Canadians have made an especially creative contribution over a long period of time. Although the game was originally invented in Scotland, curling has been played in Canada for more than two centuries. Moreover, some 70 percent of the curlers in the world are Canadian, and there are over a thousand curling clubs in existence throughout the country at the present time.

Canada's long and distinguished tradition in curling dates back to the early years of the nineteenth century. In fact, the first sports club in Canada was the Montreal Curling Club, which was established in 1807 by Scots who were involved in the fur trade, most likely the North West Company. By 1840, numerous curling clubs had been created in Canada and the first book on curling—*The Canadian Curler's Manual*—had been written by James Bicket. Interprovincial curling matches, a highlight of the game in Canada today, began in 1856. The first international bonspiel was held in 1865, and was played between teams from Canada and the United States in Buffalo, New York.

While curling was originally played outdoors, it moved indoors around 1850. By this time, Canada was considered by many in the world to be "the Eldorado of Curling." The first women's curling club was founded in Montreal in 1894, and the W. D. Macdonald Tobacco Company hosted the first Dominion Championship in 1927, awarding the Macdonald Brier Tankard. The Dominion Curling Association was founded in 1935; it was renamed the Canadian Curling Association in 1968. However, the most important event of this era was the championship game played between Canada and Scotland in 1959. It set the stage for the creation of the world curling championships, which are very popular today.

Just as other sports have their heroes and superstars, so does curling. Some of the best known Canadian curlers include Ernie Richardson, Sandra Schmirler, Ed Werenich, Brad Gushue, Kevin Martin, Jeff Stoughton, Glenn Howard, Jennifer Jones, and Brad Jacobs.

Ernie Richardson and his rink won four Canadian championships in five years, as well as four world championships in the late 1950s and early 1960s. Richardson was often described as "the best curler Canada has ever produced and the world has ever seen." This claim would undoubtedly be contested by fans of Sandra Schmirler, whose rink won three Canadian and world titles, as well as a gold medal at the Olympic Games in Nagano, Japan in 1998. Schmirler is often described as "the queen of curling," and her untimely death in 2003 is still lamented by many people in the curling community today. Ed "The Wrench" Werenich, whose team won one Brier and two world championships, is generally regarded as the man who could perform best in competitive situations and really "turn up the heat."

Not to be outdone, Brad Gushue and his rink won the gold medal at the Olympic Games in Turino, Italy in 2006, proving that it isn't just curlers from western Canada who are capable of winning international championships and Olympic competitions. Then, in 2010, former world champion Kevin Martin and his rink won the gold medal for curling at the Olympic Games in Vancouver, erasing the painful memory of a heart-breaking loss to Norway at the Olympics in 2002, when they had to settle for a silver medal. But the most amazing feat of all at the Olympics was achieved in 2014 by Brad Jacobs and Jennifer Jones. Their rinks both won gold medals at the Olympic Games in Sochi. Jones did so without losing a match during the entire competition, a feat that is rarely achieved.

In all, Canadian men and women have won more than 50 gold medals at world curling championships and the Olympic Games, far more than any other country. Interestingly, Canada can also lay claim to having "the most effective and creative" icemaker in the curling world. Shorty Jenkins is known as "the Wizard of Ice," wears "pink Stetsons, sleeps in rinks, and has changed the face of curling rinks throughout the world." He has accomplished this feat by knowing better than anyone else the specific rolls, features, conditions, and details of the majority of the world's curling rinks (and curlers).

Canada also has a long and creative tradition in rowing. Although rowing is not as well known or popular in Canada as other sports, it dates back to Confederation. And why not, given the country's myriad lakes and rivers?

In 1867, the Saint John Four won the world rowing championship at the Paris International Exposition. Shortly after this, George Brown won the U.S. single sculls championship in Boston. He was followed by possibly the greatest rower of all time, Ned Hanlan, who won six world championships and lost only six of three hundred races between 1860 and 1880. Hanlan paved the way for such outstanding Canadian rowers as Jacob Gill "Jake" Gaudaur, who won a world championship and whose forefathers were of Indigenous as well as French-Canadian and Scottish descent. Then there is Lou Scholes, who won the Diamond Sculls in England, much to the consternation of the Henley Committee and British rowing enthusiasts, as well as Joe Wright Jr. and Jack Guest, who won the Diamond Sculls representing the Argonauts Rowing Club and Don Rowing Club respectively.

It was rowers such as these who set the stage for Roger Jackson and George Hungerford to win a gold medal in pairs for Canada at the Tokyo Olympics in 1964 in a shell borrowed from a team from the University of Washington, the only gold medal won by Canadians at the Games that year. These rowers, in turn, opened the doors for outstanding rowers like Silken Laumann, who won a bronze at the 1984 Olympics, and incredibly again in 1992 after a devastating injury, not to mention a silver medal in 1996. Marnie McBean and Kathleen Heddle won a number of gold medals in rowing at the Olympics in 1996. Gold medals continued to pour forth for Canadians at international competitions when Ashley Brzozowicz and Krista Guloien took the gold in pairs in World Cup rowing in 2010, and Adam van Koeverden was crowned Olympic and world kayak champion in 2011.

SKATING, SWIMMING, TRACK AND FIELD, AND SKIING

Skating is another sport where Canadians have excelled. This is especially true of figure-skating. Here, as well, there is a long tradition, dating back to Louis Rubinstein from Montreal, who was Canada's first real figure-skating hero. He was the star of the Victoria Rink's figure skating club in Montreal, and was amateur champion in the United States in 1885 and 1889, as well as world champion in 1890, the first year the world championships were held. Numerous world and Olympic title holders and international skating stars followed in his footsteps, including Petra Burka, Donald Jackson, Otto and Maria Jelinek, Karen Magnussen, Toller Cranston, Kurt Browning, Elvis Stojko, Jamie Salé, David Pelletier, Scott Moir, Tessa Virtue, and Patrick Chan. Their achievements were capped in 2015 when Meagan Duhamel and Eric Radford won the gold medal in pairs at the world championships in Shanghai, China. It was a fitting conclusion to winning gold medals in all six of their previous international competitions.

According to many, Toller Cranston was the most artistically creative of this group. A well-known visual artist as well as an outstanding skater, Cranston transformed figure skating with his choreographic approach to the long program, and influenced an entire generation of skaters. Nevertheless, Canada's greatest and most-loved figure skater is undoubtedly Barbara Ann Scott. She won the European, world, and Olympic championships within a period of six weeks in 1948, a feat unmatched by any other skater. With precedents like this, small wonder Canadians took to the CBC program *Battle of the Blades* like ducks to water. Talk about a highly creative program in the best Canadian sense! Linking up several outstanding Canadian hockey players and superb figure skaters in a series of competitive events set to music, it attracted millions of viewers. And speaking of hockey players, figure skaters, and skating to music, 2010 saw the creation of *Score: A Hockey Musical*, which had its gala premiere at the Toronto International Film Festival. "Only in Canada," they say!

It is not only figure-skating where Canada has recorded many international successes. This is also true of speed-skating. The first Canadian speed skater to win a world championship was Jack McCulloch of Manitoba. He won the Canadian speed skating championship in 1893, the U.S. Nationals in 1896, and the world championship in Montreal in 1897. Other Canadian speed skaters to achieve international distinction were Charles Gorman of Saint John, Fred Robson of Toronto, who held nine world speed skating records between 1899 and 1916, and Frank Stack of Winnipeg, who was a world record holder in the early 1930s.

Since that time, Canada's reputation in this sport has grown even further. Gaétan Boucher from Ste.-Foy, for instance, won a silver medal at the Olympic Games in Lake Placid, New York in 1980, as well as a bronze medal and two gold medals at the Olympic Games in Sarajevo, Yugoslavia in 1884. Catriona LeMay Doan won numerous gold, silver, and bronze medals at the Olympic Games and international competitions, as did Jeremy Wotherspoon. As remarkable as these feats were, they were topped by Cindy Klassen, who won five medals—a gold, two silver, and two bronze—at the Olympic Games in Turin, Italy in 2006. She also won a gold medal and the all-around title at the World Championships in the same year. More recently, Christine Nesbitt won a gold medal at the 2010 Olympics and world championships in the sprint, 1,000 meters, and team pursuit in 2011.

If Canadians have performed very effectively on ice at the Olympic Games and world championships, they have also performed effectively in the pool. As far back as 1912, George Hodgson of Montreal won two gold medals in swimming at the Stockholm Olympics. Many years later, Graham Smith won six gold medals at the Commonwealth Games in 1978, and Canadians won 11 medals at the Olympic Games in Los Angeles in 1984, including two gold medals by Alex Baumann, a gold, silver, and bronze medal by Anne Ottenbrite, a gold medal by Victor Davies, and a silver medal by Carolyn Waldo in synchronized swimming. Waldo also went on to win two gold medals at the Olympics in 1988 in this exquisite sport, the same year that Sylvie Bernier won a gold medal for diving.

According to many experts, Canadians invented synchronized swimming in the 1920s, when a group of Canadian women developed what they called "fancy swimming" while they were preparing for their Royal Life Saving Society diplomas. The first competition in the sport occurred in

Montreal in 1924. Then, in 1938, Peggy Seller, a water-polo player and diver, devised a standard set of rules for this sport. In the 1940s, the term "fancy swimming" was changed to "synchronized swimming." It debuted in the Olympics in 1952, and became an official addition to the Olympic roster in 1984.

However, it is probably Marilyn Bell who is Canada's favourite swimmer. As a 16-year-old, Bell vaulted into international prominence when she became the first person to swim across Lake Ontario, a distance of some 60 kilometres. In so doing, she beat the highly favoured American swimmer, Florence Chadwick, who had to be pulled from the water halfway across the lake. Bell went on to swim the English Channel and the Straits of Juan de Fuca before her all-too-brief but phenomenal career came to an end.

Canada boasts a long and impressive tradition in track and field as well. At one time or another, the country has been touted as being home to "the greatest marathon runner in the world" and "the fastest man in the world." What Ned Hanlan did for rowing and Barbara Scott did for figure-skating, Tom Longboat did for running. He was born in 1887 on the Six Nations Reserve near Brantford, Ontario, and was given the name Cogwagee. In 1906, he won the Bay Race in Hamilton and became an instant celebrity by defeating the best runners in the world. He went on to win the Boston Marathon in 1907, setting a course record. He competed in the Olympics in 1908 but, unfortunately, collapsed after twenty miles. Nevertheless, in 1909, he defeated Alf Shrubb in a marathon race at Madison Square Gardens in New York and was declared "professional champion of the world."

As in many other sports, Longboat established a creative base for future generations to follow. And follow they did. In 1925, Fanny "Bobbie" Rosenfeld won the first woman's 220-yard run in Canada. Then, at the Olympic Games in Amsterdam in 1928, she was one of the "matchless six"—six Canadian women who outperformed all other women at the Games—winning a silver medal in the 100 metres and a gold medal as the lead runner in the 4-by-100 metre relay. She also excelled at discus and the long jump, was an outstanding basketball and baseball player, and an excellent golfer. In recognition of her accomplishments, Rosenfeld was voted Canada's outstanding female athlete of the first half of the twentieth century. Another great performer at the same Olympic Games in 1928 was Percy Williams. He won gold medals in the 100 and 200 metres and was proclaimed "the fastest man in the world."

These feats helped to open the doors for many other runners in the decades to follow. Abigail ("Abby") Hoffman won many medals for Canada in track and field events, and competed effectively for Canada in four successive Olympics in the 1960s and '70s. Not to be outdone, Bill Crothers, Bruce Kidd, and Harry Jerome won many short and long distance races for Canada at Canadian and world competitions, as well as at the Olympic Games. Ben Johnson won a gold medal in the 100 metres at the 1988 Olympics but was unfortunately stripped of his medal because of illegal drug use; and Donovan Bailey won gold in the 100 metres at the 1996 Olympic Games.

Not surprisingly given the country's long winters, skiing is another sport where Canadians have excelled and been inventive. In 1958, Lucile Wheeler of Sainte-Jovite, Quebec won gold in both the world giant slalom and downhill in Bad Gastein, Austria. Two years later, Anne Heggtveit, whose father Halvor was a champion cross-country skier, won the slalom at the Winter Olympics in Squaw Valley, California. She was also the world title-holder in the slalom and alpine combined. This paved the way for a number of outstanding skiers who came later, including Nancy Greene, who won gold and silver medals at the Olympics in 1968; the "Crazy Canucks"—Ken Read, Steve Podborski, Dave Irwin, Jim Hunter, and Dave Murray—who earned more than a hundred Top 10 World Cup finishes between 1978 and 1984, 39 of them in the top three; Kerrin Anne Lee-Gartner, who won gold at the 1992 Olympics; and Chandra Crawford, who won gold at the Olympics in 2006. These achievements were sustained and enhanced at the 2014 Olympic Games in Sochi, where Mikaël Kingsbury won a silver medal, and the three Dufour-Lapointe sisters—Justine, Chloé, and Maxime—won gold and silver medals as well as a twelfth place finish respectively.

Canadians have also excelled in bobsledding, where Pierre Lueders and David Bisset paved the way and Kaillie Humphries and Heather Moyse won gold medals at the 2010 and 2014 Olympics. In 2015 Humphries became the first woman to compete in international competitions against men in the bobsled, and later the same year was accorded the prestigious Lou Marsh Award as Canada's best athlete.

As these examples confirm—and confirm convincingly—there is in Canada an intimate connection between sports and "the land." In most cases, this connection extends back several centuries. It seems as though Canadian athletes do better in sports where there is a strong link to the country's climate, geography, and seasons, especially winter sports such as hockey, curling, figure-skating, speed-skating, skiing, snowboarding, and the like. But this is not a hard-and-fast rule, particularly given the fact that Canada and Canadian athletes won 78 gold, 69 silver, and 70 bronze medals at the Pan Am Games in 2015.

Canada's achievements at the Olympics and Paralympics in Vancouver in 2010 were especially noteworthy. Not only was a great deal of creativity and ingenuity manifested at these Games in everything from their planning and execution to paying tribute to the Indigenous peoples and staging the opening and closing ceremonies, but, as well, Canadian athletes performed extremely well. Who will ever forget the unbelievable performance by Alexandre Bilodeau in the men's moguls, or the moving tribute he paid to his older brother Frédéric who suffers from cerebral palsy? Also never to be forgotten were the courageous performances of Joannie Rochette, who won a bronze medal a few days after her mother died suddenly of a heart attack. Canadians won a total of 14 gold medals, the most ever achieved by any country.

The Olympics were followed by the Paralympics, where Canadian athletes also won a record number of gold medals, including three gold medals in cross-country skiing for Brian McKeever, the blind skier who was guided by his brother, a gold medal in curling by Jim Armstrong and his team, and a remarkable five gold medals for skier Lauren Woolstencroft, who was born with both legs missing below the knee and her left arm missing below the elbow. But the greatest achievement of all during these Games was surely the breakthrough that occurred in the size of the audiences watching, as well as the commitment made to recognizing these individuals as great athletes and not people with disabilities.

FESTIVALS, FAIRS, AND OTHER RECREATIONAL ACTIVITIES

A great deal of creative energy goes into planning, organizing, and marketing recreational events and activities in Canada, mostly during the spring, summer, and fall. Gardening, golfing, camping, canoeing, cottage life, and visits to arts galleries, museums, and historic sites and monuments are extremely popular, especially as most towns and cities now have well-developed recreational facilities, programs, organizations, and tourist centres. The country also has one of the largest, most extensive, and best organized park and conservation systems in the world, due largely to the vision of Parks Canada and the country's federal, provincial, and municipal governments.

In fact, some argue that Canada was the first country in the world to create a national parks system, although the United States is usually credited with this achievement. Nevertheless, Canada has more than 35 national parks in various regions of the country, with many new parks and marine areas in the advanced planning and development stages in such places as Wager Bay, Northern Bathurst Island, Great Slave Lake, the North West Territories, and Nunavut.

Winter recreational activities are growing rapidly in popularity. There are many reasons for this. One is the popularity of downhill and cross-country skiing, snowshoeing, and snowboarding, spurred on by the construction of outstanding ski and winter resorts at Whistler in British Columbia, Collingwood in Ontario, and Mount Tremblant and Mount Ste. Anne in Quebec. Another is the enduring appeal of curling, a sport that Canadians enjoy at every age. Yet another is the popularity of snowmobiling. Indeed, it was the invention of the snowmobile that really transformed Canadians' attitudes toward winter recreation.

Nowhere is the popularity of winter recreational activities more in evidence than in the Laurentian region of Quebec. Many well-known Quebecers have made contributions over the years. One of the most famous was Herman Smith "Jack Rabbit" Johannsen. He was born in Norway, was an avid skier, and came to Canada at a very early age and settled in Montreal. He cut numerous trails for alpine and cross-country skiing through the Laurentians, including the famous Maple Leaf Trail, and organized countless recreational activities and events. Living to the age of 111, he is recognized as one of the truly great creative pioneers of winter recreation in Canada. Also noteworthy are Joe Ryan's development of Mont Tremblant, one of eastern North America's most outstanding ski resorts; Emile Cochand, who created the continent's first mechanical ski lift; and especially Antoine "Curé" Labelle, a priest who created Le P'tit Train du Nord, which carried skiers on special trains to popular ski destinations in Quebec between 1920 and 1940. After decommissioning, the railway's right-of-way was converted to the longest linear park in North America, with 42 kilometres of cross-country ski trails and 114 kilometres of snowmobile trails.

Moving indoors, board games are another popular winter recreational activity. It may come as a surprise, but Canadians have made many creative contributions to the invention and development of such games. The best-known is perhaps the creation of Trivial Pursuit, mentioned earlier. However, Canadians have also invented many other board games, such as Pictionary, Balderdash, Yahtzee (originally called "the Yacht Game"), and table hockey. Then there is crokinole. Although not well-known today, it was very popular at one time, and was invented sometime in the mid-nineteenth century near Stratford, Ontario. Eckhardt Wettlaufer, a craftsman from Perth County, Ontario who is believed to have been of Mennonite or Amish origin, created the first crokinole board that we know of; it dates from 1876. Crokinole in recent years has made something of a comeback, both in Canada and the U.S.

Some believe Canadian creativity in creating board games is tied up with the need to find interesting things to do during the long winter months. And what better way to do so than by playing these games on kitchen tables, in basements, or in family and recreation rooms, waiting for spring to arrive?

Canadians also enjoy many festivals, fairs, and community celebrations throughout the year. During the spring, there are maple syrup festivals in Ontario and Quebec, apple blossom festivals in Nova Scotia, Ontario, and British Columbia, and the internationally famous tulip festival in Ottawa. Summer festivals, too, are usually held outdoors and include a variety of culinary, recreational, and related activities. Many are organized by local churches and social groups, and feature the best—and the worst!—in local cooking. In British Columbia, Ontario, and Quebec, for example, lumberjack festivals celebrate the country's timber traditions. These festivals include competitions to see how quickly trees can be scaled and stripped of their bark, as well as log-rolling contests on lakes and rivers. In Atlantic Canada, and especially Nova Scotia, where many residents trace their origins back to the Scottish Highlands, popular Highland festivals feature hammer- and pole-throwing contests, as well as a great deal of Highland music and dances like the Scottish fling.

Summer also brings with it two of the country's oldest, largest, and most unique events—the Calgary Stampede in July and the Canadian National Exhibition in late August and early September.

Billed as "the Greatest Outdoor Show on Earth," the Calgary Stampede is one of the biggest rodeos and agricultural exhibitions in the world. Commencing with a huge parade, the Stampede includes bronco and bull riding, team rodeos, chuckwagon races, and a variety of culinary delights. The Canadian National Exhibition, which takes place in Toronto, is one of the largest annual exhibitions of its kind in the world. Its roots can be traced back to 1878, and it was officially named the Canadian National Exhibition in 1912. The midway features what in years gone by was one of the finest amusement parks in North America, although permanent amusement parks have since eclipsed it. In addition, the "Ex" features numerous grandstand shows and activities as well as special events like the marathon swim involving Marilyn Bell that we mentioned earlier.

And how is this for a festival? Every second summer, a Sound Symposium is held in St. John's, Newfoundland that involves numerous composers, musicians, visual artists, and technicians. The objective is to celebrate sounds of all kinds, as well as to turn the city and its environs into a virtual "audio-visual lab." One of the major events is a "fog horn symphony," written by a different composer for each festival. Performed in St. John's harbour, it is scored for the horns and bells of all the ships and vessels anchored there. Audiences love it.

In the fall, fairs are commonplace in many communities throughout the country. The vast majority have strong agricultural roots and feature displays of livestock and farm equipment, horse races and performances, cattle-pulling contests, and much else, bringing to mind one of Canada's most popular musical compositions, Godfrey Ridout's *Fall Fair*. In recent years, many other activities have been added, such as displays of creative art and craft work, cooking competitions, and presentations by different community groups. These fairs are increasingly complemented by other types of special events, such as *Oktoberfest*, especially in communities like Kitchener-Waterloo with large German populations.

There are also a number of well-known festivals held in the winter, most notably the Carnaval de Québec in Quebec City, the Winterlude Festival in Ottawa, and the Sourdough Rendezvous in Whitehorse in the Yukon. Quebec's Carnaval is a pre-Lenten celebration that ran initially from 1894 to 1900. Revived in the 1950s, it became bigger, better, and more creative than ever. Bonhomme Carnaval, a talking snowman, is its principal symbol and host. He resides in an ice palace near the Château Frontenac Hotel, and presides over a variety of events such as ice-sculpture competitions, boat races on the ice across the St. Lawrence River, toboggan rides and runs, and other attractions. In recent years, Carnaval has been complemented by an "ice hotel" constructed entirely of ice and snow. Winterlude, in Ottawa, also encompasses a variety of winter events and activities, such as skating on the Rideau Canal. Finally, the Sourdough Rendezvous includes dogsled, snowmobile, and snowshoe races, as well as contests for flour packing and pancake making.

In recent years, film and television festivals have also become extremely popular. Indeed, Canada hosts two of the largest film festivals in the world, in Toronto and Montreal. Taking place in the fall, they attract large numbers of film buffs, movie stars, directors, screenwriters, and countless buyers and sellers of films and film properties from different parts of the world. Canada is also home to the largest television festival in the world, the Banff Television Festival. Begun in 1979, this festival is generally regarded as "the place to be" for the world's top television talents, with more than 40 countries and 900 television programs competing for the Rockie Awards.

In recent years, Caribana (now called the Toronto Caribbean Festival) has become one of Canada's largest and most popular multicultural festivals. It is a colourful festival with many highly decorated floats and fantastic costumes made of beads, satin, peacock feathers, sequined chiffon fabric rolls, purple taffeta, telescopic rods, and other glittery materials. It also features performances by many outstanding steel bands and other musical ensembles. Held in Toronto in early August, it attracts visitors from Canada, the United States, and other parts of the world. Similar multicultural festivals are held in other parts of the country, including Vancouver and Manitoba, where the Folklorama Festival is extremely popular.

With the large influx of people from Asia, Africa, Latin America, the Caribbean, the Middle East, and other parts of the world, there are now many Buddhist, Hindu, Jewish, Muslim, Sikh, and Chinese festivals celebrated in Canada over the course of the year. These festivals are usually combined with special holidays and events like Chinese New Year, Ramadan, Yom Kippur, Diwali, and so forth. They attract a great deal of attention among Canadians in general and not just the specific ethnic communities associated with them, thereby adding richness and vitality to Canada's rapidly evolving recreational landscape. Sports not historically popular in Canada have also assumed greater prominence because they are played by members of Canada's more recent immigrant groups. Especially noteworthy in this regard are ping pong, water polo, badminton, and athletic activities like acrobatics and Taekwondo. Interestingly, Taekwondo has a history in Canada dating back four generations. It was brought to Canada by a Winnipeg-area Korean family who were all black belts, masters, or grand masters.

This increasing variety of recreational activities makes it possible for Canadians of all ages and walks of life to express themselves in interesting, innovative, and creative ways. This has done a great deal to make creativity the birthright of all Canadians.

CONSERVATION OF THE NATURAL ENVIRONMENT

It is impossible to examine sports and recreation in Canada without becoming aware of the strong connection between these activities and the natural environment. Canadians have been involved with the natural environment in many other ways over the course of their history, especially attempts to preserve and protect it. In fact, Canada boasts an impressive array of people who have been passionately concerned about conserving the country's natural legacy. Most notable in this regard are Léon Abel Provancher, John Macoun, Ernest Thompson Seton, Jack Miner, Archibald Belaney (Grey Owl), Charles Joseph Sauriol, David McTaggart, Maurice Strong, Farley Mowat, Wade Davis, and David Suzuki.

Most of these individuals have stirred controversy in one form or another, but have made indispensable contributions. Léon Abel Provancher was a Catholic priest born in Bécancour, Quebec in 1820. An outstanding naturalist, he is considered by many to be "the father of natural history in Canada," largely because of his two-volume book, *Flore Canadienne*, which was published in Quebec in 1862. John Macoun was also an important student of the country's flora and fauna. Born in County Down, Ireland in 1831, he came to Canada at a very early age. He was appointed official "Explorer of the Northwest Territories" by the Government of Canada in 1879, was Dominion botanist for several years, and worked for the Geological Survey of Canada for more than three decades. He was a prolific collector and cataloguer of the country's flora and fauna, with more than 100,000 samples of his collected plants housed in the National Herbarium in Ottawa. Ernest Thompson Seton was also born abroad, in his case in England in 1860. He was an outstanding wildlife illustrator and naturalist, and was often called "Black Wolf." The author of countless animal stories, he was appointed official naturalist to the government of Manitoba in 1893. Viewed by many as a key contributor to the Boy Scouts movement in North America as well as a strong advocate for Indigenous rights, he lived close to nature all his life, and undertook an epic 3,000-kilometre canoe trip across northern Canada in 1907.

Nevertheless, the country's best known early environmentalist was undoubtedly Archibald Belaney. Born in England in 1888, he came to Canada early in life and claimed to be of mixed Indigenous and European descent, although some contend he was actually born in Mexico and not England. He was enamoured of Canada's natural environment, and adopted the name "Grey Owl" soon after his arrival in Canada. He married an Indigenous woman, assumed a First Nations identity and dress, and worked as a wilderness guide and forest ranger. He was also a prolific writer of books like *Tales of an Empty Cabin* and *Pilgrims in the Wild,* and a tireless lecturer who emphasized the importance of preserving Canada's wilderness areas.

Like many other Canadian naturalists, Jack Miner was also born in another part of the world—Dover Center, Ohio, in 1865. His family moved to Canada in 1878. Miner came to be called "Wild Goose Jack," and was well-known for the sanctuaries he created for geese, ducks, quail, pheasants, and other birds, banding over 50,000 ducks and 40,000 geese over the course of his life. His most famous sanctuary is the Jack Miner Bird Sanctuary, which is still in operation at Kingsville, Ontario near Point Pelee National Park.

Charles Joseph Sauriol, David McTaggart, Maurice Strong, Farley Mowat (who was discussed earlier), Wade Davis, and David Suzuki are contemporary counterparts to these environmental pioneers. Sauriol was born in 1904. He was dubbed "Mr. Conservation" for the remarkable role he played in acquiring lands for the creation of conservation areas, largely in and around Toronto and southern Ontario. He was responsible in one way or another for the creation of the Don Valley Conservation Area and Black Creek Pioneer Village, as well as Bruce's Mill and another nature preserve near Clairmont, Ontario.

David McTaggart was one of the original creators of Greenpeace International and an outstanding environmental activist. (Robert Lorne Hunter was also involved in the founding of this remarkable organization.) Founded in 1971 when a handful of concerned citizens set sail from Vancouver in a hired fishing boat to protest an underground nuclear test by the U.S. on the Alaskan island of Amchitka, Greenpeace was unsuccessful in stopping that specific test, but garnered considerable publicity with the result that later tests in the area were cancelled. It now operates in more than 40 countries, and is committed to protecting biodiversity and preventing pollution in all parts of the world.

These achievements have been parallelled in recent years by the pioneering achievements of Maurice Strong, Wade Davis, and David Suzuki. Strong, a highly successful Canadian businessman and diplomat, was also extremely active in the environmental movement. He played a major role in launching the modern environmental movement through his appointments as secretary-general of the first UN Conference on the Environment in 1972, first executive director of the United Nations Environmental Programme (UNEP), and secretary-general of the Earth Summit in Rio de Janeiro in 1992.

Then there is Wade Davis. He is well-known as an explorer, anthropologist, and ethnobotanist, as well as for the highly creative approach he has taken to preserving indigenous languages, cultures, and what is now called the world's "ethnosphere." More recently, he has turned his attention to conserving a pristine part of northern British Columbia that is called "the Sacred Headwaters" by the Indigenous peoples. This area, which is close to three key salmon rivers (the Stikene, Skeen, and the Nass), was opened recently for industrial development by the government of British Columbia, to the dismay of Davis and his followers.

David Suzuki is well known for his pioneering work on environmental protection and preservation. He is the host of the highly successful and long-running CBC television series, *The Nature of Things*, as well as founder in 1990 of the David Suzuki Foundation. The foundation is committed to "finding ways for society to live in balance with the natural world that sustains us" through clean energy, measures to reduce climate change, and initiatives to ensure sustainable fishing, farming, forestry, and industry. In 1997, Suzuki channeled the royalties from his book, *The Sacred Balance: Rediscovering Our Place in Nature,* into the development of the foundation. Though no longer connected to the foundation in a formal sense, he still speaks out passionately and frequently on a variety of environmental issues and problems.

With prominent Canadian environmentalists like these playing a major role over the years, it is easy to see why people elsewhere in the world were so distraught over Canada's performance on environmental matters in recent years. It is disconcerting to realize that Canada is one of the world's biggest polluters, that Canadians are responsible for one of the largest per-capita ecological footprints on the planet, and that the Canadian government dragged its feet on a range of environmental issues for many years, especially the Kyoto and Copenhagen climate accords. Given this situation, there is no doubt that a great deal of creativity will have to go into ensuring that Canada and Canadians develop more effective environmental plans, policies, and practices in the future. A good place to start will be the follow-up to the United Nations Climate Change Conference in Paris in 2015, to which the country's new Liberal government sent a large delegation. Canada will need to capitalize on the remarkable achievements of its environmental pioneers if it is to play a leadership role in this area in the years ahead.

CHAPTER NINE

Embracing the Future

Without doubt, creativity is Canada's greatest asset. While natural resources have played a vital role in the country's development—so much so that Canadians were often described as "hewers of wood and drawers of water" in earlier periods of history—it is clear that creativity is the most essential resource of all.

Without creativity, it would not have been possible to come to grips with the colossal size, cold climate, and formidable geography of the country. Nor would it have been possible to create a sovereign and independent nation in the northern half of the North American continent, one that enjoys an extremely high standard of living and excellent quality of life. In order to achieve these things, Canadians have had to be highly creative over many centuries.

KEY CHARACTERISTICS OF CANADIAN CREATIVITY

As we have seen, Canadian creativity is not limited to the telephone, basketball, standard time, or the discovery of insulin. On the contrary, it is spread liberally across virtually every domain of the country's cultural life, from food, clothing, shelter, transportation, and communications to the arts, sciences, education, sports, recreation, and the environment.

This creativity is the product both of people who have lived in Canada for a long time as well as recent immigrants. It is manifested by groups and organizations as well as by individuals. It is the birthright of women just as surely as men. We find it expressed in small towns and rural areas and in large cities, and it is limited to no one region of the country. Everywhere you go, you will find Canadians working to translate their creative visions and ideas into concrete realities.

Much of this creativity is tied up with the particular environmental, historical, and geographical circumstances that Canadians have had to confront and overcome over the centuries. This makes "place" a major factor in explaining the specific sorts of creativity that have manifested themselves in Canada. In earlier periods, creativity was channelled mainly into activities that had to do with *survival*, and consequently expressed itself in such things as food, clothing, shelter, and the need to create a transportation and communications system capable of moving people and products over long distances and linking the diverse peoples of the country together. Necessity has indeed been the mother of invention in Canada! More recently, a substantial amount of this creativity has been channelled into areas that are concerned with *well-being*, and therefore the creation of an effective social security system and some of the finest educational, political, artistic, scientific, and recreational institutions in the world.

What might be called clustering has always been an important aspect of Canadian creativity. Just as numerous economic and political developments followed from the construction of steamships, railroads, canals, roads, and the introduction of agricultural and industrial improvements in the nineteenth and early twentieth centuries, many opportunities are arising today from major breakthroughs in stem cell research, information systems, and digital technology. This matter requires close scrutiny. It is one thing to invest in creativity that yields one-time-only benefits, quite another to invest in creativity that yields cumulative benefits over long periods of time.

Relationships between the "foreground" and the "background" have also played an important role in the cultivation of Canadian creativity. This is why context is so crucial in explaining the specific nature of the country's creativity. There are many cases where creativity has resulted from background developments that may not have been creative in themselves, but which nevertheless formed an essential prerequisite for remarkable feats of creativity. This is equally true of creativity that builds on prior achievements. An excellent example is the incredible amount of creative ingenuity displayed by Canadians in popular music in recent years. This creativity did not appear "out of the blue," so to speak, but rather capitalized on a rich tradition of popular music in Canada that stretches back several generations.

One of the most fascinating things about Canadian creativity is how much it has benefited not just Canadians but people in other parts of the world. When James Naismith invented basketball in the nineteenth century, for example, who could have guessed the sport would become one of the most popular in the world? Similarly, when Jean Vanier invited a handful of mentally challenged people to live with him in his home in France many years ago, who would have thought this would led to the creation of *L'Arche*, one of the most respected and cherished social organizations in the world? And what is true of the creative achievements of Naismith and Vanier is also true of those of many other Canadians, past and present. While Canadians can be justifiably proud of the valuable contributions they have made to peacekeeping, multiculturalism, the fighting of two world wars, and the realization of many national and international milestones, their contributions to improving the well-being of countless people around the world have been far greater.

FUTURE DIRECTIONS AND PRIORITIES

While Canadians must continue to develop their creative capacities in all the different areas they are apparent in today, they will also need to develop many new capabilities.

Doing so is imperative, since the world is changing rapidly and is a far different place today than even a few decades ago. Climate change, huge disparities in income and wealth, the movement across national borders of refugees in numbers not seen since the 1940s, escalating violence, terrorism, and conflict—such challenges underline the fact that without the development of new creative capabilities, not only in Canada but in other countries, too, the world could easily become even more difficult and dangerous in the future.

Here at home, Canadians will need to demonstrate much more creativity in addressing not only the global problems mentioned above, but also a wide range of domestic issues. These include the environmental crisis, crumbling infrastructure, regional disparities, escalating inequality, skyrocketing medical costs, and persistent unemployment, homelessness, and poverty, especially among children, young people, and marginalized and minority groups.

Particularly important in this regard is stimulating the Canadian economy and generating more entrepreneurial, commercial, technological, and investment activity, while at the same time reducing Canada's huge ecological footprint by decreasing carbon emissions, creating alternative forms of "green" energy, protecting fragile ecosystems, producing goods with longer life spans, and so forth. This is looming larger and larger as one of the greatest challenges of the twenty-first century.

All these advances, and others, will require a quantum leap in Canadian creativity—a leap that won't be possible without more effective education in early childhood and the widespread use of the arts in unlocking the creative capabilities of Canadians of all ages and in all parts of the country.

Making cultural activities and the arts an integral part of daily life will also have significant implications for health care and the country's aging population. Creative activities have been shown to especially benefit those suffering from illnesses such as dementia, Alzheimer's, Parkinson's, multiple sclerosis, and other ailments. Increasing numbers of community centres and retirement homes are introducing the arts into their planning and programming, since these activities help people cope with old age and its problems in more imaginative and inventive ways.

But it is on the international scene that Canada can and should make its greatest creative mark. Over the centuries, Canadians have built up a huge reservoir of creative expertise in resource development, transportation and communications, health care, distance education, multiculturalism, public administration, and many other fields. What Canadians have learned over the years could prove extremely valuable to countries in the developing world that desperately need such expertise. While Canadians have much to gain economically from making their expertise available to other countries, they also have much to give in social and humanitarian terms. Consider how the world would benefit if Canada's creative capabilities were utilized far more extensively in other parts of the world in coming to grips with a host of difficult economic, social, cultural, political, and environmental problems.

Canadian creativity will be required in all these areas if the world is to become a safer and more secure, sustainable, and harmonious place. For what this examination of Canadian creativity over the centuries has revealed—and revealed convincingly—is that Canadians are an incredibly creative people and Canadian creativity has a great deal to contribute to the realization of a better Canada and a better world. Creativity, Canada's greatest asset, will surely be in even greater demand in the future. There is no doubt about this nor any substitute for it.

Selected Readings

Readers who are interested in or require specific bibliographic information for the various chapters in the book will find it provided on a chapter-by-chapter basis as well as alphabetically on the publisher's website at www.rocksmillspress.com.

Brown, J.J. *The Inventors: Great Ideas in Canadian Enterprise* (Toronto: McClelland and Stewart, 1967).

Brown, J.J. *Ideas in Exile: A History of Canadian Invention* (Toronto: McClelland and Stewart, 1967).

Canada Heirloom Series. *Wayfarers: Canadian Achievers,* Vol. V (Mississauga, ON: Heirloom Publishing Inc., 1998).

Canada Heirloom Series. *Visionaries: Canadian Triumphs*, Vol. VI (Mississauga, ON: Heirloom Publishing Inc., 1996).

Carpenter, Thomas. *Inventors: Profiles in Canadian Genius* (Camden East, ON: Camden Publishing House, 1990).

Downey, James, and Claxton, Lois. *Innovation: Essays by Leading Canadian Researchers* (Toronto: Key Porter Books, 2002).

Hacker, Carlotta. *Inventors* (Calgary: Weigl, 2000).

Hughes, Susan. *Canada Invents* (Toronto: Owl Books, 2002).

Humber, Charles, J., ed. *Canada: From Sea unto Sea* (Mississauga, ON.: The Loyalist Press, 1968).

Mayer, Roy. *Inventing Canada: One Hundred Years of Innovation* (Vancouver: Raincoast Books, 1997).

Melady, John. *Breakthrough! Canada's Greatest Inventions and Innovations* (Toronto: Dundurn, 2013).

Nader, Ralph, Nadia Milleron, and Duff Conacher. *Canada Firsts* (Toronto: McClelland and Stewart, 1992).

McGoogan, Ken. *50 Canadians Who Changed the World* (Toronto: HarperCollins Publishers, 2013).

Nostbakken, Janis, and Jack Humphrey. *The Canadian Inventions Book: Innovations, discoveries and firsts* (Toronto: Greey de Pencer Publishers, 1976).

Spencer, Bev, and Bill Dickson. *Made in Canada: 101 Amazing Achievements* (Toronto: Scholastic Canada, 2003).

Trottier, Maxine. *Canadian Inventors* (Toronto: Scholastic Canada, 2004).

Van Ruskenveld, Yvonne and the Department of the Secretary of State. *About Canada: Innovation in Canada* (Ottawa: Ministry of Supply and Services, 1988).

Wojna, Lisa. *Canadian Inventors: Fantastic Feats and Quirky Contraptions* (Alberta: Folklore Publishers, 2004).

Wojna, Lisa. *Canadian Firsts: Inventions, Sports, Medicine, Space, Women's Rights, Explorers, Science, Research, Arts, World Affairs* (Alberta: Folklore Publishers, 2008).

Index